dumb girl

**A JOURNEY FROM CHILDHOOD ABUSE
TO GUN CONTROL ADVOCACY**

dumb girl

HEIDI YEWMAN

SHE WRITES PRESS

Copyright © 2025, Heidi Yewman

All rights reserved. No part of this publication may be reproduced, distributed, or transmitted in any form or by any means, including photocopying, recording, digital scanning, or other electronic or mechanical methods, without the prior written permission of the publisher, except in the case of brief quotations embodied in critical reviews and certain other noncommercial uses permitted by copyright law. For permission requests, please address She Writes Press.

Published 2025
Printed in the United States of America

Print ISBN: 978-1-64742-942-3
E-ISBN: 978-1-64742-943-0
Library of Congress Control Number: 2025905820

For information, address:
She Writes Press
1569 Solano Ave #546
Berkeley, CA 94707

Interior design and typeset by Katherine Lloyd, The DESK

She Writes Press is a division of SparkPoint Studio, LLC.

Company and/or product names that are trade names, logos, trademarks, and/or registered trademarks of third parties are the property of their respective owners and are used in this book for purposes of identification and information only under the Fair Use Doctrine.

NO AI TRAINING: Without in any way limiting the author's [and publisher's] exclusive rights under copyright, any use of this publication to "train" generative artificial intelligence (AI) technologies to generate text is expressly prohibited. The author reserves all rights to license uses of this work for generative AI training and development of machine learning language models.

This book is dedicated to those who've endured tragedy and abuse, found strength in the unimaginable, and to those who fight for a safer world. May this memoir honor your pain, celebrate your resilience, and inspire a future where compassion triumphs.

contents

author's note ix
prologue xi

PART ONE

1   prison 3
2   d-b-a-d-g 13
3   columbine 17
4   vigil at the park 27
5   ask 32
6   sniper 38
7   no-press press conference 47

PART TWO

8   testify 55
9   kennedy 64
10   nra debate 70
11   gun guy 79
12   understanding 89
13   giving/taking 94

PART THREE

14   bored 101
15   christian columbine 109

16	crying in the car	116
17	touching trauma	122
18	anniversary	130
19	virginia tech	139
20	the scare	144

PART FOUR

21	board	151
22	not-cancer	158
23	chaos	166
24	sad	173
25	conference	179
26	tennis	185
27	arizona	191
28	month with a gun	204

PART FIVE

29	fundraising	217
30	truth and trust	223
31	christian	228
32	crisis	236
33	stupid	243
34	awards	251
35	becoming	257
	acknowledgments	269
	about the author	271

author's note

This book is a memoir. It reflects the author's present recollections of experiences over time. Some names and characteristics have been changed to protect the privacy of individuals, some events have been compressed, and some dialogue has been recreated.

Content Warning: *This memoir contains references to gun violence and childhood physical and sexual abuse that may be distressing to some readers.*

prologue

Jane Fonda stood on a warmly lit stage twenty feet from me. Behind her was a massive garish red-purple-pink-yellow-painted image of what was either the inside layers of a flower or a vagina.

She was part of an ensemble of sixteen Hollywood celebrities performing a rendition of Eve Ensler's play *The Vagina Monologues* in Santa Monica, California, and she was talking about her vagina. Her ability to talk about such a personal thing as her vagina was astonishing to me. And really, everything about her was larger than life: She was eighty years old but looked forty; her skin had a youthful glow; her dancer's posture exuded confidence; and her made-up blue eyes were expressive and intense. Her voice was captivating and almost sensual, kind of raspy and full of gravitas.

"Think about it," she said. "It's moist, it's a wetland, it's a place where people come for fun. And when things go south, forget about it."

I hung on her every word.

It was February 2018, the height of the #MeToo movement where women across the world were collectively refusing to hold the shame of being sexually harassed and abused. The event was one of many that Hollywood celebrities used to break the silence by sharing their own experiences of rape, harassment, and abuse. The play was both a celebration of women's sexuality and an

dumb girl

examination of violence against women, produced by Deborah Kagan.

Two days earlier my husband, Dave, and I had had lunch with my friend Jeremy Kagan, who happened to be directing the performance. He'd deemed us "special guests."

Tonight, once the lobby doors had opened to the five-hundred-seat theater, I'd made a beeline to the second row of seats, which were cordoned off with yellow tape that said "Reserved for special guests." As we ducked under the yellow tape and took our seats, I could feel the anxious excitement of the mostly female patrons who poured into the auditorium. Some greeted friends with enthusiastic hugs while others scanned the room for celebrities who might be attending. Not being from LA, I got the feeling that "celebrity scanning" was a tradition, and I was not immune. Laverne Cox, a star of *Orange Is the New Black*, sat two rows behind us, and I kept sneaking peeks at her.

As the lights dimmed, the buzz of voices quickly softened as renowned personalities, Oscar-winning actors, and comedians—Rosario Dawson, Marisa Tomei, Wanda Sykes, Wendie Malick, and Cheri Oteri, among others—walked onto the stage to perform their monologues.

I sat motionless as I absorbed the sometimes emotional, sometimes funny, and profoundly gripping monologues performed that night. The women onstage explored everything from body image to genital mutilation to consensual and nonconsensual sexual experiences to menstrual periods to prostitution and more—all through the eyes of women. The monologue about childhood sexual abuse and denied innocence took my breath away.

At the end of the play, Jane, who's been public about her childhood abuse as an eight-year-old, stood center stage.

"This has been a powerful night and the stories you've heard have been shared from a place of vulnerability, pain, and truth," she said. "There is power in sharing our stories and power in the

prologue

collective. We are experiencing a moment of clarity and of shared vulnerability with the #MeToo movement, and my guess is that this room is full of people who can say 'Yes, me too.'" She paused briefly. "I didn't plan to do this, but there is power in knowing you're not alone. So if you have been sexually abused, raped, harassed, assaulted, catcalled, or hurt, I want to give you an opportunity to say 'Me too.' I invite you to stand if you say 'Me too.'"

A stunned silence fell over the auditorium.

Dave grabbed my hand in my lap and squeezed. I wasn't sure if it was a squeeze of support that he loves me, a squeeze of affirmation that I'm part of #MeToo, or a squeeze to say "You should stand."

Heavy feelings of dread and anxiety cascaded through my body. I hesitated, not wanting to be the only one in the room who stood. I heard rustling behind me but didn't dare look back to see if other women were standing. I feared Jane and the other celebrities, standing up on the stage just feet from me, would judge me for not being brave enough to stand without making sure it was safe first.

I couldn't look up or back. I couldn't even move.

Suddenly, a wave of shame engulfed me; I didn't want to admit to a room full of strangers or to Jane Fonda that I'd been a victim.

And then a second wave of shame hit me for not "owning" my past, for not leaning into the moment and declaring "My past does not define me."

I had two options: one—stand and publicly proclaim "I've been molested, raped, assaulted, harassed, and taken advantage of." Or two—lie and stay sitting and publicly proclaim "No, I don't identify with the stories I've just seen, heard, and been moved by."

The choice was physically painful. I felt it in the tightening of my jaw, the building heat behind my eyes, and the ache in my stomach.

dumb girl

I can't do it, I thought. I wasn't ready to stand—not then, not there, at least not in the way that was being asked of me.

But then I looked down at Dave's hand, interlaced with mine. He was the primary witness of the painful and long-lasting effects of the physical, sexual, and emotional childhood abuse I'd endured. He'd lovingly held me countless nights over the years as I woke up screaming from visceral and painful nightmares and flashbacks.

I couldn't *not* stand, not with Dave sitting next to me knowing all that he knew.

So I stood.

But not in power.

I stood in reluctance, in embarrassment, and out of obligation. And as I stood, I fixed my eyes on Jane's fashionable black high-heeled boots, unable to meet her eyes and see what I assumed I would see reflected in them: pride and admiration of the rising crowd. Because I didn't feel pride.

I only felt shame.

That experience left me disappointed in myself—full of doubt about my internal strength, mortified that I'd ever thought of myself as brave.

But it was also a catalyst.

I was pissed. Pissed that I still carried the shame, sadness, guilt, and anger caused by the abuse from my childhood; pissed that after years of therapy I was still embarrassed about it; pissed that I couldn't join in a spontaneous moment of solidarity because the ghost of my abuse still inhabited my body; pissed that even after my two decades of advocacy work and all the ways in which that work had taught me to stand in my own power, I could still feel so unsure and weak—compelled to curl up and hide.

So I decided there was only one thing to do—tell my story so publicly that I'd no longer be able to control it. I'd spent a lifetime protecting myself from shame by only telling my story to a select few friends over the years, when I felt safe. Well, no more.

prologue

I decided then and there: I need the stories to leave my body; I no longer want to hold on to who and when and where people find out what I've been through. I want to celebrate the power I have, the lessons I've learned, and the empathy that is such a big part of who I am. I want to be able to meet Jane Fonda's eyes and feel an authentic connection with a room full of women who say "Yes, me too!"

I'm ready to stand, now, here, and in a way that feels empowering for me and for others who also want to shed the shame, embarrassment, and indignity of abuse.

I'm ready to tell the world, loud and clear: "It happened to me, and I will no longer live in shame."

PART ONE

chapter 1

prison

I was surrounded by a dozen or so convicted murderers and rapists serving life sentences at a men's prison in San Luis Obispo, California.

Thirty minutes earlier I'd gone through an extremely sensitive metal detector where a tall, very serious guard with a neatly trimmed mustache "processed" me and took my scarf away because "it could be used to strangle you." He replaced the scarf with a large panic button I was instructed to wear on my beltless pants in case there was an emergency, aka a riot, where the guards needed to locate and save me. It was a little surreal. I'd been warned ahead of time not to wear an underwire bra, because "the prisoners could stab you with it in a riot." So here I was.

It was the first time I'd ever been inside a prison, and as I walked through the corridors I became hyper aware of myself. My footsteps felt louder than they should, as the *click, click* sound of my loafers echoed off the barren hallway. I kept my gaze fixed ahead, avoiding eye contact with inmates who passed by as I nervously walked through several heavy metal doors that each buzzed and clanked, shutting behind me and my escort.

After stern guards checked and rechecked my ID at several checkpoints, I finally arrived in a small drab classroom where I sat on a cold gray metal chair and waited for the prisoners to

dumb girl

arrive. Even though the room was cold, my palms were sweaty. I wondered, *Why have I just flown a thousand miles to sit in a room with men who are guilty of horrendous crimes?*

I knew the answer, of course: I had written a book called *Beyond the Bullet* several years earlier about nineteen people who'd lost a loved one to gun violence. After one of this prison's inmates, who was part of a restorative justice program, had stumbled upon it, he'd asked the program director if my book could be part of their twelve-month curriculum.

When the director reached out to me and asked if I'd come and share what I know about crime victims from interviewing and writing the book, I'd immediately said yes.

It had seemed like a good idea at the time.

The prisoners arrived one at a time and appeared anxious as they came over to me and introduced themselves. They clearly thought I was "a famous author," and they were nervous to meet me. I repressed my instinct to relieve their anxiety with a handshake or hug, as I'd been told it was best to avoid physical contact with them. The awkwardness of not greeting them in my authentic, relaxed, and physical way made me feel insincere. I compensated with lots of nodding, a big smile, and soft eye contact.

After the facilitator introduced me, I noticed how each prisoner nervously held his copy of the book—I'd sent signed paperbacks for all of them a month earlier—each of which was now battered and dog-eared from numerous reads. I listened intently, trying not to look at the large muscular tattooed arms bulging out of some of their baby-blue CDCR PRISONER–stamped uniforms.

I shifted uncomfortably in my unforgiving, cold metal folding chair as each prisoner in the tight circle took his turn telling me how grateful he was to have received my book and explaining which story he most related to. One guy, who had a hard and stiff body but soft eyes, told me he most related to Michelle, a woman

prison

in the book who was consumed with anger for years after her teenage son was killed at a party.

"Reading your book has made me think a lot more deeply about the teenager I killed," he said. "I now understand that taking his life impacted not just him, but it's impacted his family, his friends, the community, and even how police do their job; they police differently now, all because of what I did."

Another guy confessed that during his parole hearings he hadn't understood why his victim's mom was still so angry, even though he'd killed her daughter decades earlier. "After reading your book, now I get it," he said through sobs. "Her pain will never go away, and she will always hate me, and I have to live with that. She'll never forgive me, and I know I don't deserve forgiveness."

I held back tears as the large man next to him, who was just a little too big for his chair, gently put a comforting hand on his shoulder. Their shame was palpable, and I understood the power of naming it and saying it out loud.

The men read stories from the book to me as if I hadn't heard them before, their voices reflecting the anguish, guilt, and remorse of those in the book. It was a surreal experience—painful but beautiful. I was overwhelmed with gratitude that I could experience, firsthand, the impact those nineteen stories had on men who'd been caged for twenty to thirty years, men who were just teenagers when they'd committed their awful crimes.

Their honesty, vulnerability, and humanity struck me in a way I had not anticipated, and my defenses melted away. Most of these men would never walk free again—being a part of the restorative justice program wouldn't reduce their sentence, give them privileges, or make their daily lives any better—yet they were voluntarily participating in a program where they had to explore and confront the pain they'd caused.

I admired their bravery in being willing to examine their past. I felt their anguish. I felt compassion for them.

dumb girl

I also felt guilt as I thought about the people I'd interviewed for the book. I wondered, *Am I breaking some kind of covenant with those nineteen people who've confided their unimaginable pain to me?* I was sitting in a room with perpetrators similar to the people who'd murdered their loved ones.

The dichotomy made my head spin; suddenly, it was hard to concentrate. My heart was heavy for the victims in my book *and* for the guys sitting across from me who were pouring their hearts out to me, a stranger who was validating their existence, their regret, and the deep pain they feel every day.

But I was familiar with experiencing this kind of emotional contradiction—withholding a multitude of seemingly deeply conflicting feelings all at once. After all, I'd been doing it my entire life.

It starts when I'm five.

I'm sitting in my bedroom doing my homework when my dad punches me in the nose. The pain is intense as blood drips down into my yellow Mickey Mouse trash can. But the shock of what's just happened is equally overwhelming.

I love my bright-yellow second-story bedroom at the back of our house. My twin bed is covered with a yellow-and-white checkered bedspread and yellow canopy, making me feel like I'm a princess in a Disney movie. There's a small brown 1920s-style school desk in the corner, a family heirloom that resembles Laura Ingles's desk from one of my favorite TV shows, *The Little House on the Prairie*. From my room, I can see our backyard and the neighboring suburban houses, which become inspiration for the elaborate stories and fun family outings my dolls will go on.

But when Dad appears at my bedroom door today, I'm not playing with my dolls, I'm sitting at my "Little House" desk lost in concentration, practicing writing my name on ruled paper and trying to stay inside the red-and-blue lines. I started kindergarten

prison

just a few weeks ago, and I'm excited to finally have big-kid homework and big-kid teachers.

Dad's six-foot-three angular frame fills the doorway. I look up and smile at him.

With an angry bite in his voice, he asks, "What are you looking at?"

"Just you," I cheerfully reply in my innocent five-year-old voice.

"Well, don't look at me," he barks. "Do your homework!" And then he leaves in a huff.

I retrace the *H* in my name and wonder, *What's he so mad about?*

A few minutes later, Dad walks back into my room and I look up at him again.

"Don't look at me!" he screams. "Do your homework!"

Tears sting my eyes as I lower them to my paper. He disappears. I desperately try to understand why I can't look at him when he comes into my room, but it makes no sense to me.

He returns once again, and I try really hard not to look at him despite feeling his presence in the doorway. I really, really try, but slowly, slowly, my gaze shifts from the sheet of paper with my half-written name . . . up to him. I think maybe he needs to tell me something.

I'm wrong.

He flies across the room, yanks me out of the desk by my thin arm, and holds me so close to his face that I can smell his breath and feel the heat of his anger. With one quick motion, he pushes me back slightly and punches me in the nose.

I feel a sharp pain and hear a pop in my ear. I crumple to the floor, feeling my nose running along with my tears. As I bring my hand down after wiping my nose with the back of my hand, I see the blood.

So does he.

He grabs my arm again and yanks me over to my trash can

in the corner of the room and barks, "Don't drip blood on the carpet!"

He holds me over Mickey, and we both listen to the metallic *ping, ping, ping* sounds of blood dripping onto the bottom of the tin can and the echo created in the sudden silence.

He quickly stands up and says, "Stay there, I'll be right back," and abruptly leaves.

I continue to hang my head above Mickey while I taste the saltiness of my blood. I don't know where he's gone, and I wonder if I should look at him when he comes back.

A minute later, he returns, and he's carrying a wad of toilet paper from the bathroom. I can feel the change—the softening in his mood. He gently leads me from the trash can, sits me on the bed, and holds the toilet paper up to my nose.

"I'm really sorry, but you shouldn't have looked up," he explains.

"Okay, I'll do better next time, Daddy," I promise as I lean into his warm embrace, grateful for his sudden kindness.

My nose heals, but Mickey's big black eyes and infectious smile are forever stained by drops of dried blood, memorializing that day.

A few months later, Dad, Mom, my two older brothers, my little brother, and I are sitting in our van at a stoplight. The light turns green, and we inch forward. Suddenly, there's an earsplitting crashing sound of glass breaking and metal crunching.

The world around us goes out of focus as our yellow-and-white van spins like a top. Butterflies enter my five-year-old stomach like on a merry-go-round, and the world seems to whizz by in a fuzzy dream, at least until the spinning slowly comes to a soundless halt.

For a moment, the van is quiet and still, and time stops.

prison

Gradually, awareness creeps in. I realize I'm now on the front bench of the van, lying awkwardly on the laps of my older brothers, Doug and Philip. The quiet is interrupted by Dad yelling and Mom moaning as she touches her bleeding head. I don't know what happened or why Mom is bleeding, but everyone seems upset. I feel upset too and somehow know the appropriate response for what just happened is to cry.

I try, but I can't. I've never been in a car crash before, and I don't know what shock is.

Two hours ago, the six of us, Mom, Dad, Doug, Philip, Robby, and I piled into our yellow-and-white striped 1962 Ford van to drive across town to see my aunt and uncle's new baby. On our way to their house, Robby and I instinctively crawled over the front bench to our assigned seats on the back bench, where we entertained ourselves by making faces and waving at the cars we passed, the goal to get them to laugh or wave back. Robby's bright-red hair and two-year-old cute round face covered in freckles always seem to do the trick.

"The boys," Doug and Philip, who are thirteen and nine respectively, get front-bench privileges for being born before us "little kids." Because Doug is eight years older than me, I view him as a pseudo parent, more than a brother or peer. I think he's cool because he's nice to me; is good at basketball, track, and tennis; and looks like Shaun Cassidy, the 1970s blond teen heartthrob, singer, and actor.

Philip lacks the athletic prowess and muscle definition Doug was gifted. His bigger-than-life personality makes up for his goofy smile from genetically missing teeth and perpetually sunburnt and peeling nose from days spent at the local swimming pool and tennis courts, under the intense Colorado sun.

When we pulled up to my aunt and uncle's house, I was

dumb girl

excited to see my brand-new baby cousin despite my disappointment in still being the only girl in the family. I'd brought two of my dolls' dresses but was not allowed to dress up my baby cousin and carry him around like I do with my dolls. I made do by putting the dresses on his new teddy bears while "the boys" and the adults carefully passed his tiny body around and coddled him.

When it was time to go, Dad got behind the wheel and Mom took her customary position with her head resting against the passenger side window, dozing off while the local news station played on the radio.

Ten minutes later, the world was spinning. And then it stopped.

An ambulance with very serious men in uniforms arrive. They carefully move Mom onto a stretcher and into an ambulance while Philip, eyes wide and scared, gingerly crawls in next to her.

One of the men leans down and explains, "We're taking your mommy and brother to the hospital for observation."

I don't know what "observation" means. Dad doesn't explain but says he's going with them. I desperately want to go in the ambulance too and don't understand why Philip gets to go and I don't.

Doug, Robby, and I sit on the curb watching a dirty and rusted tow truck back up to our smooshed van. The air is hazy, despite it being a sunny fall afternoon, and smells like burnt marshmallows. A large man with a big mustache and badge waits with us for our uncle to come get us, which doesn't make sense since we just saw him.

Only later do I learn the whole story: We were hit by a drunk driver. Apparently, he had a fight with his wife, got drunk, got in his car, ran a red light going 65 miles per hour, and hit us and another car before landing upside down in a ditch. He died in the crash.

prison

Mom gets a few cuts on the side of her head. Her cuts heal, but she never stops being startled whenever she sees a car approaching on the passenger side of the car. Philip is uninjured.
Dad suffers back pain for the next sixty years.

Seat belts don't become legally mandatory in Colorado until 1987, thirteen years after our crash, but they become an important part of our van rides post-accident for the next few years. We're repeatedly told to put them on, but most of the time, Robby and I take them off, knowing Mom and Dad can't see they're off unless Philip tells on us.

I don't like wearing seat belts because they make tickle fights with Robby harder. But when we're caught not wearing them we get yelled at—and sometimes even get kicked out of the van.

We're on our ninety-minute drive up Interstate 70 to our family cabin in the Rocky Mountains, and it's cold and snowing. I poke Philip in the back of the head out of boredom.

He turns around, looks me in the eyes, and says, "Knock it off."

I poke him again because . . . well, I'm bored and I'm six.

He yells out, "Heidi doesn't have her seat belt on!"

Dad pulls the van over to the side of the road, opens the door, and makes me get out as he yells about how important seat belts are to my safety.

Then he drives away.

This has happened before, and each time I've been so convinced Dad won't come back to get me that I've memorized the route so I'll be able to walk to the cabin or back home, whichever is closest. I'm really good at knowing where I am, which town we've just passed, and which town is coming up. And I've made contingency plans. I keep my coat, hat, and mittens near me so I can easily grab them when I get kicked out, and I've created a story to tell the adults at the next town when they ask why a six-year-old is walking alone on Interstate 70 in the snow.

dumb girl

This time, though, I forget to grab my coat, hat, and mittens. And as usual, it's unclear to me if Dad is coming back. I'm terrified, but I know it's my fault. *I'm a bad girl for not wearing a seat belt*, I think. I feel I deserve to be abandoned.

When Dad finally comes back for me, I feel immense gratitude and appreciation that he still loves me despite me being a bad girl. Flooded with gratitude and fear, I hop back into the van with tears streaming down my cheeks, which is met with scorn.

"Don't be such a D-B-A-D-G, Heidi," Dad says as I shut the door and climb onto the warm back bench next to Robby, who looks at me with big, anxious, empathetic eyes.

chapter 2

d-b-a-d-g

D-B-A-D-G was the family mantra for me growing up. It meant "Don't Be a Dumb Girl."

Simple. To the point. Self-explanatory.

It meant don't be dumb. And it meant don't be a girl. It was a reminder that I wasn't a boy, I was less than, and I could do better.

Everyone in my family used it with me—even my mom. I leaned into the mantra physically, spiritually, and emotionally.

I was reminded not to be a dumb girl constantly throughout my childhood. It was said in a cruel way, a funny way, a serious way, a sarcastic way, and a loving way, and each time I felt the words deeply.

DBADG became a noun or a verb—as in "Heidi, stop being a DBADG," or "Heidi, don't DBADG on the roller coaster," or "Why are you throwing like a DBADG?" But mostly it was just stated simply: "Heidi, DBADG." It didn't make sense grammatically, but it made sense to me. I worked hard not to be the dumb girl I was assumed to be. I learned not to react with a scream when I saw a spider or large bug, or complain when I was cold or hungry or had to pee, or cry if I was hurt or scared or sad, or really to show any kind of "weakness," which was considered a girl trait.

That included sucking my thumb.

dumb girl

☙

I'm five and three-quarters now and Dad has decided I'm too old to suck my thumb. Which is how I've ended up lying here in the dark with a bulky black ski glove on my right hand.

I know Dad is right—I need to stop. I'm in kindergarten, and I've heard kids at school making fun of thumb-suckers.

And I've tried to stop. I've tried to muster up the self-control not to suck my thumb. I've tried to think of clever strategies to make my thumb less tempting: I've slept on my side, wedging my hands between my knees. I've put my hands together under my head. I've prayed to God to help me have the willpower to stop. I've sucked on my sleeve like Robby does and I've counted sheep, but nothing has worked.

Every night for the last few weeks I've allowed myself to suck for just five minutes and promised myself I'll stop right before going to sleep. But morning after morning, Dad's delivered the disappointing news that he found my thumb in my mouth the night before when checking on me.

Now it's not just me trying to stop; Dad's involved, which means failure equals punishment. His solution? I wear a ski glove on my right hand while I sleep.

I don't like wearing a glove; it's making my hand all sweaty, and only wearing one glove feels uneven. I lie here for what feels like hours, but I can't go to sleep.

Finally, I give in to my need to suck and take the glove off. Nothing feels quite as good or comforting as falling asleep with my soft and familiar-tasting thumb in my mouth in my warm, safe bed.

I'll only suck for five minutes and then put the glove back on, I promise myself.

But the next thing I know, I'm waking up and the glove is not on my hand. It's next to me. I failed to put it back on my hand before falling asleep. I pull the covers off, swing my feet over the edge of the bed, and pick up the glove, my head heavy from failure and disappointment in my lack of willpower.

I cautiously walk down the stairs for breakfast, trying to figure out what I'm going to say to Dad. I sit next to him at the kitchen table, trying to decipher his mood while we wait for Mom to bring over the pancakes. The smell of bacon fills the room.

I sense his frustration with me. "Daddy, I'm so sorry I took the glove off. I was just gonna suck my thumb for a minute, but I accidentally fell asleep. I'm so so sorry and I promise that tonight I'll do better and won't forget," I beg. "Please don't be mad at me."

He shakes his head in disappointment, plunges his fork into one of Mom's pancakes, and says, "Just don't suck your thumb in the first place and then you won't have to remember to put the glove back on."

I nod in agreement, and we eat in silence.

This goes on for a week. Me trying. Me failing. Me begging for forgiveness and asking for another chance, like an addict begging for another chance at self-control.

Finally, Dad's fed up. He comes into my room as I'm getting ready for bed, putting on my favorite pink-and-white flannel Barbie nightgown.

"I've figured out a solution to your problem," he announces. "You'll wear the glove, but this time you won't be able to get it off, because I'm going to tape it on."

I picture Scotch tape. He uses duct tape.

He sits next to me on my bed as I watch him pull the sticky edge of the thick gray tape away from the roll, wrapping it around my arm repeatedly from my wrist to my elbow. He then uses his teeth to hold the tape as he rips it away from the roll. It's tight and uncomfortable and I realize there's no way I'll be able to get it off.

For the next several nights, my bedtime ritual begins with a prayer on my knees with my elbows propped up on the edge of my bed, followed by duct tape being wrapped around my right arm before I crawl into my bed with my favorite, yellow teddy bear, where I struggle to go to sleep.

Every morning is agony as Dad peels the heavy, sticky tape off my skin.

"It'll hurt a lot less if I rip it off fast," he explains. "Just pretend I'm taking off a Band-Aid."

I close my eyes in an attempt to somehow shield myself from the sting that's about to happen.

He yanks the tape; the sting bites me. Closing my eyes didn't help. I squirm and moan and start to cry.

"Don't be a DBADG," he says as he continues to rip.

The deep-red marks that remain and the lingering pain prove to me that he's wrong, it's not just like taking off a Band-Aid. But that doesn't stop me from leaning into his warm hug once the tape is off as he praises me for breaking a bad habit.

At five, I don't have the vocabulary to describe the discouragement I feel for not being able to stop sucking my thumb without Dad intervening, and I certainly don't feel brave for enduring the painful process of removing the duct tape from my thin and sensitive skin each morning.

What I am unaware of but will later—much later—come to understand is that I'm at the beginning of building an inner grit I'll depend on throughout my tumultuous and abusive childhood, and a determination that will help me in my adult years as I advocate for others who've experienced profound pain.

chapter 3

columbine

My adult life is divided into two parts: before and after the shooting.

It was April 20, 1999. I was a stay-at-home mom in Vancouver, Washington, keeping busy with Aaron, an active two-year-old, and his five-year-old big sister, Sami.

That morning was especially busy: a late wakeup forced me to skip my morning shower and make a quick bowl of cold cereal for the kids (Aaron promptly spilled it all over his Bob the Builder shirt). When breakfast was done, I struggled to convince Sami to put on her coat as we headed out the door for the twenty-minute drive to her preschool, which was going to start in fifteen minutes. Frustrated by her unbending stand of independence at this particular moment, I finally gave her a choice: "Okay, so how 'bout you choose either the yellow coat or the pink coat and it just stays next to you in the car?"

Uncrossing her arms, she barked, "Fine!" grabbed the pink coat, and headed out to the garage with the confidence of a five-year-old win.

Three months into his new PR job, Dave, my husband of nine years, happened to be working from home on that cold, rainy April morning in 1999. He followed me out to the garage

dumb girl

and put Aaron into his car seat. The roll of his eyes at the chaos we created by having two kids made me laugh and relax before he kissed me and said, "Nice parenting back there. You think you'll be back around eleven?"

"Yeah, I'll grab groceries at Safeway after Aaron's music class and then head home," I said as I put the key in the ignition and leaned over to kiss him again. "Love you."

"Love you too," he said before I shut the car door, turned the key, and backed out of the garage.

When I walked in the door later that morning with Aaron on my hip and a grocery bag in my hand, Dave greeted me with a kiss and said, "I think your high school is on TV."

Sure enough, it was. My heart sank as I sat on our couch, my elbows on my knees and hands on my cheeks, watching student after student run, with hands over their heads, out of the same doorways I'd used every morning and afternoon when I'd gone to Columbine High School thirteen years earlier.

I couldn't keep my eyes off the live feed, and I was horrified by the unimaginable nightmare I saw unfolding on-screen. I watched a bleeding student fall out of a second-story library window and land in the arms of two SWAT members. I saw a handmade sign in another window that read "1 bleeding to death." It consumed me.

I thought of the four teachers who had meant the most to me at Columbine, all of whom were still teaching there, and prayed they'd survive.

That evening, through a series of emotional phone calls with Mom and Dad, I learned that Dave Sanders, my former basketball coach, had been killed inside the school. He was the "1 bleeding to death."

I was devastated. That night I lay in bed visualizing the library, where most of the students died, the library I'd gone to dozens and dozens of times. I tried to imagine what I would have done, where I would have hidden, and what it must have felt like—the chaos, the fear, the blood, the pain. I tried to envision what the kids who died looked like. It was inconceivable.

Earlier that evening, Jefferson County Sheriff John Stone had said on TV that the fire sprinklers and alarms had gone off for hours, flooding the library. He had explained that the bodies had to remain in the bullet-ridden, flooded library while the police scoured the building for bombs and booby traps. That fact in particular really bothered me.

I couldn't stop thinking about it.

Later that week, I flew to Denver from my home outside Portland, Oregon, to attend the large public memorial and pay my respects to Coach Sanders at his funeral.

My oldest brother, Doug, went with me to the large outdoor memorial service held at a Cineplex parking lot a half mile from Columbine, along with sixty-five thousand other mourners, including Vice President Al Gore. The Secret Service agents with sniper rifles overlooking the crowd from the roof of the movie theater unnerved me. I couldn't take my eyes off their large evil-looking rifles and found it ironic that we were there because young men had guns, and now we were being kept safe by more guys with guns.

Five days later, my other older brother, Philip, and I sat at Dave Sanders's funeral inside a former Kmart that had been repurposed into a church. The walls were a colorless tan and the lack of natural light from windows gave a somber and cave-like feel that matched the mood of the thousand heartbroken mourners in the room.

We listened to students tell the story of Coach Sanders's selflessness and heroism as he warned and directed students and staff to safety before being fatally shot. I thought about the kindness and patience he had shown me in my sophomore year when he was my basketball coach.

I'd been struggling to maintain my position on the varsity team and was briefly demoted onto his JV team to get more playing experience. I was reeling from what I saw as an embarrassing downgrade, and he took me aside and explained, "This isn't a bad thing. This is an opportunity for you to shine, to lead, and to have court time where you can turn into the great player you are destined to become." And then he gave me advice I'd use throughout my life: "You're trying too hard. You've got to just relax a little and let things develop naturally rather than forcing it. I think you'll see improvement once you stop trying to control everything on the court."

It was a hard thing to put into practice as a sixteen-year-old, but he was right, and once I followed his advice, I got better. I stopped turning the ball over and became a triple threat, averaging twelve points, ten assists, and ten rebounds a game. I soon earned my spot back on the varsity team.

At the funeral, student after student told similar stories of how Dave Sanders had touched their lives in the classroom and on athletic courts and fields. As I sat there seeing so many former teachers and classmates broken with heartache and inconceivable pain, I vowed to myself that I'd do everything in my power to stop more senseless shootings like this from happening. That day, I turned from stay-at-home mom to activist mom—a woman highly motivated to make the world a safer place.

What I didn't realize at the time was how transformative this pivot would be in my journey to confront and heal from my own complex trauma.

"It just needs one more spoon of sugar," Robby tells me as he sips from the white Styrofoam cup of lukewarm coffee into which I've just put six heaping spoonfuls of sugar.

columbine

I fill the spoon, dump the sugar in his cup, and stir it with the coffee-stained silver spoon. "Perfect!" he says, smiling, just before a petite lady with a wrinkly face and white bun catches us and shoos us out of the room.

"The coffee is only for adults," she scolds us. "Scoot!"

St. Matthew Presbyterian Church is not just where I'm learning to drink coffee with lots of sugar; it's also our family's spiritual home and the center of our social life. When we are not at home, school, or our cabin, we're at church. Mom and Dad are deacons who sing in the choir, usher, help plan Sunday school, sit on several committees, and are family friends with the minister and his wife.

We frequently throw noisy and festive church parties at our house where the adults drink lots of wine, tell stories I don't understand, and laugh at jokes I don't think are funny. We also host numerous Bible studies where at the end of the night I'm required to kiss the dozen or so mostly male adult church members goodnight, one by one. I'm often uncomfortable, aware of my prepubescent nakedness under my thin, translucent nightgown.

In church we learn not to lie, steal, cheat, or take the Lord's name in vain. Mom and Dad add a couple more rules: We're not allowed to say "shut up" or "stupid."

Growing up in a family with three brothers, I find it extremely difficult not to say "shut up." Telling them to "be quiet" when they annoy me just doesn't have the punch I need to express how I'm feeling.

One day as we're coming home from church, Robby is being particularly annoying to me and I can't get him to stop. We're sitting in the jump seat at the back of our wood-paneled station wagon, which doesn't have a lot of room. He keeps looking at me and touching my leg, so I tell him to stop touching me. Because he's five, he responds by putting his finger a half inch from my leg and says over and over, "I'm not touching you, I'm not touching you."

dumb girl

After I tell him to be quiet over and over again and it doesn't work, I finally yell, "Shut up!"

Dad shouts back from behind the wheel, "Heidi, what have I told you about saying bad words? I'll deal with you when we get home."

When we arrive home, he yanks me out of the car, drags me upstairs to the bathroom, grabs a thin bar of lime-green Dial soap sitting next to the sink, and runs it under the water before aggressively inserting it into my mouth. He mumbles under his breath, "This hurts me more than it hurts you," as he moves the bar side to side and in and out of my mouth, scraping it against the back of my teeth.

The bitter chemical taste makes me gag, and I try to steady myself by grabbing the avocado-green and harvest-gold floral towel hanging on my left. The bitterness and fear overwhelm me, and despite my attempt to keep my emotions at bay, tears start rolling down my cheeks.

"Stop being such a DBADG," Dad insists. He yanks the soap out, scraping my one new front tooth that's started to grow in, and throws it onto the counter, where it splits in two. He grabs the handle of the door, looks back at me and says, "Now stay here and think about what you've done," before he walks out, slamming the door behind him.

I'm suddenly transported back to when he punched me in the nose, three years ago, when I was five. I don't trust that he won't come back, won't be angry if I wash the soap out. *What if he hits me again?* I think. But I need to get the soap out.

I lean over the sink, and as quietly as I can, let the soap drip out of my mouth.

I don't dare turn on the tap for fear he'll hear it and return. Paranoia engulfs me. I sit on the counter, trying to figure out how to get the awful taste out of my mouth.

That's when I see the toilet. I tiptoe over to it, carefully lift

columbine

the lid, put my face in the bowl until my tongue reaches the water, and then lap it up like a dog, quietly spitting it out until the bitterness of the soap is gone.

But now I'm paralyzed—afraid to make any noise, leave the bathroom, or do much of anything. Dad is capable of worse punishments than jamming a bar of soap in my mouth. I'm trapped physically and emotionally, and the fear of not knowing what he'll do if I do "it" wrong is terrifying.

I sit in that bathroom for a long, long time.

A year after the Columbine massacre, I found myself in Washington, DC, for the Million Mom March.

I spent part of the morning before the march at the White House, talking to President Bill Clinton and First Lady Hillary Clinton about the massacre and legislation that could have stopped it. Three hours later, I stood behind a stage with my VIP pass hanging from a lanyard around my neck, just feet away from Susan Sarandon, Courtney Love, and Bette Midler, listening to a woman on stage yell to the crowd, "We love our children more than you love your damn guns!"

How am I even here? I wondered.

The Million Mom March was a grassroots march and rally held on Mother's Day 2000. A staggering 750,000 people had come together to call on Congress to pass stricter gun control laws. Many of us were there because of the tragedy at Columbine. I was one of the state organizers.

I'd been anxious to "do something" about gun violence since Columbine. The march was "something," and it felt big. I'd been asked to lead a group of moms from Oregon to Washington, DC, after one of the organizers read an op-ed I'd written for *The Oregonian*.

I had quickly become part of a network of women across the

dumb girl

nation who were organizing buses, planes, trains, and cars full of people to attend the march. We had three months to get organized, so I'd made hundreds of phone calls, printed and posted thousands of flyers advertising the march, and held logistic meetings at the local library. The kids' nap time and after dinner became my "work time." I felt part of something that mattered, and I was inspired by other passionate women across the country who, like me, wanted change.

Now, listening to the impassioned woman speaking onstage, I thought about Columbine—and Jamal.

An hour earlier, as I left the White House and headed over to the main stage on the National Mall, I'd noticed a woman wearing a T-shirt with a photo of a child and a date above and below the photo.

I quickly realized the photo was probably of her child, who'd been shot and killed.

I wondered what her story was.

As I continued, I came upon another woman who was sitting on a bench under a tree, waving a church fan to cool herself down. She was wearing a similar T-shirt. It had a photo of a small boy with big eyes and an infectious smile, and under the photo it said "Jamal, 1992–1998."

I approached her timidly and said, "Excuse me. I've noticed your shirt and was wondering if you could tell me about Jamal?"

She looked up at me while she took a drink from her water bottle and said, "Yeah, he was my only son, and he was shot in a drive-by shooting when he was playing on our front porch. He was six."

I silently gasped and bowed my head. "I'm so sorry."

"I just hope we can stop all this madness," she said. "I don't want anyone else to feel this kinda way. He was a good boy and didn't deserve to die, especially like that."

columbine

"Yeah, I think today's a good start in ending all this terrible violence," I agreed, and then added, "I'm so glad you're here. I really appreciate you telling me about your son. I think stories like yours will make a big difference."

"Thank you too, for being here. I sure hope it makes a difference," she said before rifling through her bag.

Sensing she was ready for the conversation to end, I said, "Hope you have a great day," and continued walking to the stage. My heart broke for her, and I was in awe of her for having the strength to get out of bed every day. She was living my worst nightmare.

As I got closer to the stage, I passed dozens of women with similar shirts, different photos, different dates. Their outward and public display of their loss and pain took my breath away. Their eyes were haunted, and they held themselves as though they'd been defeated, but at the same time they gave off an aura of defiance, a proclamation that their child was loved and their life had been unfairly cut short.

The five-hour march was more of a massive rally on the mall, just steps from the Capitol. Politicians gave passionate and polished speeches about bills they'd be introducing or supporting. Choirs sang about peace and love. Celebrities delivered angry rants questioning the lack of action by Congress. Ministers prayed for peace and action, and mothers gave emotional testimonies about dead children and unrealized potential.

It was an exhausting yet exhilarating day. By the end of it, I understood that it wasn't so much about the event—it was about what all 750,000 of us would do when we returned to our communities to stop gun violence.

I felt inspired and ready to continue the fight.

When I got home the next night, I thought again about Jamal's mom, and I hugged my kids in a way I'd never hugged them

dumb girl

before. The missed showers, the spilled cereal, and the struggle to put on coats and shoes suddenly didn't matter anymore. I imagined she wished she still had these inconveniences and frustrations.

As I grappled with my newfound awareness that life is not guaranteed, I began to appreciate Sami and Aaron in a way that was deeper and more wholehearted than it had been. I resolved to never take them or Dave for granted, and to fully embrace the chaos and ups and downs of parenting.

And I vowed I would do everything in my power to make the world a safer place for my children.

chapter 4

vigil at the park

As I stood on the large gazebo stage in the middle of our city park, I noticed a dozen or more bearded men, many in camouflage clothing, walking around the park with handmade signs that read "Guns don't kill people, people kill people" and "Gun control is using both hands." The organizer told me, "Just ignore them. They come to stuff like this all the time—it's just part of the deal."

Her confidence only slightly quenched my worry, which was that the gun guys might be armed.

In the months since the Million Mom March, I had become fully engaged in all things gun control. I'd written letters to the editor and appeared on numerous local TV shows to talk about Columbine, the Million Mom March, and my efforts to stop gun violence. The media was interested in my story—a local activist who had graduated from Columbine. They seemed fascinated by how I went from a stay-at-home mom to a gun control activist who willingly contended with vitriol and animosity. "Not very mom-like," one reporter said to me.

Some of the stay-at-home moms in my neighborhood were less than impressed. They grumbled at the attention I was getting after reading about me in the newspaper and seeing me on TV. One mom, who'd graduated from an Oregon high school

dumb girl

where a fifteen-year-old student killed two students and injured twenty-five others after killing his parents, said, "My high school was shot up, but you don't see me going on TV." Her comment stung and made me feel ostracized, but I was too busy juggling a toddler and a preschooler and fielding media calls to care, and her jealousy felt petty and small.

A couple of months after returning from the march, I'd been invited to help lead a rally/vigil for gun violence victims in a local park. I had no idea what I was doing but it felt important, so I said yes.

It hadn't occurred to me that there would be protesters.

About three-quarters of the way through the event, a minister was giving an emotional speech about the toll gun violence has on families when the gun guys started yelling while slowly and combatively moving toward the stage. I couldn't quite make out what they were yelling but it disrupted the minister's speech, and I became nervous. There was confusion about how to proceed with the program, and the hundred or so people in the crowd were all looking around anxiously.

I froze, unable to act—just like when Robby's coat caught on fire.

Robby and I shiver, huddled up next to each other, waiting for the wood stove to relieve us from the bitter cold. We sit next to the fire holding our hands up to the flames to get warm and to avoid Dad, who's clearly agitated by the cold and the endless chores he needs to do to "open up the cabin." Sitting by the fire keeps us out of his way and safe from irritating him more.

I'm nine and Robby's six, and our family has driven up to our cabin to go skiing. As usual, the heat was off when we arrived.

The first thing Dad does when we get to the cabin is turn on the old furnace, but it takes hours to warm up and it's freezing in here. So he's started a fire in our Ben Franklin stove—an

vigil at the park

old-fashioned black wood stove sitting on a pallet of broken red bricks framed by four black-painted two-by-fours in the corner of the small living room—to jump-start the heating process.

Now Mom's unpacking the food and Dad's shoveling a path to the outhouse. Doug and Philip are busy bringing everything in from the car—skis, ski boots, food, and water—and taking the various duffle bags of warm winter clothes upstairs.

"Heidi," Mom calls, "go help the boys bring in the rest of the groceries."

I do as I'm told; Robby stays next to the fire.

Two minutes later, as I'm walking into the kitchen carrying two paper bags of canned foods and perishables, I hear Dad yelling. I quickly put the bags on the table and run into the other room to see what the commotion is all about.

Dad is ferociously patting the back of Robby's coat to kill the flames as smoke engulfs his backside. Robby's eyes are the size of saucers, and his mouth is open in disbelief. I see what's happened: He's wearing a blue polyester goose-down jacket, and being six years old, he got too close to the fire, causing the nylon to overheat and melt. The fire singed the lining and exposed the goose feathers, which caught on fire.

Dad quickly puts the fire out, but as he does the rage from the fire seems to transfer into him.

"What the hell are you doing, Robby?" he screams. "You can't get that close to the fire! What are you, an idiot? The fire is hot, and if you get that close, things catch on fire!"

He slides Robby's sleeve up to his elbow, sarcastically yelling, "See, the fire is hot, and it can burn you!" Then he grabs his small arm, just below the elbow, and plunges it toward the fire, holding it just inches from the flames.

Robby struggles to back away, but his six-year-old strength is no match for Dad's. His small body and legs desperately try to retreat from the heat as Dad maintains his tight grip on his tiny

dumb girl

arm and moves it even closer to the flames, turning Robby's body into a rope in a cruel game of tug-of-war.

Robby starts screaming and crying, "*No! No!* Okay, I get it! Please stop! I won't do it anymore! It's hot, it's hot!"

Suddenly Dad lets go, and Robby falls backward onto the floor. Dad stands up, slowly adjusting the front of his jacket, and looks down at Robby with disdain.

"Now do you understand? Fire is hot!" he says. "And now we have to get you a new jacket or fix this one!"

Robby slowly nods in defeat as tears run down his red cheeks.

I freeze, unable to move. I feel sorry for Robby and wish I'd been with him to warn him not to get too close. I would have noticed his jacket smoking and would have had him move before it caught on fire.

I stand almost in a trance until Dad walks by me and barks, "What are you looking at? Go get the rest of the stuff out of the car!"

I snap out of it and turn to go fetch more groceries from the car, thankful to have an excuse to escape the chaos. Mom, choosing not to or unable to comment, continues quietly unpacking the groceries, staying out of the way of Dad's anger. Doug and Philip do the same.

The next day, Robby's arm is red, with blisters, and his jacket has four pieces of duct tape to cover the singed nylon and leaking white down. The big silvery square in the middle of a sea of blue on his back makes it much easier to find him on the ski slopes and skating rink that winter. To me, it's a reminder to always stay vigilant to minimize the harm Dad can inflict at any moment, as well as a broader warning: Conflict is dangerous, and to be avoided at any cost.

The feelings of panic, uncertainty, and intimidation that Dad's volatile behavior instilled in me stayed with me well into my adult life. I had long made it a practice to avoid conflict; now

vigil at the park

here I was, surrounded by a bunch of angry, possibly armed men in a park. *What am I doing here?* I asked myself.

Suddenly the minister started singing "God Bless America," which seemed to confuse the gun guys, who were angrily walking toward the stage. I could see in their faces the existential conflict they faced: *Do we continue disrupting this event or stop to join in singing a song that is fundamental to our identity as American patriots?*

Their hesitation was noticeable as they frantically looked at each other trying to figure out what to do. The air turned thick with tension and time stopped.

And then a few people joined the minister in singing; and then a few more. As the crowd started to recognize that the minister was "disarming" the protesters, they joined the chorus, singing loudly and proudly in defiance and unity. When the song ended, the gun guys retreated, and they stayed silent as the minister finished his speech. The rest of the event went on without interruption.

I was amazed at the minister's fortitude and creative problem-solving. It was inspiring to witness someone defuse a group of loud protesters by finding commonality—in this case, a patriotic song they wouldn't want to interrupt.

I was grateful he was the one who was speaking when it happened; I knew if I'd been at the microphone, I would have frozen and everything would have fallen apart. I longed to be that quick on my feet and was frustrated with my tendency to freeze when angry and hot-tempered men were around me.

I hoped, with practice, it was something I could overcome.

chapter 5

ask

I didn't know there'd be so much opposition to my efforts to stop kids from being shot to death. I honestly thought everyone would be against kids being mowed down in their school by a teenager who had easy access to a TEC-9 or sawed-off shotgun.

I was wrong.

I loved working on the gun issue but hated the confrontations. Being in the gun control debate arena was problematic for me because it seemed to require hating the other side. Some people, like the minister at the vigil, handled the angry gun guys with grace and civility, but that was not the way most of the debate was carried out.

Time and time again I saw my friends and advocates get into screaming matches with the gun guys. One friend routinely called them "fucking morons" when she was unable to convince them that they should give up all their guns, which always made me deeply uncomfortable. To her, they were the enemy—but to me, yelling and telling people how stupid they were for their views on guns seemed fruitless and unproductive.

As I became more involved with gun violence prevention advocacy and was forced to navigate an increasing number of tense situations and conversations, I often thought of Carole

ask

Price, whom I'd seen speak at the Million Mom March on behalf of a campaign called Asking Saves Kids (ASK).

When Carole, a thin dark-haired woman with deep frown lines, got on stage in front of 750,000 people to talk about her son, John, she started her speech with "Nineteen months ago, I had to bury my thirteen-year-old son."

She went on to explain that he had gone to a friend's house to play video games and was shot and killed by the nine-year-old brother of his friend. The boy had found their dad's gun.

"When my son went to the neighbor's that day, I'd called to make sure they weren't watching R-rated videos," she said. "It never occurred to me to ask about guns. It's a safe, middle-class neighborhood." She shook her head sorrowfully. "Please ask if there are guns in homes where your children play. I wish I had asked and wonder if my son would still be alive if I had just asked the question."

I was riveted and thought about my two kids at home. Like Carole, I thought I was a good mom who was doing everything I could to keep my kids safe. And like her, I'd never thought about guns in other people's homes before.

She ended her speech with words I'll never forget: "It might be uncomfortable to ask the question, but I can tell you from personal experience, it's a lot more uncomfortable to pick out a casket for your child."

I immediately thought of Michelle.

Michelle lives up the street. We're eleven and in fifth grade together. She's an only child, which fascinates me because she gets all her parents' attention. Her house has a calmness to it that feels soothing and safe, unlike mine. She clearly got her mellow temperament, blond hair, and delicate features from her mom. Besides that, she has a really cool dog, a Great Dane, who's allowed to drink straight from the kitchen faucet. My dog drinks out of the toilet.

dumb girl

In the spring quarter of fifth grade, we're assigned an astronomy project that requires us to partner with a classmate. Every night for two weeks, Michelle and I lie on my backyard lawn, looking up at the dark sky, plotting out the constellations and noticing the changes in the locations of the planets as our assignment requires. As we lie on the cool grass, we talk about classmates, school, soccer, and teachers. We share secret crushes we have on boys and giggle about the funny things our parents do and say as we ponder the vast universe above.

A couple of months later, on a Sunday morning after church, Philip, Robby, and I go to Safeway to buy some groceries Mom asked us to pick up (as well as some candy she definitely didn't ask us to pick up).

Philip is acting really weird and won't let me out of his sight. This is unusual, as we normally split up to get the items on the grocery list so we can quickly get done with this boring chore and change out of our church clothes. Everywhere I go, Philip goes; every aisle I go down, he goes down; and when I say, "I have to go to the bathroom—I'll be right back," he grabs my arm and says, "No, we're almost done. Just wait until we get home."

His attention to me is smothering and irritating. "No seriously, I have to go real bad," I insist. "If I don't go, I'm gonna pee my pants."

"I said no," he barks. "Stop being such a DBADG!"

That evening, Mom and Dad call me into the family room and sit me down at the round table in the corner, which is used for game night when church friends come over but is currently full of random junk, including an abandoned UNO card deck, a Chinese checkers board with two missing pieces, and a dying plant in a harvest-gold crochet cover.

It's weird that we're sitting here. The chaos of the table combined with Mom's and Dad's serious and sullen faces and the

ask

intense eye contact is disconcerting. I'm both scared and curious. They have my full attention.

Mom gently puts her hand on my bare leg and proceeds to tell me that Michelle was abducted and killed last night at her country club, a twenty-minute drive from our house.

They tell me I am safe.

They tell me the police have found and arrested the man who did it.

They tell me they didn't know he'd been arrested until after they got home from church, and that's why Philip wouldn't let me out of his sight.

They tell me it's very sad, and they tell me I can talk to them anytime I need.

They tell me other things, I'm sure, but my mind goes numb as I study Mom's face and the tears that slowly roll down her cheeks. I know crying is the correct and expected response, but like when we were hit by the drunk driver, I can't make the tears flow.

"Do you have any questions?" Mom asks.

I have a million, but I can't formulate any of them into words.

I want to know how she died, why she died, where she died, was she with her parents when she died, why didn't they stop it, and why would someone want to kill her, to start.

A few weeks later I ask Mom what happened to Michelle. She explains, "She'd been swimming at the pool with her mom and dad, and around eight at night she went by herself to use the bathroom in the women's locker room. A maintenance man forced her into a small room in the basement, hit her on the head with a metal pipe, and put a plastic bag over her head. The police were called, and they found Michelle's body at two in the morning in a maintenance room, bound and gagged with a plastic bag over her head."

dumb girl

"Oh, okay," I say, not knowing what to say. "I . . . I don't understand. Why would someone do that to her?"

"I know it's hard to understand," she explains. "Sometimes bad things happen, and it's not fair. It's sad and scary, so you just have to remember the good times you had with her and hold on to those memories."

I'm shocked. Shocked that something like this can happen to an eleven-year-old like me and shocked that Mom seems to think it's all okay now. It doesn't feel like it's all okay. After Mom gives me a hug, I go to my room and pet my cat, Tigger, hoping my stomachache will go away and I'll stop shaking.

I don't go to Michelle's funeral—in fact, I'm not even aware a funeral has taken place until long after the fact. My friends and I don't talk about her death, and neither does my family. When school resumes in the fall, the teachers don't say anything. It feels like she's just another student who's moved to another state because of her dad's job. Several months later, her parents divorce and sell their house, and a new family moves in. The existence of Michelle and her impact on my life simply vanishes.

But her memory continues. I think of Michelle every time I walk by her house or trick-or-treat at her house or look at the constellations and planets in the sky. And it continues, far into my adult life.

Until Michelle, I'd never experienced a death or known anyone who'd died. Because I don't have a way to process Michelle's death and have no way to understand or talk about why what happened to her happened, a morbid curiosity about death grows inside me, along with a great sadness and loneliness that I silently carry with me into adulthood.

After hearing Carole's story at the Million Mom March, I resolved to never let our kids play in a home where guns were accessible. I

ask

figured I couldn't stop all bad things from happening, like what happened to Michelle, but I could absolutely stop my kids from being killed in a home where guns weren't locked up.

I had a chance to put my new resolve to the test a few weeks later, when four-year-old Sami was invited to a birthday party at a house up the street.

A few days before the party, I called the mom and asked my usual questions—"Who'll be watching the kids?" and "Do you have a trampoline?" and "What kind of pets do you have?"

Then, in a tentative voice, I said, "I just have one more safety question. Sami tends to get into things she's not supposed to, so . . . do you have guns in your home?"

"Yeah, we have guns," she said. "But they're stored in a gun safe and the ammunition's stored in a separate safe."

"Okay," I said. "Thank you." I was so relieved that she'd given me such a calm, reasonable answer. I had no idea what I would have said if her response had been "Yeah, we have guns! What about it?"

"I'm so happy you asked," she added. "I'm surprised no one had asked me that before."

What I was amazed by was how easy the conversation had turned out to be. Going in, I'd felt like I was asking a taboo question like "How much money do you make?" What I'd learned from that mom was that it was possible to have a nonconfrontational conversation about a controversial subject. The question wasn't about gun ownership, it was about child safety.

The approach of the ASK campaign made me feel in control, allowed me to be proactive in keeping my kids safe, and gave me a way to talk to other parents and neighbors who were extremely pro-gun. There was no "enemy." Hate and anger were not required in order to protect my children's well-being.

chapter 6

sniper

For three weeks in October of 2002, the Washington, DC, metro area was terrorized by two gunmen who drove around and randomly shot and killed people who were doing normal, everyday activities like pumping gas, mowing lawns, waiting for a bus, or walking to work. The shootings were known as the DC sniper attacks.

After three weeks of paralysis, police finally arrested the DC snipers, who turned out to be two men who had modified their Chevrolet Caprice to be a "rolling sniper's nest," allowing the shooter to fire from the trunk through a small hole above the license plate while his accomplice drove away undetected. All in all, they'd killed ten people and injured three using a Bushmaster XM-15 rifle.

It was premeditated mass murder three thousand miles away, but it turned out there was a relatively local connection: The Bushmaster XM-15 rifle the shooters used was traced to Bull's Eye Shooter Supply, a popular gun store and shooting range in Tacoma, Washington, 135 miles north of our house.

Once the two gunmen were captured and the dead were buried, I was invited by the director of the Seattle gun violence prevention group, Washington CeaseFire, to speak at a press conference in front of Bull's Eye. The purpose was . . . well I didn't know the

sniper

purpose and didn't quite understand why they had reached out to me. It probably had something to do with my connection to Columbine, my being on local TV several times, and my being part of my local, newly formed Million Mom March chapter.

I hadn't been a part of a press conference before and had never met the organizers, but I didn't hesitate to say yes. If there was any chance my participation could help stop future shootings, I was all in. I didn't know what I'd be doing or what I'd be saying but trusted the organizers to guide me and figured I'd just be in the background anyway.

That's not exactly what happened.

The day of the event was a typical Pacific Northwest fall day—cold and dreary. I had dressed in heels (for confidence), nice gray slacks, and a light sweater thinking I'd be inside. But the press conference was very much not inside. Instead, I stood on a cracked and uneven sidewalk in the rain, on a busy street in an industrial area of town—void of trees and cute coffee shops—in front of a gun store with a massive two-story mural of an angry buffalo with a scope for an eye.

Four burly men in heavy raincoats who held large network TV cameras arrived shortly after us, along with three smartly dressed reporters, one of whom had perfect hair neatly swept into a professional updo held in place with what I imagined was a lot of hair spray. She held an umbrella, which, given the light rain, I thought made her smart.

As the organizer, DeAnna, welcomed the small crowd of reporters and cameramen and started her remarks, several intimidatingly large black-and-dark-gray pickup trucks with oversized tires drove slowly by. A scruffy-bearded passenger with a green camouflage baseball hat leaned out of one of the windows and yelled, "Fuck you, gun grabbers!" before he and the driver sped away, leaving behind a black plume of diesel exhaust.

dumb girl

I suddenly felt vulnerable and unsafe and out of my depth as it dawned on me that the truck guys were probably armed. Then another truck came by, then another and then another, each driver loudly revving their engine, yelling, interrupting the first and then the second speaker, and each time leaving plumes of nasty-smelling black diesel fumes.

I began to tremble—from the cold, the fear and anxiety, and the lack of control I was feeling. I felt just like I had as a child at Mom and Dad's fireplace store: confused, powerless, and unable to control the situation.

Dad has put me in charge of the phones. I'm ten and have no training, and I accidentally keep hanging up on people. All the adults are mad at me. I don't know why, I don't know what to do about it, and when I ask for help, I'm brushed off.

When Robby and I heard Mom and Dad were buying a store a few years ago, we hoped it would be a candy store or toy store. I had grand visions of gaining friends and admirers as I gave out free candy and gum to my classmates. When I learned it was a fireplace store, full of fireplaces, barbeques, and accessories, I was heartbroken.

The name of the store is logically The Fireplace House. It's twenty miles north of our house in a depressed Denver community full of gas stations, billboards, liquor stores, and warehouses. When Mom and Dad first bought the store, Robby and I loved playing in and around the loading dock area. Our favorite thing to do was to ride up and down the soft black rubber two-story conveyor belt, playing a "Guess what I am?" game (heavy fireplace inserts, frozen animals, other objects?) with an elaborate point system we made up. We were not supposed to ride on the steep, not-made-for-children conveyor belt—Dad and his employees told us more than once that it was dangerous—but no one ever actually checked to make sure we listened to them, and the fun

sniper

outweighed our fear of getting into trouble. Dad rarely came out to the loading dock area.

The store was thriving after the first few years, so Mom and Dad decided to expand the business and add two more stores (they would later say this was "a big mistake"). The strain of running three stores, managing sixty-four employees, and balancing finances has become time-consuming and stressful for Mom and Dad, especially Dad. They are no longer home on Saturdays (the stores are closed on Sundays), and most weeknights they come home late or angry or both. They've started fighting a lot, so I avoid them a lot.

Fireplace sales are dependent on snow in the winter, which is when Mom and Dad are the busiest and most stressed. Dad explains to us, "People buy fireplaces when it's snowing," so I pray for snow—not so people will buy fireplaces but so that Dad won't be in such a bad mood.

One particularly stressful and snowy Saturday when I'm ten, the store is busy with customers who've come in to buy a fireplace insert, a tool set, or a glass screen. The phones are constantly ringing with customers responding to an ad Dad placed in this week's *Denver Post*.

Dad's tired-looking salesmen with tight, fake grins and twitchy eyes are frantically trying to manage the phones and the steady trail of people streaming through the front door. The air is full of stress and tension, so Robby and I do our best to avoid anyone who is an adult.

We are in the middle of a particularly amusing game of tag when Dad catches me running up the stairs and barks, "I need you to stop goofing around and come answer phones!"

I follow him into a small room behind the front sales counter where two cold gray metal desks sit cluttered with spilling piles of old invoices, a broken desk lamp, a half-filled Styrofoam cup of cold coffee, and three dirty black office phones. Each phone has

dumb girl

a rotary dial above a red "hold" button and five translucent square buttons that are either blinking or fully lit up. The randomness and lack of rhythm of the clear buttons blinking on and off is unnerving. The chaotic assortment of clutter on the desks doesn't help.

Dad points to one of the phones and quickly explains, "When the phone rings, push the button that's lit and say 'Fireplace House, may I help you?' and then do what the customer wants."

He then explains—very quickly because he's in a hurry and under pressure to get back out on the sales floor—the intricate details of how you put someone on hold or transfer a call and all the other things you can do with an incoming phone call, none of which I understand.

Before I can tell him that, he darts out of the room, leaving no time for questions.

I sit staring at the phones, wishing I was upstairs with Robby, who no longer has a tag buddy.

Thirty seconds later the phone rings, and one of the buttons lights up. I suddenly feel anxious. I pick up the handset, push the lit button, and say as confidently and cheerfully as I can, "The Fireplace House, may I help you?"

"Yeah, I'm interested in buying a zero-clearance fireplace for my family room fireplace," the deep voice says.

Not sure what a zero-clearance fireplace is, I mumble, "Ugh, yeah . . . I'll get someone . . . just a minute."

I gently put the handset back on the receiver and then frantically search the sales floor looking for Dad, Mom, or any salesman who can help the man on the phone. I tug on the sleeve of Steve, Dad's top salesman, who is talking in fireplace jargon to a tall man in a stylish tan suede jacket and shiny shoes. Annoyed that a ten-year-old is interrupting a possible sale, he dismissively swooshes me away with a flick of his wrist.

Defeated and with no plan, I go back to the phone, pick up the receiver, and push the button. All I hear is a dial tone.

sniper

He must have hung up, I think.

The phone rings again.

"The Fireplace House, may I help you?"

The voice on the phone sounds annoyed. "Yeah, I just called and got hung up on. I want to talk to someone about buying a zero-clearance fireplace."

"Oh, sorry. Just a minute, I'll find someone."

Again, I put the handset back on the receiver and frantically look around the sales floor, tugging on several salesmen's sleeves, all of whom motion me away because they're busy with a customer.

I go back to the phone and notice the button isn't lit anymore. *Thank God!* I think, but I'm also worried I've probably hung up on him again. I walk over to the front counter to try and busy myself, organizing random pieces of paper into neat piles, putting pencils in the brown pencil cup, and pretending I'm writing a very important message on the message pad. I don't want to answer the phones anymore.

A guy with a handlebar mustache walks into the store and spots me behind the counter. "Do you work here, young lady?" he asks before I have a chance to duck into the room with the phones.

"Yeah, my dad owns the store."

I can tell he doesn't want to talk to a kid, but after looking around and not seeing any available salesmen, he sees I'm his only choice. Exhaling in frustration, he says, "I saw the sale in the paper on glass screens and was interested in looking at one."

"Um, I'll find someone who can help you," I mutter, and dash off onto the salesfloor.

I can't believe I'm running around the store once more looking for someone to help a customer. Again, nobody is available. So I do the only thing I can think of.

I hide upstairs in the bathroom.

When I eventually come back downstairs, I see that Mr. Handlebar Mustache has found someone to help him. I breathe a

dumb girl

sigh of relief. But a deep sense of dread sets in as I head back up front and hear the distinct ringing of the small gold bell attached to the top of the door, indicating a customer is walking in. I can't handle seeing another adult disappointed in me because they're forced to talk to a kid about an adult matter. I feel stupid and useless and decide being in the room with the phones where I can't see the customers' faces is the better option.

But the phones are just as bad. I accidentally hang up on several people when trying to transfer their call to another phone. I'm yelled at because "I've been on hold far too long." And I'm interrogated with "What kind of business are you people running over there?" before they hang up on me.

Frustrated with my incompetence, I change my mind, again, and head over to the front counter, thinking dealing with customers is probably easier. *At least they don't yell at me*, I rationalize.

Just then, Dad sees me at the counter and screams, "What are you doing?"

"I'm helping customers," I whisper.

"I told you to answer phones!"

I try and explain, as I nervously chew on my nails, "I keep accidentally hanging up on them and then they yell at me when they call back."

"Well, then stop hanging up on them!" he replies. Then he says something about the order that you push the buttons and pick up the receiver in and then something about pushing the hold button, just like he'd explained earlier in the day, but this time he says it much louder.

Louder doesn't make it more understandable.

He leaves and I feel dumb for not understanding.

The rest of the afternoon is a blur of feeling stupid, fighting back tears, disappointing people, and being yelled at by Dad, people on the phone, and salesmen I keep bothering. I promise

sniper

myself, *When I grow up, I'm never going to be in a situation where I don't know what I'm doing.*

Easier said than done.

I'm sure ten-year-old me would have been disappointed to see me at this press conference a full twenty-five years later, waiting to speak on TV with no clue what I was doing.

Alice, the woman who spoke before me, was confident and eloquent. She easily rattled off statistics from memory like how 28,663 people die and 80,000 are injured every year from gun violence. And then she gracefully, without looking at her notes, told the story of how the owners of the large and intimidating building behind us broke numerous laws when they provided illegal guns to the DC snipers. And she did it all as the truck guys drove by and taunted her from the safety of their large pickups. I was impressed with her calmness. She never once flinched.

When it was my turn to speak, I took a deep breath and said, "My name is Heidi Yewman and I'm a graduate of Columbine High School. I graduated thirteen years before the massacre where twelve students and my basketball coach were killed."

I tried to hide my shaking hands, but the piece of paper with the talking points I was holding highlighted the tremble. The talking points were my lifeline; I read them straight off the paper. I knew it wouldn't exactly make for compelling TV, but ad-libbing and thinking on my feet were not things I was good at.

Another truck slowly approached and the driver hurled a loud "Fuck you!"

I could feel myself beginning to freeze—mentally, emotionally, and physically. DeAnna, who stood next to me, must have noticed, as she shifted her body, lightly grazing her shoulder on mine. The kind act grounded me, reminding me I was not alone.

After I finished reading my remarks, DeAnna invited the

small group of reporters to ask questions. Hairspray Reporter Lady responded, "Yes, I have a question for Heidi."

I assumed she was going to ask me something about Columbine or the people I'd met at the Million Mom March.

"How do you feel about the parallel press conference that's going on in Washington, DC, right now?" she asked.

I just stared at her; I had no idea what she was talking about.

Right then, another truck drove past us. This driver yelled, "Go home losers!" before speeding off.

I thought about making up something but worried I'd be way off and she'd have a follow-up question, so I just said, "Oh . . . um . . . I don't really know about that."

What I wanted to say was "Let me find a grown up."

I found out later that the DC press conference was the whole reason we were there: Another gun violence prevention group was holding one there to honor the victims while we simultaneously held one to show how an inept gun dealer had directly contributed to the carnage. I didn't know this, but the look on the reporter's face told me I *should* have known. I wanted to fold in on myself.

But then something miraculous happened: Me admitting I didn't know the answer ended up not being a big deal. DeAnna stepped in and answered for me, and the reporter quickly moved on to other questions.

That was the first time I'd experienced the freedom of not knowing something and not having to hide from it. Nobody was angry at me for not knowing how to respond; no one ridiculed me or made me feel inadequate. In fact the opposite happened—DeAnna and the other speakers praised me for attending, telling my story, and weathering an unhospitable situation. When I brought up how I'd had no idea how to answer the reporter's question, DeAnna said, "Oh, I thought your answer was perfect. We got your back."

chapter 7

no-press press conference

In 2003, a ten-year-old girl named Emily was shot and killed by her fourteen-year-old brother just a few miles from our house. The dad was a cop and "stored" his unlocked and loaded gun on a bedroom shelf, confident his kids would not touch it.

I heard about Emily's tragic death on the radio as I drove to my yoga class on a cold January morning. Tears of disbelief, guilt, sadness, and grief rolled down my cheeks while I did downward dog and child's pose.

I took her death personally, thinking I should have worked harder to get the word out about safe storage. I somehow felt it was my sole responsibility to stop unintentional shootings in my community.

It was in that yoga class that I came up with a plan to raise awareness. Since getting involved with gun safety efforts, I'd had some success promoting the ASK campaign in my community. I'd done several presentations at moms groups and PTAs, including at Sami's school. Politicians, community leaders, and the media all seemed drawn to the nuanced campaign, covering gun violence from the lens of "a mom who just wants to keep her kids safe" rather than the usual polarized debate—nobody could be against keeping young kids away from guns.

dumb girl

So after Emily's death, I reached out to the mayor of Vancouver, Washington to ask if he'd speak at an ASK press conference I was organizing. I'd never organized a press conference but figured the best way to get the message out to the masses about the dangers of unlocked guns was through the local papers, radio, and TV news. *If I could get through that sniper press conference*, I thought, *I can definitely do this*.

I called the mayor's assistant and said, "I've invited Chief Martnick, Representative Fromhold, and Dr. Koontz from the health department. We'd love to have the mayor join us for this important press conference."

"I'll check with the mayor and get back to you."

The next morning, she called with good news. "Yes, the mayor is happy to participate in the press conference. Would you like me to help you schedule a room?"

I said yes, and in short order, the other officials said yes too (mostly because the mayor said yes, which was a useful thing for me to know for future events).

I couldn't believe how easy it was to get all these local bigwigs to come—I'd thought that would be the hardest part. It felt like everything was clicking into place.

Two weeks later, we all gathered at a local office building the mayor's office had reserved. There were six of us: me, the mayor, the police chief, a priest, a state representative, and the head of the health department. I'd sent out a press release a few days earlier and followed up with phone calls to the four TV stations, two newspapers, and five radio stations in the area, confirming they'd be there. They'd all said they would send a reporter.

The six of us waited for the press to arrive in what could best be described as a room devoid of any aesthetic consideration. The fluorescent lighting cast a harsh and sterile glare on all of us. I hoped the colorful three-fold posterboard I'd made explaining

no-press press conference

the ASK campaign would at least make for a good visual for the cameras. I'd also put together a dozen press kits that included a fact sheet of US gun deaths, childhood deaths, and comparisons of the number of gun deaths to other countries, and—to help make the point that ASK was not an anti-gun program but a gun *safety* campaign—I'd put five gunlocks on the table.

I felt confident I'd thought of everything, but as the 2 p.m. start time grew closer and no reporters appeared, I began to grow anxious. The weather and local news discussions among the speakers started to wane.

Finally, Bill, one of the state reps, asked, "Did they respond to your press release?"

"Yeah," I said quickly, "they all said they were sending someone. I'm not sure why they're not here yet." That old familiar feeling of guilt gripped me.

"Don't worry," he said, "they'll show up."

But twenty minutes later, not a single reporter had shown up.

I'd been part of press conferences where fewer people from the media showed up than was expected, but I'd never been to one with *no* press.

I became nauseous and dizzy. *Is this my fault?*

As I stood there, Dad's voice popped into my head: "It's Mr. Nobody's fault!"

Dad calls all four of us kids down to the basement. I can tell by the tone of his voice that he's mad and somebody is in trouble. As I cautiously walk down the stairs, I rack my brain trying to figure out if I've done something wrong that would get all of us into trouble.

When we all get down to the basement, Dad points to a large hole in the top of an old green two-drawer wood filing cabinet he salvaged from his days in the army and screams, "Who did this?"

I look down, knowing that eye contact is not the way to go.

dumb girl

"This filing cabinet was fine yesterday and now it has a big hole in it," he shouts. "I want to know—who did it?"

The silence continues as I stare at my feet and nervously pick at the Band-Aid on my thumb.

Mom cautiously walks down the stairs. "Did you do this, Betty?" he asks her accusingly as he points to the filing cabinet.

She moves her head side to side as she looks down at the floor. To me, she seems like one of his children.

"So, what . . . ? Mr. Nobody did it?" he sarcastically asks. "I know one of you did it and I want to know who. No one is leaving until someone confesses!"

I try to think who might have put the hole in it. *Did I do it and just can't remember?* But no—if I'd done it, I'd probably remember. It must have been one of the boys or Robby.

"One of you did it and I want to know who," he continues screaming. "If no one is going to confess, then I'm going to spank all of you! I want to know who did it!"

Somehow, I know he doesn't mean Mom when he says "all of you."

Getting a spanking from Dad is extremely painful, so I can see why whoever did it isn't confessing. I really don't want all of us to get a spanking, though. We all stand in silence waiting for the culprit to fess up for what feels like forever. When the tension and suspense become too much, I yell out, "I did it!"

Everyone looks at me and then back at Dad. He tells Mom, the boys, and Robby to go upstairs and then he grabs my arm, bends me over, and spanks me—hard. I clench my butt and pull it in as much as possible, hoping that will somehow shield me from the blows, but it doesn't really help.

Afterward, I gingerly walk up the basement stairs and then up the second set of stairs to my bedroom, where I lie on my bed—on my stomach—and cry, not only because of the physical

no-press press conference

pain but also because of the unfairness of the whole thing. Our cat, Tigger, joins me, and I pet him, trying to soothe myself.

Two hours later I hear Dad's angry, booming voice call me down to the living room. Wondering what I've done now, I cautiously walk down the stairs.

When I finally stand in front of him, he asks, "Did you break the filing cabinet?"

I keep silent, looking at his feet.

"Did you?" he screams as he leans down, putting his face inches from mine.

In as small a voice as I can muster, knowing he somehow knows the truth, I squeak, "No."

He looks at me with disappointment and yells, "You lied to me to save your brothers! Lying is wrong!" He grabs my upper arm, positioning my body for leverage, and starts spanking me again. As he hits me, he says, "This hurts me more than it hurts you."

I seriously doubt it.

Standing there, flanked by the mayor and the police chief, I was silently spinning out.

Where are the media . . . What did I not do to get them here . . . What did I do wrong . . . Why did I even try this . . . Why am I such an idiot!?

Bill, the state representative, perhaps sensing my total inner freak-out, kindly offered, "There must have been a big traffic accident or some big news story they're covering that pulled them away."

"That must be it!" I agreed, grateful he'd given me an out but still beyond embarrassed.

Thirty minutes after the press conference was supposed to start, one by one, the community leaders I'd invited shook my

dumb girl

hand, thanked me for the work I do, and left to go do whatever it is important people who have important jobs do. Attending a press conference where there's no press, I'm sure, was not one. I apologized profusely to each one as they took their leave.

Deflated, I gathered up the brochures, the press kits, the large three-fold display, and the gunlocks and trudged my way to my car, promising myself I'd do a more thorough job next time.

That night when I explained to Dave what happened, tears ran down my cheeks. He lovingly wiped them away and gave me a hug before asking me, "No one died, right?"

"No, but they all just looked at me like I was an idiot." I sniffled loudly. "I should have called the newsrooms this morning to make sure they were coming."

"Yeah maybe, but you can't think of everything. Sometimes they just don't come, and you never know why," he said. To make me feel better, he recounted some past failed PR experiences of his own, then joked, "Besides, you aren't really a bona fide activist until you've experienced your first no-press press conference."

I never found out why the press didn't come. Watching the local TV news that night, I found no stories of major car accidents or an event that would have pulled all those outlets away from my event.

But I decided Dave was right: I was now a bona fide activist—and I had the figurative scars to show for it.

PART TWO

chapter 8

testify

Hostility and tension engulfed me as soon as I walked into the Capitol. The halls were lined with men wearing plaid shirts that only barely covered their protruding stomachs. They wore cowboy boots or combat boots, were in desperate need of a haircut, and reeked of musk—and not the sensual kind cologne companies advertise.

I could feel their eyes bore through me as I passed them in my freshly ironed white buttoned dress shirt and blazer with a black pencil skirt and matching patent leather high heels—an outfit I'd specifically chosen to make me feel more professional and less stay-at-home mom–like.

It was the fall of 2003, and DeAnna's group, Washington CeaseFire, which was trying to outlaw assault weapons in the state, had invited me to testify at the Washington State Capitol. Specifically, they'd asked me to testify in a Senate hearing about Columbine and how destructive the assault weapons the shooters used were on that awful day. Not allowing the general public to have access to military-style weapons seemed pretty reasonable to me; I was happy to say yes.

Not having done anything like this before, I was thrilled and nervous at the same time and had spent days preparing and

dumb girl

practicing my remarks, including during my hour-long drive to the State Capitol in Olympia.

Being an advocate for gun safety didn't match with my deep-seated desire to avoid conflict. It was the exact opposite. Working in gun control was inherently full of conflict, contention, and controversy. Intellectual and emotional fights about how to stop gun violence were common, and when I started dipping my feet into the legislative world, things became intense. The gun guys were stubborn, dismissive, and angry, and they consistently showed up to state houses across the country to show their support for bills that loosen gun laws and oppose bills that tighten them.

I wish I could say I held my head high as I walked down the hallway looking for DeAnna. Instead, I walked with my shoulders hunched, clutching my handbag harder than it needed to be held, questioning my choice of a tight-fitting skirt that my husband had called "sexy as hell" when I'd put it on that morning (I thought it just looked professional). My heels loudly echoed off the thinly tiled floor and I became uncomfortably aware of, well . . . all of me, as my eyes scanned the hall, desperately avoiding eye contact with the scary men waiting to get into the hearing room.

I soon found DeAnna, who seemed to sense my angst. She gently took hold of my arm and guided me over to the sign-in table, where I found my name and signed in before we disappeared into the hearing room.

The large hearing room had a drastically different feel than the loud and emotionally chaotic hallway. The sudden quietness and professional atmosphere made it feel safe as people in business attire sat quietly waiting for the hearing to start. DeAnna and I made our way to the front of the room and sat in the first row, right behind the intimidating stately table holding six long-stemmed microphones that looked like small black roses without leaves.

testify

After the dozen or so senators filed into the room and found their seats, two other gun control advocates and I were called up to the table. Three National Rifle Association (NRA) representatives were also called up. The hushed tones and seriousness of the room were stifling. The senators sat in large leather swivel chairs above us on stadium-like risers that were clearly built so we'd all understand who the most important people in the room were. They were literally looking down on us. I felt intimidated. Adrenaline surged through my body as I fought my instinct to make myself small.

When it was my turn to speak, I talked about Columbine and the horrifying violence that the guns used that day made possible. I closed with a story about AR-15s that I hoped would give me credibility: I'd gone shooting with a hunter friend, Kyle, on a family camping trip that previous summer in Eastern Washington. While there, he had me shoot an AR-15, a similar type of weapon used by one of the Columbine shooters. Spoiler alert: I didn't like it. For a number of reasons.

First of all, every time I pulled the trigger, the butt of the gun recoiled into my shoulder, which felt like being kicked by a mule. Kyle had not warned me.

Second, after each shot, burning-hot casings flew out of the gun, stinging my neck and bare arms. Kyle had not warned me.

Finally, I was caught off guard by the sudden realization of the God-like power the semiautomatic gun gave me—how easy it would be to take a life. Images of the Columbine shooters reveling in that power pained me as I shot at a nearby hillside. I actually had to hold back tears. Kyle had not warned me.

Afterward, he and I talked about AR-15s and assault weapons and why people have them. He explained, "People buy them for target shooting but they'd never use them to hunt with. If you showed up on a hunting trip with an AR-15, everyone would totally make fun of you. If you shot a deer with one of these guns, there'd be no meat left on the deer; it would tear it apart, and it takes the sport out of it. If you're a legit hunter, you'd never use an assault weapon to hunt."

I was the last speaker in my group, so as soon as I finished my closing argument, I collected my notes, put them in my bag, and walked back out into the hallway.

The vast majority of the gun guys had moved into an auxiliary room to watch the hearing on closed-circuit TV, so the hallway was no longer cluttered with disgruntled gun owners. A small group of us were waiting just outside of the hearing room for the rest of our group when an extremely tall, large man wearing a leather vest with an AR-15 imprinted on it above the words "FROM MY COLD DEAD HANDS" walked over to me and stood so close I could smell the tobacco on his breath. He must have been at least six foot ten.

Looking directly down at me, he said in a deep voice, "I just heard you speak in there and disagree with what you said."

I had no idea which part he was talking about and was still coming down from the mixture of adrenaline and euphoria from holding my own in an incredibly intimidating situation.

"Which part?" I asked.

"The part where you said people don't hunt with AR-15s," he grumbled as he inched even closer.

I instinctively swiped at my neatly gathered ponytail in an attempt to soothe myself as I looked up at his tobacco-stained teeth.

"I hunt with an AR-15 and no one's ever made fun of me," he said, eyes narrowed. "You're wrong about people not hunting with AR-15s."

"All I know is what my friend who's a big hunter told me," I replied. "He said if you use an AR-15, there's no meat left on the deer."

My adrenaline shot up again as I squared off with this stranger. I contemplated stepping back to create space between us

testify

but didn't want to show him I was intimidated. My physical and emotional responses were familiar and disappointing: my gaze dropped, my confident posture softened, and feelings of inadequacy and inferiority engulfed me.

Just like when I was in second grade.

I can't wait to be in third grade. Third graders are superior, have status and an aura of confidence I'm hungry for. It's the grade where you're considered a "big kid." It's a rite of passage.

Third graders seem cooler and more sophisticated, and their classes are taught in classrooms where kids sit at tables instead of on the floor. Third graders also get to learn cursive, which means I'll finally be able to read my piano teacher's weekly assignment notes. She usually forgets to use print, and I feel like a little kid not being able to read her cursive, which seems like a foreign language.

But most importantly, third grade is the year we are permitted to ride our bikes to school. Kids who ride their bikes are seen as really cool "big kids."

But I'm stuck in second grade for a little longer. It's the spring quarter, and every day my friends and I sit in the love tunnel (an industrial-sized cement tube on the playground) at recess, making elaborate plans about how and where we're going to meet to ride our bikes to school, and the route we're going to take. We call it the "bike riding club."

We can't wait.

One Saturday morning, Mom, Dad, and I drive home from my soccer game in our 1973 red Mustang Convertible and pull in to our garage. But we don't get out. Instead, Mom and Dad turn to face me in the back seat with serious looks on their faces.

"We've made a horrible mistake," Mom starts. "When you were five, we moved from Cheyenne to Denver, and because you're

dumb girl

a girl, we thought you should enter school early because generally girls are more mature and better at school."

I nod, confused about where this is going.

"We had Doug and Philip start kindergarten when they were six because they are boys. Boys do better when they start later," she explains. "We met with your teachers, and they recommended you stay in second grade for another year. The kids going into third grade are a year older than you, and we've noticed school is hard for you," Mom points out. "If we hold you back, school will be easier, and the neat thing is that you'll be the same age as all the kids in your grade! We made a mistake by putting you in school at five years old, so now we need to undo that mistake."

My eyes fill with tears. I stare at my bike leaning against the garage wall, realizing that all the plans I've made with my friends will still happen, just without me.

Mom tells me, again, "This is our mistake, and it's not something to be embarrassed by."

"What about riding my bike with the bike riding club?" I ask.

"You'll just have to wait another year."

I wipe the tears from my eyes as I feel my world crumble.

"There's one thing you need to know though," Dad warns me. "Some of the kids who are going into third grade without you might make fun of you for 'flunking out.'"

I hadn't thought of that. Until now. I guess I really am a dumb girl.

"The best way to deal with it is to beat them to the punch by making fun of yourself before they do," he says. "Doing it louder and better than they do will take away their fun. Kids make fun of you because they want the attention and they want to see your reaction. If you don't react the way they want, it isn't fun for them, and they'll stop."

I nod in agreement. If Dad says so, it must be true.

testify

∽

A few weeks later my second-grade class goes on a field trip. I sit in the fourth row of the bus in front of Jack Fisher, a boy who has the size, confidence, and demeanor of a fourth grader. He's heard I'm not going into third grade next year, and he starts making fun of me just like Dad predicted.

"You're flunking second gra-ade, you're flunking second gra-ade," he says in a sing-song voice.

I look him right in the eyes, like Dad told me, and say, "Yeah, you're right. I'm stupid and I'm dumb and a big baby who isn't going into third grade cause I'm sooo dumb!"

His eyes grow big and hesitant. "Yeah," he slowly mumbles. And then he lets it go, turning back to his friends behind him.

It worked! I can't believe it! He lightly teases me the next couple of weeks until school gets out for the summer, but I feel like I have a secret tool. It seems to take the power out of his taunts and eventually he stops.

The problem is I believe what Jack says about me and I believe what I say about myself. I'm stupid and dumb. I continue using this secret tool Dad's given me, making fun of myself before someone else can, for years—long after it's useful or helpful.

Jack Fisher is not my only problem in elementary school. There's a boy in Robby's first-grade class with the nickname The Boobie Pincher. When I'm eleven, in fifth grade, he starts running around the playground at recess pinching and twisting unsuspecting girls' boobs.

Most of us don't really have anything to pinch, but that doesn't seem to stop him from trying. I'm vaguely aware of him, having only overheard my classmates talk about him a few times, so I don't think much about him, especially since he leaves me alone.

Then one day he finds me. And he won't leave me alone.

dumb girl

When I'm standing in line to play four-square, he sneaks up behind me, reaches around me, and pinches my nipple. Then he runs away. I tell the recess aide, but she never sees him in the act, so she doesn't do anything.

"Stop being a tattletale," she tells me.

He sneaks up behind me when I'm waiting for a jump rope, when I'm waiting in line for tetherball, and when I'm walking to the swings. I become aware of where he is and, as soon as I see him coming, I run away. I'm faster than him so that works for a while. I just don't like having to be so aware, and it really hurts when he "gets" me.

I've had enough. I decide to ask Dad what I should do.

"The next time he comes up to you, look him right in the eye and say loudly and firmly 'Ned, I don't want you to pinch me anymore and you need to stop!'" he explains. "If you don't stop, I'm going to yell at you to stop, and if you still pinch me, I'm going to punch you." Dad tilts his head. "If he keeps doing it, yell at him and then punch him as hard as you can. If you get into trouble, I'll tell your teacher I gave you permission."

I can't believe Dad's telling me to punch a boy. But I'm at the end of my rope—and hey, the advice he gave me about Jack Fisher worked perfectly.

The next time Ned comes up to me, I don't run away. My palms are sweaty, and I can feel my heart beating through my chest. He darts out a hand and pinches my nipple, hard.

It hurts, but I stand tall, ignoring the desire to hunch in pain. I look him right in the eyes and yell as loudly as I can, "Stop it! If you pinch me again, I'm going to punch you!"

He reaches forward, grabs my nipple between his thumb and finger, and pinches and twists. It hurts worse than the first pinch.

Blood rushes to my face. I throw my elbow back, clench my hand into a fist, and put all my weight into punching The Boobie Pincher right in the stomach.

testify

Time stops for an instant as a look of surprise freezes on his face—his eyes get wide and his mouth opens just enough to let the air escape from his stomach. Then he doubles over.

I stand up straight, look down at him, and say, "Don't ever pinch me again!"

He never touches me again.

Now here I was, once again facing a bully—a tall bully who cowered above me and stank of tobacco and body odor. I was tired of backing down to men like him, bullies like him. I didn't want to punch him in the stomach, but I did want to stand up for myself.

His deep voice began to rise in volume, and he leaned in again, this time aggressively pointing his finger at my chin. "You are wrong about AR-15s, and you don't know what you're talking about."

My palms became sweaty and I could feel my heart beating through my chest, but I didn't back away and I didn't break eye contact.

Just then, one of the women who'd testified next to me recognized what was going on, rushed over, and said, "Heidi, they need you to come sign some paperwork about your testimony." She grabbed my arm and whisked me away to another hallway, where I didn't sign any papers because that wasn't a thing. I was so grateful to her for recognizing what he was doing and saving me. I didn't exactly stand up to him, but I also didn't back down, and that felt like a win.

The satisfaction I'd gotten when I punched The Boobie Pincher was immediate. This felt more like a first step—a starting block to building my confidence as an advocate. I left the Capitol that day feeling proud that I went, that I testified, that I'd held my own in an intimidating situation, and that I'd made at least a small step toward reclaiming my power.

chapter 9

kennedy

I saw Senator Ted Kennedy the moment I entered the lobby. His stark white hair, puffy face with red cheeks, and wide smile made him instantly recognizable, even from all the way across the room.

Dave turned to me, grinning. "Hey, you want to meet Senator Kennedy?"

"Yeah!" I enthusiastically replied.

He grabbed my hand and maneuvered through the crowd until we were on the outskirts of the small group that formed a tight circle around him. Waiters offered sophisticated bite-sized hors d'oeuvres and champagne off silver trays while we waited to enter the circle.

We were there because in 2003 the NRA came up with a blacklist for their members of organizations and individuals around the country to boycott because they allegedly supported anti-gun policies. It was a crazy-long list and included really weird organizations and people that had nothing to do with politics, like the pop groups NSYNC and The Temptations, singer Britney Spears, and former Olympian Mary Lou Retton. It was a ridiculous list—so ridiculous that when the actor Dustin Hoffman found out he was not on the list, he wrote to the NRA and asked to be listed.

kennedy

Following Hoffman's move, the Brady Center to Prevent Gun Violence decided to mock the NRA by holding a Blacklist Ball where advocates would gather to celebrate the organizations and individuals on the list who had the gall to support efforts to end gun violence. Many of the people on the blacklist attended the ball, proud to be on the side of saving lives. I, of course, wasn't on the NRA's list, but I'd been invited to the ball because of the grassroots work I'd been doing on behalf of Brady in Oregon and Washington State.

It was my first ball in Washington, DC, and I was thrilled to go. I asked a neighbor to take the kids for a few days. I bought a fancy black dress, and Dave rented a tuxedo before we headed off to DC.

Standing there in the lobby, I felt out of my depth; I'd never been around so many celebrities and politicians in my life. And in my mind, Senator Ted Kennedy was one of the biggest—American royalty tinged with tragedy: two brothers assassinated, Chappaquiddick, alcoholism, and rumors of affairs and sexual harassment. He was also a tireless advocate for gun control, along with other progressive and liberal issues I cared about. I was excited to meet him.

Finally, Dave and I saw our opening: A friend of mine, a grassroots leader from Texas, was speaking to Senator Kennedy. Dave gently nudged me. "Get in there," he whispered. "I'll get a photo."

My confidence was bolstered by the tight-fitting but classy backless dress I was wearing that night. *Professional* is what I'd thought as I looked at myself in the full-length mirror in our hotel room before heading down to the event. I took a deep breath, exhaled, and caught my friend's eye.

"Heidi!" She waved me over. "Have you met Senator Kennedy?"

We all spoke for a couple of minutes, and we took a group photo. After Dave snapped it, my friend continued talking to Senator Kennedy while I stood there, awkwardly waiting my turn.

dumb girl

Finally, Dave stepped in. "Can you step aside for a quick second so I can get a photo of just Senator Kennedy and Heidi?" he asked.

As Dave fidgeted with the digital camera, Senator Kennedy and I maneuvered into the traditional photo pose: an arm wrapped around each other, our hands on the middle of one another's backs. The warmth of his hand on my bare back was noticeable.

As we waited, I could feel Senator Kennedy making an adjustment. At first, I thought he was just moving his hand down to the small of my back.

He was not.

I felt his hand continue to move down, ever so slowly . . . down, down, down until it rested on my left buttock. And then a squeeze. And it wasn't a little pat or a gentle squeeze—it was a full, open-handed, get-as-much-flesh-as-you-can kind of squeeze. A grab.

I froze. My feet were frozen, my smile was frozen, and his hand was frozen. As the flash of the camera went off, I tried to telepathically tell Dave what was happening with my eyes, but he didn't "hear" me.

Senator Kennedy let go of my ass and looked me in the eyes and I . . . just stood there.

Looking at his white teeth.

His expression instantly made me regret wearing the dress I had chosen and question my newfound confidence. But mostly, the way he looked at me sent me back in time: it was the exact same way Dad had looked at me when I was sixteen, taking a bath.

I look forward to getting home and unwinding after school these days, especially when nobody else is home. The bath is where I find refuge because I'm frequently sore and tired from basketball or volleyball practice and just want to be alone.

kennedy

At sixteen, I have an unrelenting craving for and addiction to chewing ice cubes. There is a peace that comes to me as I slowly apply pressure on the hard ice cube with my back teeth and feel the cube buckle as it breaks into smaller manageable pieces. The tension of the ice, the tension in my jaw, and the tension of the day melt with each crunch, and I am soothed by the numbing of my tongue. The problem is it makes me shiver with cold. The antidote is sitting in almost unbearably hot bath water. So as soon as I get home, I fill a large plastic cup with ice, sit in scorching bath water, crunch the ice, and sweat until I run out of ice or the water cools down.

There is no lock on the bathroom door, however, so when Dad gets home from work, this is where he finds me.

As soon as I hear the creak of the door handle turning, I quickly bend my right knee, bringing my heel up to my butt, and rotate my leg inward to cover my pubic area and then fold my arms over my chest to cover my naked breasts. By this point, the frothy suds that covered me at the beginning of the bath have long since vanished.

He walks over to the edge of the bathtub, looks straight down at me, and peppers me with questions about my day and about practice and about school: "How'd you do on your math test?" and "What'd coach say about losing the game last night?" and "How many rebounds did you end up pulling down in the game?"

I try to answer his questions as quickly and succinctly as possible so he'll leave: "Good," and "She was mad, so we ran ten extra sprints," and "Eight."

I hate it when he comes in here. I feel exposed, vulnerable, and trapped, and I can't figure out a way to get him to go away. My overt attempt to cover myself goes unnoticed. He doesn't avert his eyes or make any attempt to make me more comfortable; he just stands there staring at me and talking to me while I awkwardly lie there, naked.

dumb girl

Looking at his white teeth.

I'm consumed with shame for not confronting him and for letting this bad situation continue while I remain mute.

But what can I do? Me asking him to not look at me would make me a DBADG.

My trance was broken when Dave took three steps toward Senator Kennedy and me to shake his hand. As they shook hands Dave said, "I just want to thank you for everything you've done," not knowing what he'd *just* done.

As we walked away, visions of me throwing a drink in his face, yelling at him, kicking him, slapping him, or doing something—anything, even punching him in the stomach like I did to The Boobie Pincher—flooded my mind. But it was too late. The moment came and the moment went. He was Senator Ted Kennedy, and I didn't want to make a scene.

Once again, I'd frozen.

I wasn't all that surprised, just disappointed that I was still in some cruel, cosmic circular pattern I couldn't seem to break. And confused, too. Was I right in being upset about this? Or was I overreacting to the senator's actions because of my own complicated past? I needed someone to put what had just happened into context—someone to tell me what to make of it and how to react to it.

As we headed to our seats in the main ballroom for the programed event, I turned to Dave and said, "Do you know what just happened?"

"No, what?"

"Ted Kennedy just grabbed my ass!"

"What?" His eyes widened. "Are you serious?"

"Yeah, he totally grabbed my ass when you were taking the picture."

kennedy

Without missing a beat, my sarcastic British husband said, "Well, what do you expect? He's a Kennedy, and he's a Democrat."

Dave didn't think it was a big deal, and I didn't want to think it was a big deal, so it became not-a-big-deal. What it did become was cocktail-party fodder. For years after, I'd tell my Ted Kennedy story with the punch line being Dave's comment about him being a Kennedy and a Democrat. It always got a big laugh and gave me a fun connection to the powerful and famous because my butt was squeezed by an American royal. Ha ha!

It wasn't until 2017, when #MeToo became a thing, that my Kennedy story became not all that funny to me anymore. It wasn't until that point that I realized I'd been *sexually assaulted* by Senator Ted Kennedy.

Dave had made light of it, I'd made light of it, and everyone who laughed at my story had made light of it, but it wasn't a joke. Being a Kennedy or a Democrat or famous or powerful didn't give you the right to grab women's butts.

I came up with a plan for the next time someone tried something like that. Next time, I would be ready.

chapter 10

nra debate

The email from Washington CeaseFire in Seattle said, "The Federal Assault Weapons Ban is sunsetting in two months, and we need to do everything we can to stop it from expiring. We just got an invitation to debate an NRA representative on a live segment on KOMO-TV in Seattle next Tuesday. Can you do it?"

My initial response was "Absolutely not."

The debate itself sounded like a great idea. But debates for me were, I thought, my weak point. I got tongue-tied, couldn't recall stats, and often realized how I should have responded only hours later—sitting bolt upright in the middle of the night. It was all extremely frustrating, and I often felt stupid, just like I had as a kid when Dad was angry with me. I knew what to say, I just couldn't say it in the heat of the moment, no matter how prepared I thought I was.

My other problem was that the idea of facing off with the NRA was terrifying. They seemed mean and angry and, honestly, reminded me of Dad.

One late afternoon, Dad takes Robby, ten, and me, thirteen, to a Denny's wannabe–type diner. It smells like maple syrup, burnt coffee, and french fries. Because it's between the lunch and

nra debate

dinner rush, the restaurant is mostly empty—just a few tables are occupied.

Once we're seated, our waitress quickly comes over to us. She is young, maybe in her early twenties or possibly a teenager; I think this because of how she chews her gum and smells like Bonne Bell Lip Smackers. She is nice and smiles and nods as she takes our order.

As we wait for our food, I watch her glide around the restaurant and marvel at her ability to multitask as she refills glasses, delivers large trays of food, and seats new customers.

Once we finish our grilled cheese sandwiches and french fries, she asks, "How are things here? Can I get you any dessert? Our brownies are pretty good . . ."

"Well, if you're going to pressure us, then sign us up for three brownies with ice cream on top," Dad says cheerfully.

They smile at each other, and she disappears into the kitchen along with our dirty plates and utensils.

A few minutes later, she returns, carefully placing our brownies with ice cream and whipped cream in front of us. A bright-red cherry sits on top. Unfortunately, she disappears before Dad gets a chance to ask her for forks. We look at each other and then at the surrounding empty tables, scanning for clean utensils we can snatch. The other tables are bare, so we wait.

And wait.

Dad's mood changes. His brows furrow and his breath gets short. He disconnects from the conversation as we sit, slowly watching our brownies cool and our ice cream soften.

My jaw tightens and my stomach starts to ache, and I anxiously pick at the edge of the table. I search for topics to talk about that will calm and distract him. "Do you think the Broncos will win this weekend? Do me and Robby get to go to the game?"

He doesn't hear me or ignores me as his eyes desperately search the restaurant, trying to find our waitress or anyone who

dumb girl

can save us from the melting ice cream and his rising irritation.

Robby and I eat the cherry and dip our fingers into the whipped cream as it slowly slides off the heated brownie while Dad fidgets in his seat.

Finally, he sees our waitress emerge from the kitchen with a tray full of food she's delivering to a family across the restaurant. "Waitress, waitress!" he bellows, frantically motioning her over to our table.

I melt into my seat, embarrassed that he has brought us to the attention of not just the waitress but the other people in the restaurant. After emptying the large tray, she quickly returns to our table and innocently asks, "Yes?"

"We need utensils!" he demands.

"Okay, I'll be right back," she says brightly as she quickly heads for the kitchen. We watch her go in and out of the kitchen a couple of times, delivering pop and then straws and then food to another table before she seats a couple that is waiting at the hostess stand. She's suddenly become very busy and has clearly forgotten about our forks.

"Waitress, waitress!" Dad yells again.

She doesn't hear him. I start to worry about what will happen when she eventually does come over.

"This is ridiculous!" Dad steams. "Waitress!"

This time she hears him and quickly comes over. My worry for her increases. He looks directly into her eyes and says very slowly, "You brought us our dessert, and it looks very tasty, but something is missing." Then his tone turns to sarcasm. "Can you tell by looking at the table what we are missing that is making us unable to enjoy this wonderful dessert?"

She scans the table, trying to find the answer to the riddle, and then looks at him and smiles, her eyes searching his face for a smile to match his sarcasm.

It isn't there.

nra debate

"Well?" he asks, his voice losing the sarcastic tone. "We ordered our desserts ten minutes ago. I asked you to get us something to eat this with and then you disappeared into the kitchen and didn't come back. Meanwhile, we just sit here, watching our ice cream melt and brownies get cold. How are we supposed to eat this without utensils?"

Her gaze drops to the floor and her shoulders hunch forward as her body absorbs his harsh tone. Robby and I sink into our seats, and I begin aggressively chewing the skin around my fingernail as we listen to him "teach a lesson" to our waitress about how to be a waitress. I secretly pray that his berating will soon end.

"I don't know," she whispers.

"Exactly!" he barks. "Go get us forks and do not do anything else. Do not help other customers. Do not deliver any other food or seat anyone else. Just bring us forks!"

She slithers back to the kitchen and quickly returns with three forks.

The ice cream and brownies have lost their taste. We eat in silence.

Our waitress avoids us until she returns and informs Dad the desserts have been removed from the bill. Her smile is gone; I can see that she feels heavy and sad.

I know the feeling.

From that day on, restaurant meals with Dad are stressful. I never know what's going to set him off: A meal that takes a little too long getting to our table or not being sat right away often pushes him over the edge. And it's not just restaurants. I hate how my jaw tightens and my stomach aches when he starts getting angry and becomes rude and short with whoever's made him mad.

NRA guys reminded me of Dad: unpredictable, quick to anger, and scary. I mostly tried to avoid them.

dumb girl

But when I told Dave about the invitation to debate the NRA on live TV, he enthusiastically said, "You totally should do it. You'll be great!"

I often wondered how it was that he saw in me things I couldn't see.

"There's no way I can go on live TV and argue with an angry man about the assault weapons ban expiring," I argued. "I'll get a stomachache, and I won't be able to think on my feet."

"I know you can do it," he said. "And I'll prep you!"

He was a presentation coach and media trainer, someone who'd spent years meticulously prepping CEOs for speeches and interviews. If he thought I could do it, maybe I could. Especially if he was willing to help me.

With his training, maybe, just maybe, I might be able to take back some of my power, control the situation, and hold my own even in the face of an explosive bully.

After a bunch of back and forth, he finally convinced me to say yes.

I was to debate Troy Mills, a short round old guy with a weathered face and permanent frown lines, which I believed came from years of anger at the government. I'd seen him at the State Capitol when I testified and on TV speaking against gun regulations. He was the archetype of an NRA member. I nicknamed him "NRA guy."

Three days before the debate, Dave and I removed our dining room table, replacing it with three chairs and a large cardboard box with a video camera and small tripod perched precariously on it. Dave had watched several prior episodes of the news program I'd be on and knew exactly what the studio looked like, where the host would sit, where I'd probably sit, how the host would ask questions, and what the general vibe of the interview would be like.

nra debate

As we sat in our pretend studio, he advised, "Try and sit in the chair next to the host so NRA guy won't be in your line of sight when you're answering questions. Ignore NRA guy in the green room just like you ignore the players on the other team before a basketball game—that way you won't be intimidated. And once you're on the set, don't look at the camera. Look at the host and look at her face. And don't forget to smile."

"What if he yells at me?" I asked. "I don't even know what I'm supposed to say, and even if I figure it out, how will I remember it?" My jaw suddenly felt tight, and my stomach started to hurt.

Sensing my panic, he smiled sweetly and reached out for my hands. "Look, this is a three-to-four-minute interview, max. All you need are three main talking points to get across and answers to the questions we know the host might ask. Remember, the host isn't a lawyer and you're not under subpoena."

His confidence in me, the warmth of his hands, and the softness of his voice instantly relaxed me.

"You don't have to answer a question, especially if you don't know the answer," he told me. "All you need to do is remember the three things you want to get across, and pivot to them if you get stuck."

We wrote down the three key messages on a whiteboard he'd brought in from his office. Then came the hard part: Dave turned on the video camera perched on the cardboard box, and we recorded a mock three-minute interview with him playing the host.

Watching the video was awful. I could see myself being assertive when I remembered the message, and I could see my body language crumbling when he interrupted me or asked a nasty question like "Assault weapons account for almost no deaths, so why even bother having a ban?" I fidgeted in my chair and picked my nails, and when I couldn't immediately recall what I wanted to say, I stammered.

dumb girl

"Everyone hates being videotaped," Dave reminded me. "And the only thing they hate more than being recorded is watching it back. You'll get better as we go along. Take your time. Breathe. Deliver the talking points."

We recorded a dozen or so mock interviews. Each time, my delivery improved, and the messages sounded more natural and conversational. My body language strengthened every time. I lost the shifting, picking, and stammering, and I started to feel like I could do it. But anxiety still persisted.

After we practiced the interview, we started thinking about adjacent issues.

"TV studios are always freezing, so you should wear layers to keep warm," Dave said. "Solid colors, no patterns, hair pulled back off your face, no jangly earrings, no gum, nails done—everything counts. You never lean back in the chair, it can look like you're slouching. You sit up straight and lean forward 20 degrees—like someone's pulling you up from the top of your scalp."

It seemed like overkill, but I went along with it. Dave also noticed that NRA guy was pretty short.

"You're wearing heels, right?" he asked.

"Probably," I responded. "Why?"

"You're five foot eight, and in heels you're closer to six feet. He's five five, tops. You'll tower over him and he'll look small," he said. "Heels, heels."

Lastly, I practiced not looking at NRA guy but at the host, which in our "studio" was our son's giant teddy bear perched on the other chair. I felt I was being rude, but Dave reminded me, "Remember when that tall gun guy tried to intimidate you after you testified last month? Fuck those guys."

I knew he was right.

The most helpful thing we did was create what I imagined to be the worst-case scenario—being yelled at, diminished, or interrupted by NRA guy.

nra debate

Dave played NRA guy. I'd begin delivering one of my messages and he'd scoff, mutter something nasty, or interrupt me. "Oh, come on," he'd say. "That's just ignorant. If she knew anything about guns, anything at all, she'd know that what she's saying is just ridiculous." Loudly, "Guns don't kill people, people kill people." Angrily, "Let me say something here." Dismissively, "You don't know what you're talking about."

I stayed calm and level, ignored him, and let his voice remain in the background as I kept eye contact with Mr. Teddy Bear while I talked. After Dave stood up and aggressively pointed at my face, I said, "Oh, come on, Dave. There's no way NRA guy's going to act like that."

"You never know," he said, "and you should be prepared for everything."

By the end of our prep, it seemed possible that I was.

Three days later we drove to Seattle. I don't remember the three-hour drive to the TV station, I don't remember walking into the building, and I don't remember the greenroom. What I do remember is being terrified but confident at the same time. The familiar sensation of a tight jaw and stomachache briefly took root before I remembered: *I know my three talking points, I know how to react if NRA guy is rude, mean, angry, or obnoxious to me, and I know how to handle myself.*

I was ready.

When I was escorted into the large studio, the cold hit me just like Dave had warned me. They kept the warehouse-like studio at a cold 64 degrees to combat the heat from the bright studio lights. I'd worn layers under my blazer so I wouldn't shiver and look like I was nervous. I was also wearing tight slacks and four-inch heels that made me taller than NRA guy—and made me feel more confident and professional.

Once on set, I made a beeline to the seat next to the host, like

dumb girl

Dave had advised, and felt power in that moment knowing NRA guy would be looking at the back of my head when he talked to the host. I sat up straight in my seat, scooting my butt to the back of the chair but not leaning against the back like Dave instructed. I could feel my power.

NRA guy leaned back in his chair and looked defeated even before we started.

In the end, NRA guy didn't interrupt me, yell at me, or try to intimidate me. I still got blocked and overwhelmed a couple of times, forgetting what I was talking about, but was able to quickly pivot to one of my three talking points. In the moment, they felt like a lifeline. It went fast and was over before I knew it. Thanks to the prep, I'd talked for probably 65 percent of the time.

After the interview, I looked down at NRA guy in my heels and smiled as we shook hands, filled with the unfamiliar feeling of holding my own and not cowering to his potential anger.

When I walked off set that day, Dave wrapped me up in a bear hug and whispered into my ear, "You destroyed his ass."

I couldn't tell you who actually won the debate. What I do know is I walked into the studio that day feeling scared but prepared, and I walked out feeling powerful.

chapter 11

gun guy

I leaned into the microphone. The crowd was yelling at me so loudly I couldn't hear myself speak. Their anger was vile, and I stumbled on my words. I clung to the podium as if it were a life ring and read my speech, desperately trying to ignore the guy standing just feet from me with a large black Glock on his right hip while holding a toddler on his other hip.

Three months earlier, California gun owners had started showing up in coffee shops and restaurants with long guns strapped to their backs. Why? To exercise their right to carry unconcealed weapons in public view.

Having a bunch of guys show up at businesses openly bearing their weapons was alarming to customers and business owners. My activist friends with the Brady chapters in California were also alarmed, so they'd organized protests. And it worked. For weeks, they'd stood in front of businesses where the open carry guys met, holding signs and chanting that they wanted gun-free dining—and many businesses, like Peet's Coffee & Tea and California Pizza Kitchen, had begun to forbid guns at their establishments.

Starbucks, however, had resisted.

Brady had fought back, collecting over thirty thousand signatures on a petition demanding Starbucks change their gun policy. I was asked to help deliver the petitions to their headquarters in

dumb girl

Seattle. But first we were to hold a press conference and protest near the site of the original Starbucks store at Pike Place Market.

So there I was on a rainy, cold gray spring morning in downtown Seattle protesting Starbucks's gun policy. Behind me stood a dozen fellow gun control advocates and Aaron, my twelve-year-old son, who proudly held a sign he'd made the previous day: "Hot Coffee not Hot Bullets." I'd decided to let him skip school that day so he could see what I do and see what using your First Amendment right really looked like. The attention to detail he'd demonstrated when making his sign and his willingness to wear a Million Mom March T-shirt while standing behind me made me feel admired and supported.

Numerous TV cameras and reporters from both local and national news stations were there to capture what we'd be saying and get the visuals—us protesting Starbucks and the open carry guys protesting us. It was a made-for-TV moment, and I well understood the gravity of it.

As I began my speech, I looked at the cameras, the reporters, the bystanders, and the protesters, conscious not to peek at my notes too much and trying not to shiver in the frigid air, which was thick with mist from Puget Sound behind us.

I quickly got into a rhythm and landed the talking points I had practiced. About midway through my speech, I said, "By allowing people to openly carry firearms in their [Starbucks's] stores, they're violating the public's trust."

"You're violating our trust!" a woman yelled in a high-pitched voice.

Wait, I thought, *that doesn't even make sense*. After a brief hesitation, I continued.

But she kept yelling and soon more people joined in, shouting, hollering, and booing. Their taunts got louder and louder as their anger swirled around me.

I felt a familiar sinking feeling.

gun guy

3

I pant hard as I frantically ride my bike home from school. My report card is due to arrive in the mail today, and I know I did terribly on both my spelling and social studies tests this winter quarter. I'm desperate to get to the mailbox before Mom and Dad.

Getting good grades has become increasingly difficult in fifth grade. I'm eleven now, and I feel like I'm trying my best, but I'm still not one of the smart kids. They seem to "get" stuff I don't.

Spelling tests are the hardest. I also find memorizing the state capitals, where they are on a map, and the routes explorers took to find America to be boring and impossible to remember. The four days of the year when we get a report card fill me with panic and fear.

I breathe a sigh of relief when I open the garage door and see that Mom and Dad are not home yet. I rush to the mailbox, cautiously opening the envelope, my eyes searching for the spelling grade. This is usually my worst grade, and I know that all the other grades will be higher.

It's a C-, and I feel a ping of relief; I thought it was going to be an F.

As I look through the twenty categories on the report card (sharing, doing his/her best, being nice to others, participating fully, etc.), I begin to relax, confident nothing will be lower than the C- spelling grade. But then I see the large "F" next to "Social Studies."

My heart sinks. I know this will be hard to explain to Dad, and I have no idea just how angry it will make him.

Tonight Mom, Dad, Philip, Robby, and I go to our usual Mexican restaurant to celebrate the end of the third quarter of the school year. The restaurant is chaotic with brightly colored decorations and too many tables for the space. It's filled with people

dumb girl

celebrating the end of the week while energetic traditional Mexican music plays in the background. It feels fake and forced and doesn't match the apprehension I'm feeling.

My plan is to bring up the subject of grades here, knowing a public place will shield me from being yelled at or hit. I also know it's important to bring it up at just the right time so I can control Dad's reaction as much as possible.

Dad beats me to it.

"So," he says casually after we place our orders, "how'd you guys do on your report cards?"

Robby and I entertain ourselves with the sugar packets, opening them and dumping the contents of each packet in our mouths, one at a time, while Philip goes on and on about his classes and how his teachers love him.

By the time he's done, our food is arriving. As the waitress haphazardly puts our dinners in front of us, I quickly announce, "Robby said he did pretty good on his report card."

That's not entirely true, unfortunately. I know he has a few C-s, and I know that will cause Dad concern. Robby's only eight, after all. Getting As and Bs shouldn't be that hard in second grade.

Mom is drinking her second margarita and not participating much in the conversation. At stressful times like this, I feel like Mom is one of our equals, not an advocate or any type of shield. It's Dad who cares about our grades, or at least reacts the most to them.

Dad's angry with Robby and the C-s, so he lectures him with direct eye contact and a raised voice. When he finishes his rant and the conversation starts to show signs of ending, I once again throw Robby under the bus.

"He probably didn't do so well because once when he said he was in his room studying, he was playing with his Stretch Armstrong," I declare.

gun guy

    Dad's voice once again becomes loud as he reprimands him, telling him how disappointed he is. I come up with three or four more statements that keep the focus on Robby until Dad notices what I'm doing and, as the waitress puts the *sopaipillas* on the table, finally asks, "Heidi, how'd you do on your report card?"

    My heart races. "Well . . . okay, I guess." I pull the folded, tattered paper out of my back pocket and hand it to Mom, hoping she'll take the conversation over.

    She puts her margarita down and unfolds it.

    As she and Dad study it across the table, I frantically search their faces for any sign of my immediate future. I'm hoping for the "I know you try hard, but you need to try harder" speech or *The Brady Bunch* Dad "I know you struggle with this, and I want to help you do better" speech. I hold my breath.

    As Dad's eyes slowly shift from the paper to me, I know I've made a huge mistake in waiting for my report card to be discussed last. I'm not going to get a simple speech. His face hardens, his eyes become small, and the air around us stands still, heavy with tension. His whole body radiates with anger.

    I look down, unable to bear his fury.

    "We'll talk about this at home," he says tightly.

    Him not saying much terrifies me. The bright reds and oranges and yellows in the decorations around the restaurant suddenly feel too bright, too bold, and alarming. My go-to strategy of acting extremely happy to change his mood isn't going to work this time. Nothing I can say will change Dad's mood.

The drive home is dark, quiet, and long. I know I'm in a lot of trouble, and I can't think of anything on the way home that will help me. Mom by this time is drunk and will go straight to bed when we get home, so she's not going to be any help. I'm on my own.

    When we get home, I go straight to my room, shut the door, get into my nightgown, quickly clean my room spotless, and lie

dumb girl

in my bed. I pray that the silent drive has calmed Dad down, and when he checks on me he'll see me "asleep" and decide being angry and waking me up is useless. I also think that if my room is clean and I look really cute, curled up in bed, he will leave me alone.

I lie in my bed perfectly still, listening to Dad scream at Robby. His booming voice—belittling him about his bad grades and his inability to keep a tidy room—is getting louder and louder, penetrating the thin wall between our bedrooms.

Well at least he can't be mad at me about a dirty room, I think.

I listen as he throws things against the wall and hits Robby. I listen as Robby cries and scrambles to stay out of his reach. I pray that he'll stop and that he won't kill Robby. I also pray that he'll get all of his anger out on Robby so there won't be any left for me. I feel incredibly selfish, useless, and scared.

Time passes, and things die down. I know I'm next.

My door swings open. He never gives himself a chance to see how cute and innocent I am as he screams, "Heidi! Get up!"

Tigger, who's been lying peacefully next to my head, makes a dash for the door.

Dad flips my light switch on, revealing an immaculately clean room. I always think Robby is dumb not to keep his room clean, because it seems to give Dad more ammunition. I will later realize having a clean room never spared me, it just made me feel in control.

The next two hours are as close to hell as I have ever been. I'm pushed, slapped, hit, grabbed, and hurt. He tells me I'm dumb, an idiot, stupid, and worthless, and he tells me he can't understand why anyone is friends with me. The night becomes a blur of me feeling scared, inadequate, unsafe, sad, small, and powerless mixed with his yelling, rage, spite, cruelty, aggression, and power.

When things don't seem like they can get worse, he yells, "Go get every single one of your spelling tests and bring them to me."

gun guy

He sits on my bed while I frantically search my desk. I hand him eight.

He narrows his eyes. "That's it?"

"Yeah, that's all I could find," I say cautiously.

"Then go get every paper and test you've gotten a D or F on, in all subjects."

I scramble to my closet, where I find dozens in a box. I hand them to him.

After he looks over them, he says, "Now, tape every one of these on your wall."

He watches me as tears stream down my face and my hands shake while taping the dozen or so D and F papers to the wall. I try to figure out where he's going with this and what it's going to teach me.

After the last paper's taped on the wall, he nods, satisfied. "Now all your friends will know how stupid you are!"

All the air leaves my lungs, and the room starts to spin.

While I try to catch my breath from the emotional blow, I think, *Fine, I'll never invite anyone over again, so they'll never see the wall.* It gives me a very small feeling of victory.

But he's not done yet. He continues to belittle me, hit me, and lecture me for what feels like hours. I wish Mom would wake up and help me, but she never comes. I don't know why.

The night ends with me crying myself to sleep in a dark cloud of pain, surrounded by proof of my many failures. At least Tigger is there; he jumps back onto my bed after Dad leaves and he sees the danger is gone.

Going forward, that wall of shame is the last thing I see every night as I fall asleep and the first thing I see when I wake up. I'm terrified to take the papers down for fear I'll get into trouble again.

I learn a lot that night, and I change things so I'll never have a repeat of it.

dumb girl

I learn to stay at least an arm's length away from Dad when he's angry—it makes it less tempting for him to hit me.

I cheat on every spelling test to ensure a good grade. I can't trust myself to do well.

Whenever a signature is required for a poor grade I receive, I forge it.

And lastly, I begin to understand that I have no control and I am, in fact, stupid.

A few weeks later, on a sunny April afternoon following an unsuccessful search for a four-leaf clover in our backyard, I'm heading upstairs to my room when I hear yelling in Mom and Dad's room. I creep slowly and quietly up the stairs with cautious curiosity to see who's in trouble now.

I reach the top of the stairs and gently squeeze through the partially open door as I hold my breath. As I round the corner, I see the back of Dad's large frame through the bathroom mirror; he's looking down at Robby, who's red-faced with tears running down his cheeks.

He looks so small compared to Dad. Which makes sense. He's eight.

His shoulders are rounded and his eyes down, avoiding Dad's glare. He looks scared. Dad's in the middle of berating him for something he's done or not done, and Robby's literally backed up against the wall.

Just then Dad yells, "I'll give you something to cry about!" and he punches Robby right in the stomach.

Robby immediately doubles over in pain and lets out an agonizing "Ughhhh" as the air from his diaphragm leaves his lungs. Dad looks down at Robby and says, "Come on, take it like a man!"

I can't believe what I'm hearing or what I'm seeing—except deep down, I do.

I back up before Dad sees me and makes me part of his

horrifying game. I quickly return to my room and busy myself with my Barbies, trying not to think about what's happening to Robby.

Later that night, I walk into Robby's room and whisper into his ear, "The best way to keep Dad from punching or hitting you is to try and stay at least an arm's length away. If you're too close, it's too tempting for him."

Robby nods. I walk back into my room feeling glad I thought to tell him and hoping it will keep him safe.

I wish I could do more to protect him.

As angry gun owners yelled at me for protesting Starbucks's gun policy, I was hyperaware that my son was standing just a couple of feet behind me. I wondered what he thought about his mom being yelled at by people carrying guns on their hips, and I wondered if he was scared.

Should I have even brought a twelve-year-old here with me in the first place? I wondered.

As I continued with my speech, the crowd inched forward. I fought to stay present and not cower to their anger and threats. The only thing I could do was to just keep moving forward with my written remarks.

When I got to my conclusion, my final plea, I took a big breath and said, "So please, Starbucks, please don't allow people to carry firearms in your store. If you do, my family can once again drink coffee without fear of death."

As Brian, the moderator, took over the podium to give a few final remarks before wrapping up the protest, I turned to Aaron.

"You okay?" I asked him.

"Yeah, that was crazy! I can't believe how much they were yelling at you." His tone and smile made me understand he didn't share my fear. I was in awe of his ability to see screaming, angry gun enthusiasts not as a threat but as part of a spectacle.

dumb girl

As I gathered up the signs, my notes, and my bag, a short bald guy with a gun on his hip came up to me and started a conversation. It was cordial and surprisingly pleasant. He asked, "Did you mean it when you said you don't trust guys who 'open carry'?"

I looked at him and then over his shoulder at the guys who'd been yelling at me. "So here's my deal," I said. "You seem like a pretty nice guy, and you seem like a guy who's probably pretty responsible with your guns."

He nodded in agreement and smiled.

"But look at those guys over there. Do you really know them? Do you know that none of them are drunk, or angry, or on drugs, or just had a fight with their wife and want to take it out on someone else?" I lifted my chin in their direction. "Surely you don't *know all* of them. You don't know what their deal is. Do you seriously trust all of them?"

He looked over to the lingering audience members and then slowly back to me. He exhaled, his eyes dropped, and his shoulders slumped as he thought about my questions—of course he didn't know them and of course he didn't trust them. The question seemed to flummox him. But then suddenly he took a big breath, puffed up his chest, looked me straight in the eyes, and defiantly said, "Ugh yeah, I trust 'em."

I shook my head in disbelief. "Okay . . . Well, thanks for talking to me," I said. "It's nice to know that we can have a civil conversation and not just yell at each other. I'm glad to know that not *all* of you are disrespectful."

I reached out my hand, he shook it, and then I walked away.

Though we ultimately didn't find a real common ground, that interaction felt like a huge win. I'd had a civil conversation with one of my nemeses and had even managed to get him to question his own hard-held beliefs, even if it was just for a couple of seconds.

In that brief moment I felt clever, kind, respectful, and smart. I felt my power.

chapter 12

understanding

I was starting to see that fearing and avoiding the gun guys was not getting me anywhere. It didn't help me be a better advocate and it wasn't particularly effective. And on a personal level, feeling scared of them wasn't good for me.

It felt like it would be more effective to try to understand where they came from and why they were so adamant about having no restrictions on gun ownership, even common-sense restrictions like for age and prior felonies. I wanted to go toward them, have conversations with them, and understand their perspectives. I figured if I could just understand their motivations and histories, maybe I wouldn't be so scared.

It wasn't the first time I'd tried this tactic.

I am desperate to understand Dad. I think if I can get to know more about where he came from and who he was as a little boy instead of the scary and unpredictable man I know now, I'll somehow be less scared of him and be able to be the daughter he wants me to be.

The stories of Dad growing up in Grand Junction, Colorado, come in small bits and pieces and never really fit together or explain why he is the way he is.

The way Dad tells it, for the first eight years of his life he

dumb girl

lived with his mom and dad and older brother. At age eight his mom was diagnosed with breast cancer and, as soon as she found out, bought a train ticket to Denver to have a mastectomy. A week before her trip in 1941, a faith healer came to town and convinced her to pray instead of going to Denver for the surgery. God would heal her, he assured her. So she prayed.

Praying didn't work. She died when Dad was eight, in third grade.

His mom's death left two boys, eight and fourteen, alone with their father to raise them. His dad knew nothing about raising boys and was responsible for putting food on the table. Dad's three aunts, his mom's sisters, all lived nearby and took over the task of raising Dad and his brother. The three sisters did their best to help a bad situation.

The middle sister eventually married Dad's dad to become the official new mom. I think it's weird that his aunt married his dad, but it's explained to me that that's just what families did back then.

She might have taken on the role of mother, but she certainly didn't become what a mom should be: warm, kind, gentle, helpful, and loving. I wonder if she was bitter about having to exchange her life for her sister's.

Dad's aunt is a schoolteacher and a mean one at that. When I write thank-you letters to her after Christmases and birthdays, she mails my letters back filled with red marks, the spelling and punctuation corrected. Apparently, she loves me, and this is her way of showing me, so I'm told.

Dad's interactions with her were similar to mine. He tells me once how she drove him eight hours to start college. He was excited and scared, never having been that far away from home before. When they pulled up to his dorm, he got his suitcase out of the car. She leaned over from the steering wheel to the passenger side window where he stood and said, "I hope you have a terrible time!" and then drove away.

understanding

    I feel sorry for Dad that he has such a crappy mom. I'm grateful that she lives in California and we don't have to see much of her. Knowing about Dad's history and the family he comes from doesn't end up helping me be a better daughter or make him less scary. Dad is Dr. Jekyll and Mr. Hyde for me.

    It's the times when he is happy that I feel like he's the greatest dad ever. I love being with him in these moments. I'm his buddy, and his nickname for me is Heidi-Pooh. When he has errands to run, I volunteer to go with him. We drive to the hardware store to get tools for projects he's working on, we drive together to get Shakey's Pizza on most Friday nights, and we drive together to get Kentucky Fried Chicken when Mom is "sick" from drinking too much wine. He enthusiastically drives me to basketball camps and tennis tournaments, and sometimes we just drive to drive. I love being in the car with him where nothing affects his mood. We drive in his red 1973 Mustang Convertible with the sun beating down on our foreheads, my hair whipping around, and me feeling free and loved. I show him the radio stations I like and sing to him "Jack and Diane" by John Cougar, "Afternoon Delight" by Starland Vocal Band, or "Rainy Days and Mondays" by Karen Carpenter.

    The care and love I feel from Dad continue on the ski slopes. When we go skiing as a family, I'm always so cold, and Dad does everything he can to help me warm up my freezing fingers and toes. His concern for me is unmistakable. On the painfully slow ski lift up the mountain, as we're pelted by snow and wind, he lovingly takes his warm black leather gloves off and puts them on my ice-cold small hands while blowing his hot breath into my cold mittens, one at a time, to warm them up. It feels heavenly to put my numb fingers back into my warmed mittens as he gently explains to me the importance of keeping my fingers and thumb together so the body heat from my hands can keep my fingers warm. At lunch, my fingers and toes are painfully numb from

dumb girl

the cold despite Dad's efforts, so he helps me take off my ski boots and gently places my frozen foot under his bare underarm to warm it up. When one foot is done, he warms the other.

The problem is his kindness and loving care of me are fleeting and I never know when I should or shouldn't lean into it. And I frequently choose wrong.

At twelve, I've been having a lot of anxiety about why I haven't gotten my period yet. All my friends seem to have gotten theirs already; why haven't I?

Mom and I talk about my period, what to do when I get it the first time, how it will feel physically, and what it means to be a "woman." She shows me where the "stuff" is for when my period comes and I ask, "How do tampons or maxi pads work?"

"We didn't have those when I was growing up, we only had belts," she says dismissively. "What I will tell you is that when you do become a woman, it will be a day to celebrate."

When mine finally comes for the first time, I'm excited to tell Mom and Dad. The second Dad gets home from work that day, I run up to him in the garage as he gets out of his car and blurt, "I've become a woman! I got my first period today."

He smiles and says, "Wow, that's great, Heidi. I'm proud of you."

And then he lets me hug him before we both walk into the house.

That night Mom cooks a "special" dinner—Hamburger Helper Beef Pasta and red Jell-O with canned fruit, which is probably what we were going to have anyway—to celebrate my "womanhood." I revel in the attention.

A month later, when I get my period again, I assume the celebration of my womanhood and ability to give life will continue and am anxious to share the good news with Dad. As soon as I hear

understanding

the vibration of Dad's car as he drives up to the house at the end of his day, I run to the garage, push the button on the wall, and watch the garage door slowly open.

"Dad!" I enthusiastically yell across the room as he slowly climbs out of his car. "Guess what? I got my period today!"

He glances at me as he walks by, looking tired. His head hangs low, his shoulders slump, and his necktie loosely hangs around his neck as I notice that the wrinkles in his dress shirt match the deep stress wrinkles in his forehead.

I bounce as I follow him into the house, ignoring his sour mood, figuring my good news about my period will brighten him like it did last month. "Aren't you excited?" I demand.

He abruptly stops and turns around, looking me straight in the eyes. "No, I'm not excited," he bellows. "It's a normal part of life and we're not going to make a big deal about it. In fact, I don't want to know about it every month."

I'm crushed. I'm embarrassed. I'm confused. But mostly, I wish I wasn't a girl. I never talk to him about my period after that, except to complain about the painful menstrual cramps that accompany it.

His response? "It's all in your head."

I feel like a DBADG.

Dad was always hot and cold—far too unpredictable for me to ever make sense of his actions. But I learned from his volatility. I learned how to read a room, how to read men, and how to talk to them in a way that doesn't threaten their ego. Because of Dad, I instinctively knew not to challenge that short bald guy's ego at the Starbucks protest and instead gently guide him to see what I saw.

I knew the importance of keeping our conversation civil.

chapter 13

giving/taking

Lonnie played dead for seven hours after her boyfriend shot her three times in the head. Miraculously, she managed to stay alive while the SWAT team negotiated with him to come out over those many hours.

She was the first person I interviewed for the book I was writing about people who'd been impacted by gun violence.

Lonnie was a forty-one-year-old glass artist who still lived and worked in the house where four years earlier, in 2001, she almost lost her life. And it was in that same house, in the same room, where I interviewed her. The room was inviting, with soft blue walls, warm lighting, and smells of lavender and sandalwood. No evil hangover was detectable that might have lingered after the violent events that had taken place there.

Sitting in that peaceful room, Lonnie described to me how her boyfriend had pushed her onto the couch, covered her face with a pillow, and shot three times. One of the bullets went through her cheek. The scar was still visible, and she told me she'd decided not to have plastic surgery to fix it because "It is who I am now. It's my star nebula. I think my scar looks like the opening of heaven."

Her bravery floored me, and I was shocked that she was willing to tell me her story, a stranger she'd only briefly met at a networking event a month earlier.

giving/taking

I'd decided to tell the stories of people who'd been impacted by gun violence because I'd grown tired of talking about statistics and wanted to show the real impact, but I was a little on the fence on whether or not I could get people to open up to me or do what it takes to write a book. Once I interviewed Lonnie, who seemed to trust me implicitly, I knew I had to finish and publish the book no matter what. *If she can share the details of her horrific near-death experience*, I thought, *the least I can do is follow up with my promise to her to tell her story.* It felt like a contract.

Yet asking strangers to tell me the details of the worst day of their lives felt nosy and meddlesome. I was so grateful to every person I interviewed but could not shake the feeling that I was taking from them or possibly retraumatizing them further.

Until I interviewed Michelle.

Michelle carried a heavy mix of sorrow and rage, along with a charitable disposition, warm smile, and haunted eyes—haunted in the same way as those of the women I'd met at the Million Mom March.

When we were introduced and I heard her name, I immediately thought of my childhood friend Michelle who'd been murdered. This Michelle, though, was a different kind of victim: It was her son who had been killed—shot at a party three years before we met. She was burdened with pain and shared in detail the frustration she'd had with the police, who she felt were not particularly interested in finding and arresting her son's killer.

About an hour and a half into the interview, as Michelle described the overwhelming emotional pain she was in, it occurred to me that she might have PTSD, post-traumatic stress disorder. Not being a therapist, I simply asked her, "Michelle, have you ever talked to anyone about what you've been through?"

She wiped her eyes with the damp and torn tissue in her hand and said, "Well . . . I've talked to God"—she looked at the

dumb girl

ceiling as she thought about it a beat longer—"and I've talked to you."

The weight of her words took my breath away.

It was at that moment I realized my questions were not intrusive, were not invasive, were not inappropriate; they were helpful. I was creating an opportunity for her to get her pain off her chest, and my listening was honoring not just her pain but her son's life. I was not *taking* from her; my being there, listening and caring, was an act of *giving*.

When Michelle is murdered, I'm just eleven. I have no way to process or understand her death, and I am desperate for answers, details, and connection with people who knew her best.

Amy was Michelle's best friend. I figure she's sad about losing Michelle; I think maybe we should be friends. (I also think maybe she'll know what happens to you when you die; Mom telling me "Michelle's in heaven" just doesn't cut it.)

One afternoon, I ride my bike to Amy's house a few blocks away, ring the doorbell, and ask if she wants to play. She says yes and invites me in. We hit it off immediately and spend most days of that summer together.

She has an impressive collection of plastic Breyer Horses, a second-floor laundry chute, which I think is the coolest invention ever, the entire five-book Judy Blume series, and the confidence to call FM radio stations and request songs from the DJ in English and Texan accents.

We don't talk a lot about Michelle but when I ask her if she misses her, she simply says, "Yes," as she solemnly looks down at the floor and then quickly recovers with a half smile before we call another radio station to request a Captain & Tennille song.

Later, while sitting together on her bedroom floor, playing with the Breyer Horses, I ask her, "What was the funeral like?"

"Sad," she says while putting a harness on Misty, her favorite

giving/taking

horse. Then without looking up she says, "No one really wants to play with me anymore, at least not since Michelle's funeral." Her sadness fills the room for a few seconds and then vanishes when she suddenly rolls over onto her knees, gently makes Misty gallop across the carpet, then lifts her in the air in a slow-motion jump while making *neighhhh, neighhhh* sound effects.

Somehow, I know not to ask Amy specific questions about Michelle's death, the funeral, the pain, or what she saw and knows. I dance around it and decide just to be there, to hang out with her, to play with her and have fun with her. It's instinctual. I guess I just do what I would want her to do if Michelle had been my best friend.

Though I won't know this until decades later, befriending Amy and maneuvering around her sadness and the void Michelle's death left is the start of my training for writing and interviewing people for my book. With Amy, I experience the power of being fully present and authentic with someone who has experienced great loss.

A couple of months after I interviewed Michelle about her son, I interviewed Sandi, whose twenty-one-year-old son (her only child), Christopher, was killed in what was known as the Seattle Capitol Hill massacre. Seven young people, including the shooter, died in that shooting.

A year had passed since Christopher's death when I drove to Sandi's house to ask her questions about how his tragic and untimely death had affected her life.

When I first arrived, Sandi showed me Christopher's basement bedroom, which was pristine: His bed was made, his books were perfectly lined up on the shelf above his desk, and his shoes were carefully placed next to his backpack on the floor. As she walked into his room, she said, "I haven't turned his light off since he died," and then she sprayed a small bottle of his musky

dumb girl

and slightly sweet cologne into the center of the room. As she took a big deep breath to inhale his scent, she closed her eyes. Her anguish was palpable.

We sat down on her back porch together to record our conversation. After just a couple of questions, she began to weep and then to sob, so much so that I couldn't understand her. I began to worry I was harming her.

When Sandi finished her story, in between sobs, about finding out at the funeral that Christopher had been secretly helping homeless teens who lived under a busy highway overpass, I reached over to the recorder and turned it off.

"I feel like I'm retraumatizing you," I said, "and it's totally not worth it if I'm causing you even more harm. I think we should stop."

Her demeanor changed instantaneously: She sat up straight in her metal chair, her eyes pleading. "Oh no!" she exclaimed. "You're not hurting me—just the opposite. I never get to tell my entire story. I go to support groups, and I talk for like ten minutes and then have to stop and let someone else go. This is the first time I've been able to tell my story, out loud, from the beginning to the end. Please don't stop."

So we continued on—her sobbing, me listening and asking questions about Christopher, their relationship, and his death. As the interview wrapped up, I was filled with a sense of connection and purpose. I felt an intimacy with her as she shared the details of her pain, her anguish, and her regrets as a mother.

And just as I had with Amy, I once again felt the power of being fully present and authentic with someone who had experienced great loss.

PART THREE

chapter 14

bored

One average winter vacation day when Mom and Dad are at The Fireplace Store, Doug is at college, and Robby is playing at the next-door neighbor's—that's when the game starts.

I am ten. Philip is fourteen.

I'm upstairs in my room playing Barbies, which involves getting Barbie, her sister Skipper, and Ken ready for fabulous outings and exciting adventures, when Philip yells for me to come with him down to the basement.

Grateful to have someone to play with besides Barbie and her perfect family, I happily walk down to the basement.

It's dark down here and the single-bulb hall light above me casts long shadows into the room, with just enough light to see the posters that still cover the walls of the room Doug abandoned for college four months earlier. The furniture, 8-track player and tapes, books, and clothes in the closet make it feel and smell like it's still Doug's room.

As soon as I step into the room, I hear Philip's quiet, detached voice from the back of the room. "Come here," he urges.

He's sitting on the edge of Doug's bed. I can see his outline and part of his face through the shadows but not much else. He pats the bed next to him as his lips form a half smile. I slowly walk over to him and sit down. He tells me he wants to play a new game called "boyfriend/girlfriend." He explains how the game works. He'll turn off all the lights and leave. While he's gone, I'll take all my clothes off and lie on the bed and pretend to be asleep. Then he'll come back, and we'll pretend he's my boyfriend, and I'll do what he says.

I don't really understand the game or the point, but I think maybe I'll figure it out later. "Okay," I say reluctantly.

He leaves and I do what he told me to do. I take off my blue turtleneck shirt along with my tan polyester pants and Holly Hobbie underwear. I pile them, inside out, onto the floor next to the bed. I lie on the bed and hope he hurries back because I'm getting cold. I lie perfectly still as I listen to his feet land on each wooden step as he makes his way down the stairs. He quietly walks over to me and stands there for what feels like a long time. I squeeze my eyes tight, pretending to be asleep.

I hear him remove his clothes and then feel him touch my stomach with his hand. He glides it slowly down from my belly button until I feel it touch my hairless vagina. Suddenly I shiver and my goose bumps intensify as coldness envelops me. He then gets on top of me, his knees on either side of my hips. I keep my eyes closed. I hear the bed springs squeak as the bed adjusts to our weight and then feel him hit something against my vagina.

Then I feel nothing. He rustles around. Then I'm floating. I am above me. Above us. Looking down. I still can't see but I'm not in my body. I don't feel anything. Don't feel him touching me, slapping me, handling me, probing me. I just float. I don't feel, physically or emotionally.

Years later, in therapy, I will learn that the technical word for "floating" is disassociation. It's how my mind protects me by shutting off the trauma into non-memory, and it's a very common experience among children who are molested. Today, I simply float until he gets off me.

bored

When I am back in my body, I feel him touch my flat chest. I don't understand why he touches me there, his fingers gently circling my tiny nipples. Then I hear him leave. I open my eyes and see nothing.

As my eyes adjust, taking in the little light there is, they focus on a poster of Cheryl Tiegs in her tiny pink bikini. She smiles at me, her teeth white and perfect. I sit up, gently get off the bed, pick up my clothes, and put them on before slowly walking up the two sets of stairs to my warm room where I continue playing Barbies, just where I left off.

Day after day we play this game. When school goes back into session, we stop or do it on the weekends when nobody else is home.

In the summer, the game is relocated to his room. His room is sunny and bright and yellow, so I can no longer hide in the darkness. I don't float as much but the feeling of extreme boredom is constant. I can see his penis. It's skinny and I hate touching it. I hate lying there, motionless, as he hits it on me. I don't like it touching me. I don't like spreading my legs and giving him access to probe me.

I search for ways not to be alone at home with him so I don't have to play his game. I find respite playing and dancing to Disney songs on tape with a girl up the street who's Robby's age. Because she is younger than me, Mom discourages me from playing with her, insisting, "You need to play with someone your own age."

Despite Mom's objections, I sneak over to her house as much as I can.

"I want to play," I say to Philip and Robby as they run past me, almost knocking me over. Shirtless, Philip points a blue plastic dart gun at Robby, who is also shirtless, as he jumps over the couch, landing with a thud on the burnt-orange shag carpet just

dumb girl

as a bright-orange dart whizzes by his head. They are both dripping with sweat.

Playing "dart guns" is not the most fun thing to do, but it's one of the ways we combat boredom.

And we're bored a lot.

Our school district has adopted the educational Concept 6 Plan, which is a way for our over-populated schools to create more classroom space by keeping the school buildings open year-round. What it means to us is we get two months off school in the summer and two months off in the winter.

Mom and Dad can't take two months off work, so we're left to entertain ourselves.

Besides playing dart guns, we watch an enormous amount of TV, which we're not allowed to do. Mom tells us, "TV will rot your brains," but the threat of brain-rot is not a big enough incentive to stop us. The TV is on from the time they leave for work until the minute we hear them pull into the driveway at the end of the day.

"I want to play!" I whine again.

"Okay," Philip says to me as he leans over trying to catch his breath, "you can play but you can't wear a shirt. It makes it harder to hit you if you don't have a shirt on. Besides," he adds, "it's the rule."

Not wanting to break the rules, I take off my shirt and he hands me a blue plastic handgun and six orange foam darts.

The nakedness of my eleven-year-old chest, with small mounds beginning to protrude, makes me uncomfortable and unable to concentrate on the game as I hide and roll and dive behind the couch, trying not to get hit by Robby's dart. I don't like playing topless, but if I don't, I'll be called a DBADG.

Nudity has been the norm in our house ever since Mom, Dad, Philip, and Doug went on their Europe trip last year. They went for three weeks, including a week in Sweden with the family Mom lived with when she was an exchange student in high school.

bored

When they returned, Mom and Dad told Robby and me about their week in Sweden.

"What's so great about the people in Sweden is they aren't ashamed of their bodies like Americans," Dad enthused. "The Swedes love being nude. We went swimming, laid in the sun, and took saunas, all without the constraints of a swimsuit. It's the most natural and freeing feeling in the world!"

"We've decided to put an addition onto the house," Mom told us. "We're going to build a sunroom off the back of the house, convert Dad's office into a sauna and shower room, and put a pool in the backyard."

Robby, Philip, and I literally jumped for joy and hugged each other as we celebrated the news.

Once construction was done eight months later, we had a pool, a big sunroom, a sauna, and a huge shower, made specifically so more than one person can shower at a time.

"The more the merrier!" Mom enthusiastically broadcasted.

So I started taking showers with Dad.

At the beginning, I didn't think much about my showers with Dad. I'd seen him naked a bunch of times, so it didn't seem weird.

But now that I'm twelve and my body is starting to change, I have questions. For one, I'm perplexed and fascinated by how his penis size changes, sometimes hanging down and small and then, near the end of the shower, longer and bigger. I somehow know not to ask about it.

We are instructed not to wear swimsuits in the sauna, "to be natural, the way God made us." It makes sense because, as Dad explains, "God made us in his image, we were born naked, and we shouldn't be ashamed of our bodies."

Mom and Dad lean into their nudity awakening so much that they hang a large sign on the wall next to the sauna that says "No swimsuits allowed after 6 p.m.!" So we swim without suits, we lie

dumb girl

in the sauna without suits, and we shower together without suits. The only place we wear swimsuits is on the pool deck because "the neighbors won't understand."

I used to be okay with all this because I liked the idea of how sophisticated and worldly it made us. I felt like we were special. But now it's becoming uncomfortable. I've become very aware that Mom and I are the only ones without a penis in this family. My skinny upper body still looks like my brothers', mostly flat and hairless, but I try to cover myself with a towel, especially my lower half as I become increasingly self-conscious.

Word about the pool gets out at school. "I just found out you put a pool in your backyard," a classmate says to me at lunch recess. "Lucky! When do Paul and Phil and me get to come over and go swimming?"

I revel in the attention, and I feel popular. I invite my friend Susan, who is in my Girl Scout troop, and instantly become overwhelmed with excitement for her to be my first friend to use the pool and sauna. I spend Saturday morning vacuuming and fluffing the pillows in the new sunroom, and I refold the brightly colored striped towels in the sauna room, placing them perfectly in line so she'll be impressed.

When she arrives that afternoon, I grab her arm, yanking her to follow me to see the sauna and new sunroom. Satisfied with her excitement over our new additions, I quickly close both sets of doors into the sauna room and we start to undress. As she starts to put on her swimsuit, I say, "Oh, you aren't allowed to wear a swimsuit." I clarify, "It's the rule," as I point to the sign on the wall.

Just then, Mom comes in and heads to the sauna. Right before she reaches for the sauna door, she takes her robe off and we uncomfortably stare at her backside, noticing the large stretch marks on her white skin that four pregnancies have left.

Susan and I look at each other, her face contorted in a question along with disbelief that Mom is now fully naked.

bored

I watch her nervously look around and realize she does not want to stay. I don't want her to leave. Panic sets in. It takes some doing, but I finally convince her that this is what we do in our house and it's perfectly normal. "It's what all the people in Sweden do," I explain in an English accent, trying to change the mood.

We open the sauna door and sit down on the bench facing naked Mom, lying peacefully with her eyes closed on the top bench. Our combined nakedness feels briefly comforting, as finally there is a girl in the sauna who looks like me—hairless and boy-chested. I can feel Susan's unease as we try to have conversations without looking at Mom's body or each other's.

The air is full of heat and moisture and anxiety. I tell Mom we're hot and want to go swimming. She haphazardly flips her hand toward us and mumbles something we can't hear over the hiss of the heater, so we quickly grab our towels, put on our suits, and run out to the pool. The dive into the pool feels particularly refreshing, and Susan and I play and splash away the next two hours.

Susan's anxiety is the first time I think that maybe what we do in our family is not sophisticated and natural, but weird and not normal. I'm surprised that Dad doesn't make her shower with him like he does with me, and the afternoon leaves me to question the normality of it all.

A few days later, Susan comes up to me at school and bluntly announces, "I don't want to be your friend anymore."

When I ask her why, she says, "Because you bite your fingernails."

I don't figure out until years later that my fingernail biting has nothing to do with the loss of that friendship. But I never invite another friend over, for fear of what would be required of them.

The game has changed since we got our swimming pool. Philip hunts me whenever we're in the pool alone.

It starts as soon as we dive in. I know what he wants, so I race ahead of him as he grabs at my foot. I frantically kick, my

dumb girl

heart pounding, as I glance back at him, seeing that I've escaped him but just barely. I get to the edge of the pool, hoist myself out, take two quick steps along the pool, and dive back in, distancing myself while he continues the chase.

The challenge of out-swimming him, out-diving him, and evading him in the pool is usually a lost cause. He's four years older than me, bigger than me, faster than me, and smarter than me, so my deceptive strategies to get away from him usually fail and I end up trapped in the corner of the pool, him putting his finger inside me. He seems obsessed with my vagina. He tells me, "This is what boyfriends and girlfriends do." I don't like it and I hate that I have a vagina.

There comes a point where he no longer has to tell me he wants to play the game in the pool. I know by the way he looks at me or starts chasing me or grabbing me in places he likes to touch. I grow a radar for vibes he's transmitting and become sensitive to his moods, his looks, and any slight signals he gives off.

I don't want to be a dumb girl and I don't want to be a girl—at all. I eventually figure out that if Robby is in the pool with us, Philip won't touch me or try and touch me. So, when I sense that "pool time" is coming, I convince Robby to come with us. I try my best to only swim with Robby and be as close to him as possible when Philip's in the pool.

The basement, the pool, his room—it continues over and over, for months and then years, him telling me we are going to play boyfriend/girlfriend, me taking off all my clothes and him coming in to do what he wants and me being really bored.

He tells me I shouldn't tell anyone about the boyfriend/girlfriend game. "We have lots of secrets and things we don't tell Mom and Dad about," he insists. "This is just another secret like that. Dad wouldn't like it if he found out."

I don't want to get into trouble, so I never tell.

chapter 15

christian columbine

Reverend Don Marxhausen officiated at Dylan Klebold's funeral, one of the Columbine shooters. And for that, he lost his job. I spoke to him on the phone as part of my research for my book five years after he was forced out of his position.

He had a kind and gentle voice, the kind of voice you'd expect from a minister. We talked for an hour, at first about common acquaintances (he knew several people from my childhood church) and then about his painful experiences in the aftermath of the Columbine massacre.

He told me that when Dylan's dad called him asking him if he'd officiate at the funeral, he didn't hesitate to say yes, despite the Klebolds being universally and viscerally hated by the community. He wanted to use the opportunity to humanize the Klebolds and give them much-needed closure and redemption. He also felt Dylan's parents deserved to have a funeral for their beloved seventeen-year-old son, and he'd been the Klebold family's pastor prior to the massacre, so, in his mind, it made sense that he'd officiate at the service.

dumb girl

"He was their son," he said. "I believe in a forgiving God, and I felt for the Klebolds, who were mourning the loss of a child. They are God's children and deserve grace."

His congregation did not agree. And he was forced to resign. His frustration and pain felt fresh and distinct.

I understood the rejection of his congregation; after all, he gave comfort and guidance to the parents of a child who caused unimaginable pain to an entire community. They were angry, hurting, and needed someone to blame. I understood the limitations of a church community. I'd grown up in a church similar to Reverend Marxhausen's, one that provided me with love and acceptance—and at the same time, confusion and rejection.

At thirteen, I find refuge at church—specifically, my church youth group—as I try to navigate the conflict in my family and not be the outlet for Dad's anger, Mom's frustrations, and Philip's sexual desires.

Mom and Dad's focus has turned to saving The Fireplace House, which has begun to lose money. They are stressed out a lot. They spend their Saturdays and most weeknights at the store. When they're at home, Dad's angry and distracted. Their fights get louder and more intense, and Mom's drinking turns from social to escape.

At church, I'm told over and over that Jesus will save me and solve all my problems—I just need to pray hard enough and be devout enough. So every Sunday morning, I walk into the tan classroom-style portable building behind the main church for Sunday school, where a couple dozen of us teenagers sit on cold metal folding chairs facing a projection screen filled with words a guitar player sings passionately.

Singing is the highlight. I love the inspiring religious messages in the words. I love how the better singers add harmony to the slow and emotional songs. And I love how the slow songs gradually build

christian columbine

tension and climax at the end, leaving me on the verge of tears. The feeling of euphoria and community through singing is addictive.

After twenty minutes of singing, we break into small groups, usually by grade, and go into classrooms where a twenty-something-year-old leader reads a Bible verse and explains what it means in today's world.

I'm desperate for answers to why I'm so sad and anxious and what I can do to feel better, so I appreciate the straightforward formulas we are given: "Pray at least twice a day, start by thanking God for all you have, then ask forgiveness, and then, maybe, ask for something you want, but not every time, because you have a better chance of God granting your wish if you have more to thank him for than ask for."

I believe it completely and work to be the best Christian I can be. I pray before I go to sleep and pray when I get up every morning, like I'm told. I start with thanking God for my life, my family, and for all the good things I have, like basketball skills. I then tell him how sorry I am for all the bad things I've done, like stealing two cookies or gossiping about a friend, followed by asking for forgiveness for the things I've probably done bad but can't remember. Then I tell God how I don't deserve his love and clarify how grateful I am for any small amount of love he can give me. And, since school is still really hard for me, I bargain profusely with him to help me be smarter.

Because we are told over and over how much God loves us and how great it is going to be to live with him in heaven for all of eternity, I begin to covet the afterlife. I'm miserable and can't find a way out of it, so joining Jesus for eternity sounds like a great solution. I wonder, *If heaven is so great, why not just go there now?* I don't see the point of being here on Earth if God wants me to be with him and I want to be with him.

I ask Dad about it as we drive to the hardware store one Saturday afternoon. "Yeah, heaven is wonderful, but it's like this," he

dumb girl

explains. "Heaven is dessert and life on Earth is a peanut butter and jelly sandwich. Why would you throw away the PB&J and go straight for the dessert when you can have both?"

I guess that makes sense.

My Christian and life role model at thirteen is Linda Parker. She's a tomboy, she's a Christian, she's four years older than me, and she's the coolest person I know. She's also Philip's girlfriend. She gets me in a way nobody gets me and spends time with me. She loves playing sports, especially basketball. She loves Jesus and refuses to wear dresses. Until Linda, I didn't know you could not wear dresses. She's the polar opposite of a DBADG.

I tag along when she and Philip drive up to go skiing. The three of us sing at the top of our lungs to upbeat Christian music that loudly plays from her car's cassette player on the drive up to the mountain and then again, a cappella-style, while we're on the ski lifts. She and Philip have lots of inside jokes, do imitations of people from church, get into snowball fights, and goof around a lot. She is funny and relaxed, and I love being around her. She's a great skier and, like me, she gets a thrill out of bombing down the mountain as fast as she can but always stops to help me if I wipe out. I feel her kindness and compassion for me, and I admire her adventurous spirit and love of life.

One of the things I enjoy most about Linda is the time we spend aimlessly driving around South Denver in her burgundy hatchback, just the two of us talking about God, basketball, what high school is going to be like, and her advice on boys. I figure she's an expert, since she's dating Philip. I desperately want to ask her if he plays boyfriend/girlfriend with her but never have enough guts.

I look for answers in Philip's locked green plastic file box in the back of his closet, where he keeps letters from girlfriends, stuff from church retreats, certificates and awards from school,

christian columbine

a couple of wooden cross necklaces, a small diary, and old report cards. It's private, and I know I'm not allowed to look in it, but I know where he keeps the key, so, when he's not home I unlock it and read the letters and diary entries.

It's the letters from girlfriends, especially Linda, I'm most interested in. I search the letters trying to find some kind of evidence they're physically intimate. Do they kiss? Does he touch her boobs? Does he touch her anywhere else? Is it boring for her too?

I can't find anything in the letters or his diary and just assume she must not be doing "stuff" with Philip or else why would he still be doing "stuff" with me? I secretly wish she would.

Around this same time, there's a lot of talk in my church youth group about the importance of "becoming a Christian and accepting Jesus into your heart." I'm taught that the only way to avoid going to hell when I die is by saying a specific prayer to God that includes telling him I understand he sent Jesus, his only begotten son, to save me from my sins. To avoid hell, I need to tell Jesus I'll accept him into my heart.

I say, "Count me in."

Many of my church friends, including Linda, tell me that accepting Jesus as their personal Savior was the most monumental and spectacular moment of their life. They describe how everything changed for good the moment they did "the prayer," accepting Jesus into their hearts. I want everything in my life to change for good but am worried I'll mess it up by saying the wrong thing and he won't come into my heart.

One cold winter day, Linda and I are driving around, and I ask her about "the prayer." As she carefully maneuvers around a snowplow on our right, she describes when, where, and how she did it and how it felt afterward.

Sensing my curiosity and hesitation, she offers to pray "the prayer" with me. I reluctantly agree, not convinced that Jesus wants to be in my heart. We pull in to an empty parking lot that's just

dumb girl

been plowed, bow our heads, and close our eyes while holding hands. The calluses on her fingertips from playing basketball rub against the soft skin on the back of my hands.

She prays to God, thanking him for all his glory and for the opportunity to serve him, thanks him for bringing me into her life (which makes me smile), tells him I want to accept his son, Jesus, into my heart as my personal Savior, and asks that he listen to me and my request.

I immediately get butterflies in my stomach and become flushed as I ask Jesus to forgive me for my sins, tell him I believe he died for my sins and rose from the dead, ask him to come into my heart and life, and tell him I trust him and will follow him as my Lord and Savior. When we end the prayer with an "Amen," I expect to open my eyes to a sky that is bluer, air that is purer, sunshine that is brighter, and be filled with peace and elation.

I feel nothing.

Linda looks up at me and asks, "So how do you feel?"

"Wonderful!" I lie. "I feel the love of Jesus in my heart," I tell her, enthusiastically.

I want to feel what I'm supposed to feel more than anything I've ever wanted. I want it for me, and I want it for Linda. But mostly I want to feel what everyone told me it would feel like. I want Philip to stop making me play boyfriend/girlfriend, I want Dad to stop being so angry, I want Mom to appreciate me, and I want school to be easier.

But nothing seems to have changed. Perhaps Jesus doesn't want to be in my heart, or I said the prayer wrong. All I know is it didn't happen, and it must be because something's wrong with me.

Linda seems satisfied with my lie and gives me a huge hug in celebration of my now being a certifiable Christian. I lean into the hug, desperate for connection—for salvation.

But those things evade me and will continue to do so into adulthood.

christian columbine

༄

At the community memorial I attended four days after the Columbine massacre, seventy thousand of us stood shocked—in a large movie theater parking lot—mourning in our ski jackets while holding umbrellas to shield us from the cold April rain. The collective agony of the crowd was almost unbearable.

Reverend Marxhausen was one of the speakers at the memorial, but the only one I really remember is Franklin Graham, the son of famed evangelist Billy Graham. He was there to speak on behalf of evangelicals around the country.

I was looking for words of comfort and messages about forgiveness, mercy, and grace; I was looking for a way to comprehend how four days earlier two students had gone into a high school, shot and murdered twelve fellow students and a teacher, and injured twenty-three others. It felt unfathomable.

But what Graham went on and on about was how this was the time and place to give your life to Christ. This struck me as incredibly insensitive and not what the shocked and mournful crowd, including nineteen hundred teenagers who'd just been traumatized, needed or wanted.

This was not the time for a sales job. It was the time for empathy, love, healing, understanding, and compassion. Graham's words, which felt decidedly un-Christian to me, reinforced that church was not the place for me. Listening to him, I felt simultaneously repelled by his message and inspired to look for a community where empathy, love, healing, understanding, and compassion would be at the core. I didn't know it at the time, but the gun violence prevention world is where I'd eventually find my "religion" of compassion.

chapter 16

crying in the car

D awn Anna's daughter, Lauren, was killed at Columbine. She was eighteen, a volleyball player, and was shot dead while studying in the library.

I felt a connection with Lauren. Like me, she was the captain of the varsity volleyball team at Columbine, she'd been coached by Dave Sanders, and she'd studied in the library during her lunch break. The only difference was that I'd done those things thirteen years before the massacre.

The interviews I did with Lonnie, Michelle, and Sandi gave me the confidence I needed to continue interviewing people who'd lost loved ones to gun violence. My interview with Dawn Anna gave me permission to take care of myself when interviewing them.

Dawn Anna met me and my photographer friend Kathy one cold fall Saturday afternoon at a Village Inn in South Denver. Kathy and I had met a year earlier, playing on the same competitive volleyball team back home. We'd hit it off immediately as we shared similar experiences playing college volleyball, being from large families, and having two young kids. She didn't hesitate when I asked her to be my photographer.

Eight years had passed since Lauren's murder. Dawn Anna told us how she found out about her daughter's death, how she

crying in the car

reacted, and the details of arranging a funeral for an eighteen-year-old whose bright future had been violently cut short. She shared details of her years of sorrow and her daily agony ever since Lauren's death.

"After this interview," Dawn Anna said near the end of our time together, "I'm going home to finally take Lauren's athletic T-shirts out of her drawers, sort through them, and give them to charity. There's something about giving away her T-shirts that make her death feel more real," she explained. "It's a rainy day and it's time."

Dawn Anna's grief was palpable, and I felt it deeply. Listening to her put a lump in my throat; it physically hurt to swallow. In particular, hearing about their closeness and Lauren's last words to her mom broke my heart. But to be professional, and channeling my childhood DBADG, I didn't allow myself to cry during the interview.

Before we walked into the Village Inn, I'd told Kathy, who cried at the drop of a hat, "The rule is, you can cry, but you can't cry more than the person talking about their kid's death." For my own part, I worked hard over the two-plus-hours-long interview to keep my eyes dry.

I took pride in my ability to hold back emotions. I didn't yet know that it came with a profound cost.

After the interview, we hugged Dawn Anna goodbye and watched her get into her car and pull away, driving toward a task she'd been avoiding for eight years. When her car was out of sight, Kathy and I got into our rental car and drove toward the highway in silence. The familiar tightening in my throat and the developing headache behind my eyes grew as I continued to hold back tears, tears desperate to be released.

After entering the highway and driving a couple of miles, I made a quick decision and pulled off the road at the next exit. I drove to a small empty road sandwiched between a chain-link fence and an abandoned ranch and put the car in park.

dumb girl

Kathy looked at me. "What are you doing?" she asked gently.

I looked over the steering wheel at the snowcapped mountains in the foreground and admitted, "I just need a minute." Then as my headache started to pound, I turned to her and asked, "Is it okay with you if I cry?"

The moment the question left my lips, I thought, *Why do I need her permission to cry?*

But I knew the answer—I didn't want her to think I was a DBADG.

My throat feels tight and I feel a sharp pain right behind my eyes as I hold back tears. But my knee is bleeding and throbbing from the saw blade Dad just threw at me, and he's already warned me not to be a DBADG.

It all started six months ago when Cyrano started getting into the trash.

Cyrano, our black-and-white collie, has figured out there are treasures of leftover food in the four large plastic trash cans stored in a gated area on the side of the garage. Dad built a gate to keep her out of the trash, but the latch never works correctly. She easily nudges open the gate with her long nose, sneaks in, tips over the trash cans, drags the white bags of trash to the middle of the backyard, and feasts on the dirty napkins, rotting corn cobs, used Band-Aids, chicken carcasses, and whatever smelly thing happens to be in there.

As soon as Mom notices the mess, Robby and I are told to clean it up. It's smelly, slimy, and gross, and I hate cleaning it up because it feels so unfair—especially since Dad's the one who didn't fix the latch on the gate, allowing Cyrano to get into the trash, in the first place.

The snow makes it worse. A foot of snow doesn't stop Cyrano or give Robby and me an excuse for not having to clean up her mess. It's nearly impossible to pick up small pieces of trash like

crying in the car

little pieces of tinfoil, broken eggshells, napkins, and toilet paper with mittens or gloves because they get dirty and wet and gross from the various sauces and rotten sludge stuck to the trash. So I pick them up with my bare fingers while I cry from the pain of my freezing fingers and the anger I feel toward Cyrano and Dad for making me be out here.

I've learned to work quickly and yell at Robby to hurry so we can finish before the cold makes my eleven-year-old fingers lack the ability to finish digging out the last of the frozen pieces of trash from the snow and ice.

But I've grown tired of having to pick up trash, and my attempts to convince Dad to fix the gate have been unsuccessful. So the other day, I decided to fix it myself.

On Saturday morning, I walked down to the basement to get the tools I thought I'd need to solve my problem. I grabbed a hammer, a saw, a few nails, and a screwdriver off Dad's workbench, then went to the trash area and tried to figure out why the latch wasn't working and how to fix it. But I'm eleven; the problem was beyond me. I quickly became frustrated and lost interest, leaving the tools on the ground next to the gate because working on my cartwheels seemed like a better use of my time than putting them away.

And today, while Robby and I were playing in the large pile of leaves we'd just raked up, we heard Dad's angry voice boom, "Heidi and Robby, come here!"

We scrambled to him, knowing by the sharp tone of his voice that we were in trouble.

He pointed at the tools. "Were you using these?"

"Yes, I was trying to fix the gate," I reluctantly admitted.

"Well, you can't just leave them outside, or they'll get rusty and ruined," he screamed.

He abruptly turned away from us and grunted loudly in frustration. Then, with his back to us, he leaned over, picked up the saw, and hurled it back at us.

dumb girl

I jumped back but not quickly enough. The blade hit my knee. I grabbed my knee in pain and started to cry.

"What are you crying about?" Dad thundered. "I'll give you something to cry about. Stop being such a DBADG!"

And now here I am, trying with every fiber of my being not to let any more tears escape so I don't get into worse trouble.

"Pick up these tools and put them away and don't leave them out again!" Dad yells. "And pick up all this trash!" He walks away without a backward glance.

I slowly pick up a used, ketchup-stained paper napkin from the ground that Cyrano dragged out of the trash and use it to wipe the blood from my knee.

Robby and I pick up the trash in silence, apart from the sobs I can't seem to control. Good thing Dad's not around to hear them.

"Is it okay with you if I cry?" I asked Kathy a second time.

She looked at me quizzically. "Sure."

Staring out at the snowcapped mountains, I let out soft, quiet, reflective tears that then turned into loud sobs as I felt the energy and weight of Dawn Anna's emotions leave my body.

I was embarrassed for Kathy to see me cry and worried she'd make fun of me or judge me.

But she didn't. Instead, she cried with me.

In that moment, she validated a part of me that I'd been working to discount, ignore, and reject. She also gifted me the experience of crying without penalty.

In that moment, I learned that crying in front of other people did not make me a DBADG.

Going forward, taking time to cry became part of our interview process. It became as important as making sure the recorder had batteries in it and Kathy had all her camera lenses with her. We learned the importance of self-soothing by expelling some

crying in the car

of the energy we'd inevitably absorb, and it became our coping mechanism for interviews. After every interview, we'd drive a few blocks, pull over, and then cry.

It worked wonders, and I wished I'd learned earlier in my life just how cathartic crying could be.

chapter 17

touching trauma

It was a cold December night, colder than usual or maybe it just felt that way. I put on my winter coat and headed across the street with the keys I'd been given to a house that was no longer a home. My job was to get two kittens and a week's worth of clothes for Amelia, a seven-year-old girl who no longer had parents.

The paramedics, the cops, and the detectives had all left; the two bodies had been bagged, tagged, and taken to the medical examiner's office and the house had been released back to the family.

As I slowly opened the front door, I was struck by the stillness and the lack of contrast. There seemed to be no shadows, no light, just gray—gray that envelops a space after evil comes and goes. I expected a smell, a smell of death, a smell of gunfire, a smell of chaos, a smell of a family that just that morning lived, cooked, put on perfume, and lit candles, but there was none.

As I walked through the house to the garage to search for the cat carrier, I imagined the family that had woken up, made breakfast, and sent Amelia off to school that morning. I imagined the fight the mom and dad had had, and I imagined the dad grabbing his gun, shooting his wife dead, and then turning the gun on himself. I tried to keep my head down so I wouldn't see

touching trauma

the blood splatters, brain matter, or flesh on the walls or floors, because looking around seemed like an invasion of their privacy. I walked on my tiptoes, partly out of respect and partly to avoid stepping on . . . well, leftover carnage.

After finding the cat carrier in the garage, I quickly went upstairs to look for the kittens who I was told were most likely hiding under one of the beds. What stopped me in my tracks was the 11×16 dark wood–framed family photo on the wall at the top of the stairs. The mom, the dad, and seven-year-old Amelia with two ponytails and big bows, all smiling smiles of better days, a time of happiness and maybe even optimism. I looked closer, looking for what was behind their eyes. Were they really happy, or was what happened here today already in process? How did they get from wide smiles in front of a photographer to a murder-suicide that orphaned a young child?

After briefly studying the "happy family," I went into the parents' room to search for the kittens. As I kneeled down next to the bed, I saw a basket of half-folded clothes and the inside-out pair of the mom's pink underwear on the floor next to her pajama bottoms. I imagined she'd changed out of her pajamas that morning and was folding clothes when she was summoned downstairs.

She never made it back. Never finished folding the laundry, never picked up the underwear, never finished her morning routine, never finished raising her daughter. A life interrupted.

How did I get here? I asked myself.

When I was interviewing people for my book, one of the questions I asked each person was "How did you find out your son/daughter/husband/dad was killed?" I discovered that how you're told about a loved one's death can lessen the sting of the news or make it even more devastating.

But how does that work? If my husband's killed in a car crash, who would tell me? And how? And then what would I do?

dumb girl

Looking for the answers to these questions, I found an organization in my community that touches trauma every day. It's called the Trauma Intervention Program (TIP), and for thirty-plus years it's been a critical service in my city.

Curious, I attended TIP's intensive sixty-hour training and became a TIP volunteer. Once trained, I signed up for the mandatory three twelve-hour shifts each month. Over the next several years, I was called to give immediate emotional and practical support to people directly impacted by a suicide, a natural death, an unexpected death, a crime, a fire, a drowning, or a car accident. TIP called it providing "emotional first aid."

I was drawn to trauma and those experiencing emotional pain. I knew that made me a bit of an oddball and figured it was probably me trying to come to terms with all the death and trauma I'd experienced growing up. All I knew was I could feel an internal strength growing that told me I was good at listening and helping people as they experienced or talked about their trauma.

It was Karena, a friend who spends her days in prisons running restorative justice programs for convicts, who put my attraction to trauma into perspective. She told me, "I do this work, 'emotional injury work,' because of all the trauma I experienced as a kid, and I feel like I need to always be 'touching' trauma. It's what I know. Being around emotional pain is weirdly familiar and soothing."

Her explanation was revolutionary to me. Hearing it, everything clicked into place for me. *That's it*, I thought. *That's why.*

One July morning before my ninth-grade year, I learn that Linda Parker, my mentor, my role model, my friend, is in the intensive care unit (ICU) fighting for her life.

The previous night, I'm told, she and a group of friends snuck into a public swimming pool at 2 a.m. Why? Because they could, because they are teenagers, because it's 1982 and "pool hopping" is a popular, harmless, and fun activity.

She dove into the pool, swam a few strokes, and then suddenly went under the water and didn't come up. Her friends jumped in, pulled her out, gave her mouth-to-mouth resuscitation, and called 911. She was rushed by ambulance to St. Anthony's Hospital, the same hospital where her younger brother, just three years ago, had his leg amputated after a trash truck ran him over.

She was placed in the ICU, put on life support, and is now in a coma.

All our family activities, concerns, and worries abruptly stop as we focus on Linda's perilous situation. Our dinner conversations are consumed with updates and processing the tragedy of her "accident." Philip keeps vigil at her bedside for three days, praying, holding her hand, and talking to her.

I'm given permission to go with Philip to see Linda in the hospital once she's stable. I'm warned she is surrounded by big scary machines and has lots of tubes coming out of her, helping her stay alive. I try to imagine what that looks like, but the closest I can come up with are the antiseptic soap-opera hospital scenes I've seen on *General Hospital*, where a woman, in full makeup and perfect hair, miraculously and easily wakes from her coma. I pray the same thing will happen to Linda.

Once in the hospital, we quickly head to the elevator and go up to the ICU. The elevator door opens, and I immediately notice the dim lighting, the cool temperature, and the smell of disinfectant. And I feel a heaviness and seriousness in the air. I follow Philip and wait as he hesitates at the threshold of the thin blue curtain door that separates us from Linda. He takes a deep breath and then walks in and over to Linda's mom, whose face is red and puffy as she sits holding Linda's hand.

I follow, avoid looking at Linda in the bed, and give her mom a hug that lasts longer than a hug with an adult usually lasts. Once

dumb girl

she releases me, I look at Linda, who appears to simply be asleep. Her skin has a translucent bluish look to it and her hair is slightly matted, nothing like the beautiful woman on *General Hospital*.

Machines next to her bed hum, beep, and moan as they breathe for her, keeping her alive. I notice all the tubes and wires coming out of her arms, legs, mouth, and nose, not knowing what they are for but grateful that I was warned. Deep sadness permeates the room, her nurses solemnly hurrying in and out checking monitors and adjusting clear bags of liquid that hang from poles above her bed.

I stand, just staring at her, willing her to wake up. It doesn't feel real and feels too real all at the same time. Philip leads a prayer as he, Linda's mom, her sister, and I hold hands. We cry and sniff and breathe along with the machine that breathes for Linda.

I visit Linda two more times that week. Philip stays there the whole time, praying with her family and sitting and talking and singing to Linda.

Eight days after her dive into a pool at two in the morning, the doctors tell Philip and her family that Linda is brain-dead and won't be coming out of the coma. The following day, along with her family, Philip holds Linda's hand and cries and prays while the doctor turns the life support machine off. They watch her die.

My world shatters. My role model, my mentor, my confidant, is dead.

Her death leaves a hole in me that I can't describe. Her death is tragic and unfair. Her death is the beginning of my disbelief in the power of prayer. Her death affects my family, our church, and my faith deeply.

A few days after she dies, there is a wake at her house.

Mom explains to me what I'll see at the wake, how to act, and what others will be doing. "Linda's body will be there, and you can choose to see her or not," she says. "I won't be looking at Linda because I prefer to remember her as an athletic, alive, strong, sweet, kind girl, not the girl who's in the casket."

The choice is distressing, but I want to see her one last time.

Linda hated dresses. I never saw her in a dress, and she took great pride in being a jock. She once said, "I wouldn't be caught dead in a dress." I hope they bury her in her favorite outfit, her high school letter jacket and jeans.

I make my way to the small basement room where the shiny white casket sits. Cautiously, I look down at Linda, who is wearing a frilly blue dress. I exhale in disappointment.

Dad appears next to me and lovingly puts his arm around my shoulder. "You can touch her if you want and say a few words if that's something you want to do," he whispers. He then reaches out and places his hand on top of her hand and says something about how we are sad and how we'll miss her and how she means a lot to our family.

I swallow hard and look up, trying to keep the tears from coming, trying not to be a DBADG. I reach out and touch the back of her hand, which rests peacefully on her chest. The calluses on my fingertips from basketball feel rough on the back of her delicate hand.

I expect to feel warmth, like a few days ago when I held her hand in the hospital. She isn't warm.

Sensing my confusion, Dad whispers, "Linda isn't in there anymore. This is just her body. She's with God now."

I nod in agreement as I study her unnaturally styled black hair and her plastic-looking face, which is heavy with makeup that covers her freckles and natural skin tones. *Linda didn't wear makeup*, I think.

"She's in a dress, but her mom told me that she has on her basketball shoes," Dad murmurs.

Well, at least that's something, I think.

dumb girl

Her funeral—a blur of sad songs, agonizing prayers, and despondent teenagers heartbroken over their friend's tragic and untimely death—leaves me overwhelmed and numb.

A few days later, Mom, Dad, Robby, and I go to a small Mexican restaurant where we eat tacos, enchiladas, and rice and process the last two weeks.

I'm not sure why or how Mom and Dad recognize the need for all of us to share what we've been through, but miraculously, this time, they do. They encourage us to each share our experiences, our thoughts, our feelings; they allow us to ask questions that were deemed too inappropriate to be asked before the funeral.

During this conversation, I find out what an autopsy is, and that Linda got a virus in her heart that "attacked" it when she was swimming, and the lack of oxygen deprived her brain of life-sustaining function that fateful night. I find out that a book called *When Bad Things Happen to Good People* by Harold S. Kushner gives a much better explanation of why Linda died than the old ladies at church who said, "God wanted Linda to be with him." I find out the details of the agony Philip, who is only eighteen, has been through and how kind the Parkers have been to include him so fully in all the discussions and decisions about how and when to "pull the plug."

We talk for hours, until the restaurant closes and we are asked to leave. I allow myself to cry, and the dinner leaves me feeling heard, noticed, appreciated, and informed.

What my parents gave me after Linda's death—that's what I wanted for Amelia and her aunt.

That's why I spent half an hour in a house where a murder-suicide had just occurred, trying to find two kittens and get a week's worth of clothes so the aunt of a now orphaned seven-year-old wouldn't have to go into the house where her sister

touching trauma

and brother-in-law had died so violently. And that's why, after bringing the clothes and successfully captured kittens to Amelia's aunt's house, I stayed to help her aunt figure out how to tell Amelia that her parents were dead.

I'd spent the afternoon with Amelia keeping her busy at a neighbor's house while the police tried to contact her aunt and worked to figure out what had happened while gathering evidence. She'd made it clear that she knew her parents were hurt, but she fully expected them to return to her after the doctors at the hospital "fixed" them.

As Amelia's aunt and I sat together, I coached her on how to be clear with Amelia that her parents couldn't be "fixed," and how to answer questions she might ask in the upcoming days and months. I encouraged her to be honest, giving Amelia only the information she asked for.

Explaining how to talk to a child about a life-changing and devastating loss was, for me, instinctual. I'd been that child, I'd experienced tragic loss, and I knew what I had needed in that moment. And, of course, I was very good at controlling my emotions when I needed to. I'd been doing it my whole life.

chapter 18

anniversary

I shivered as the cold wet marble slab radiated through my decades-old Columbine letter jacket while I focused on the dark clouds that swirled above us. I could hear Dave Sanders's granddaughter, who was lying next to me, cry. And I could hear the faint coughs of the crowd who stood around us, watching us pretend that we were dead.

We were there doing a "lie-in" on the steps of the Colorado State Capitol to commemorate the ten-year anniversary of the Columbine massacre, demonstrate the toll of the shooting, and call for stricter gun control.

My book *Beyond the Bullet* had recently been released and I'd been invited to speak alongside Columbine parents and victims of other mass shootings, which felt like the honor of a lifetime.

After a handful of emotional speeches, thirteen of us had formed a circle with our bodies to represent those killed at Columbine. We'd wrapped blue-and-white ribbons around our necks, the official colors of Columbine High School, and held hands while others, representing the twenty-three injured in the massacre, knelt next to us.

And then we lay there, listening to Tom Mauser, whose son Daniel was murdered in the shooting, slowly read the names of

anniversary

each person who was killed or injured. He wore the Vans sneakers Daniel was wearing the day he was killed.

As I lay there, my attention turned to the US and Colorado state flags that flew at half-staff, and I thought about the tragedy of it all. I thought about the students who'd died, I thought about Dave Sanders—and then, somewhat inexplicably, I thought about Mom.

Mom does all the right "mom" things, but I don't feel connected to her emotionally. She isn't who I go to when I'm sad or scared or angry or confused. She manages us kids and provides for us but not in an affectionate way. I get my sense of connection from Dad, despite his unpredictable anger.

She's a good mom in a June Cleaver "Leave It to Beaver" kind of way: She keeps a good house, provides well-balanced meals, and teaches us to be polite and tidy, share, clean up after ourselves, and always be pleasant. The enduring phrase of my childhood, besides DBADG, is "If you can't say something nice, don't say anything at all." This includes "I'm sad, mad, frustrated, or unhappy."

Mom gives love through food. She feeds us well-balanced meals every day and tries to make eating fun or at least not boring, giving names to everything we eat. We don't just eat tuna casserole; we eat "special Wisconsin casserole" or "special cabin cake" or "special Grandma pea soup." Everything starts with the word "special," and she presents it to us in a high-pitched, over-enthusiastic fake voice as if she's trying to convince us that it is indeed special.

Holidays are Mom's specialty. Not just the big holidays, but the little ones too. On St. Patrick's Day, everything we eat is green from food coloring, including green milk in our cereal, green eggs, green Jell-O, and green corn bread. On April Fools' Day, she prepares hamburgers, french fries, and Jell-O for breakfast and pancakes for dinner, and she makes sure to put something

dumb girl

weird in our lunch bag, like a couple of nails from Dad's workbench or something impractical, such as a small jar of nutmeg. I appreciate her lightness and silliness in these moments.

At Thanksgiving, she teaches me how to make Thanksgiving dinner. I complain and pout as I watch Doug, Philip, Robby, and Dad play basketball out in the driveway while the two of us prepare the meal. I don't think it's fair that I have to be inside cooking and baking with her while my brothers and Dad are having fun outside. It makes it worse knowing she's chosen me because I'm a girl, a DBADG.

My anger and frustration with Mom bubbles up on a family Jeep trip the summer I turn twelve.

Dad's relatives are from all over the Colorado Western Slope, so instead of having a family reunion at a local park or dance hall, twenty adults and twenty kids of various ages squeeze into eight Jeeps near a small town on the Western Slope to venture out onto a winding dirt road through a bunch of ghost towns.

Our "Jeep" is a 1980 four-wheel drive Ford Bronco. I prefer the rugged look and feel of the real Jeeps, with their open tops, over our Bronco, which seems too nice and too new and not like a vehicle you're supposed to drive when you go "jeeping." They don't call it "Ford Bronco-ing," after all. I do like how us kids sit on the tailgate, our feet dangling off, as we carefully and slowly drive through creek crossings, around huge rock obstructions, and over rocky terrain.

Mom is annoying me more than usual on this trip. Through the lens of my hormonal preteen eyes, she seems bossy and showoffy with the other moms. I begrudgingly help her and the other moms and daughters prepare the lunches and snacks, vaguely aware that my brothers and male cousins are not required to help. It annoys me and I blame her.

Today, our caravan of Jeeps meanders through three ghost

anniversary

towns. We look out at old broken-down, abandoned wooden structures that were once stores, bars, cabins, and mines. We're only allowed to go into a few of the buildings, steering clear of the ones that look like they could collapse at any moment. Mom is easily impressed and points every little thing out to me. She gives me the history of the town, who used to live there and why, and she explains the process of gold ore mining in 1897. I couldn't care less about any of it.

After the third town, we begin a steep ascent up several hills, where we eventually reach the summit of 12,840 feet. The clear, majestic mountain landscape of Colorado is breathtaking, and we all take a moment to appreciate it. There are steep drop-offs, and it seems like I can see all the way to the Pacific Ocean if I just squint hard enough.

As we look out across the vastness, my gaze shifts down to my feet on the edge of the steep cliff and I start to think about what it would be like to just jump. My mind floods with visions of me leaping to my impending death. I picture myself plunging down the side of the cliff, Mom and Dad gasping as they cover their mouths, realizing what I've done. As I fall, I yell back to them "I love you, Dad!" but I don't say "I love you, Mom."

I feel freedom and power in the thought of being able to say what I want to say, but never can, with such a grand gesture. I fantasize Mom will wish she'd been nicer to me, nurtured me, and been less annoying. I envision them at my funeral looking down at me, again with Mom overcome by sadness because she didn't treat me better when she had the chance.

The feeling is intense and deep but short-lived, as I'm eventually interrupted by someone calling my name to load up so we can head to the other side of the mountain.

The north side of the mountain still has snow on it, left over from the winter and a recent storm. The dirt trail we are on is steep,

dumb girl

narrow, and intense with barely enough room for one vehicle. The sign at the start of the trail reads, "You don't have to be crazy to drive this road—but it helps. Jeeps only."

We slowly make our way down the narrow stretch of steep switchbacks, which is famous for being one of the most dangerous roads in the country. It's cold on this side of the mountain, and because we are up so high, Mom, Robby, and I, along with a few cousins, have chosen to ride inside the warm Bronco with the tailgate closed. I was irritated before about having to be in the Bronco, but now I'm grateful to be in a heated vehicle and not be in one of the open-topped Jeeps.

Dad closely follows two Jeeps, unaware that their tires and weight are compacting the new snow into a slippery ice trail. As we slowly crawl down the cliff's edge, we start to skid. I anxiously watch out the passenger side of the window, instinctively leaning away from the frightening drop-off as I will the vehicle not to plummet off the nine-hundred-foot drop. Luckily, we only slide a few feet before Dad gains control by pumping the brakes.

Mom and one of Dad's cousins jump out of the Bronco, deciding to walk down the hill. Dad continues, steering the Bronco a little closer to the hillside and away from the drop-off. I instinctively bite my nails and worry. He has about two feet on the left before he hits the mountain wall and two feet on the right before we careen off the nine-hundred-foot cliff. He really has no choice but to follow the icy tracks created by the other Jeeps.

As Dad continues down, he again loses control. The Bronco starts sliding, but this time gaining speed as Dad ferociously pumps the brakes over and over. Dad's second cousin yells, "What are you doing? Slow down!" His eyes in the rearview mirror are big and full of fear.

The rest of us are silent as we continue gaining speed, getting closer and closer to two of my cousins, who are walking ahead

anniversary

of us, enjoying the beautiful scenery and crisp, clean air. Dad quickly rolls down his window and yells for them to get out of the way while honking the horn and frantically pumping the brakes.

They jump out of the way just as we pass by, barely missing them—only to realize that there's a hairpin turn a hundred feet in front of us. The two Jeeps ahead of us have already made the turn, so there is nothing to stop us from careening off the cliff if Dad doesn't get this rolling death trap to slow down before we get there.

A hundred feet, eighty-five feet, sixty feet, fifty feet.

"Dad, you need to stop the car!" I scream.

"I'm trying!" he barks back, pumping the brakes up and down as hard and as fast as he can.

Then, with forty feet left until our fiery death, Dad miraculously brings the Bronco to a stop.

In unison, all four doors fly open and everyone jumps out. Both groups of relatives from up the hill and from below come running to see what happened. Dad breathlessly explains how he couldn't stop.

"Yeah, the packed snow and your Bronco being heavier than the Jeeps makes it almost impossible for you to go down the trail without slipping," Dad's cousin says, shaking his head. "It's a miracle you were able to stop. I thought you were a goner."

All the men pat Dad on the back and tell him what a great driver he is to be able to get the Bronco under control before the hairpin turn.

The problem now becomes how we are going to get the Bronco down the hill and around the hairpin turn. It's not like we can just leave it there, and we definitely can't drive it back up the hill.

Someone suggests putting dirt on the trail to make it less slippery. No one has gloves or mittens, so several of us push dirt onto the snow with our feet. It's time-consuming and cold, but I think it's a good strategy so am happy to help.

dumb girl

The next decision is who will drive the Bronco, knowing there is a real chance the driver might lose control and not make the hairpin turn.

Dad, of course, volunteers. It's his car and his responsibility.

Mom says nothing.

Suddenly, I realize that there's a real possibility Dad could die. Tears fill my eyes. I don't want Dad to die, and I don't want Mom to be my only parent.

Everyone who was previously in the Bronco volunteers to walk. Mom is particularly enthusiastic about not being in the Bronco. Dad shrugs, knowing it's something he has to do on his own.

As he turns to get into the car, I follow him. Once out of earshot from the others, I ask, "Dad, can I come with you?"

He frowns. "I don't know, Heidi. It's pretty scary."

"I know, I just want to be with you. You're a good driver and I know you can do it," I plead.

He thinks for a minute, then shakes his head. "Sorry Heidi, this is something I need to do on my own."

Suddenly I'm overcome with emotion. I fall into his arms and bury my head in his chest knowing this might be the last time. I can smell his fear.

"I'll be fine. Don't worry," he says as he turns me around by my shoulders to go back to the group.

Defeated and rejected, I use the heel of my hand to wipe away my tears as I slowly walk back up to Mom, Doug, Philip, Robby, and the rest of the cousins.

Mom doesn't recognize my distress.

We watch Dad lean over to release the emergency brake and then slowly begin his descent. It feels like he's moving an inch at a time, away from us, as he carefully rolls closer and closer to the hairpin turn. We collectively hold our breath, listening to the rhythmic thumping and squeaking of the brakes and the crunching from the tires rolling over the snow and ice.

anniversary

I stand next to Mom, hating myself for not insisting Dad let me go with him, envisioning what it would feel like and look like to be with him in the Bronco. Mom, who doesn't seem particularly concerned, breaks the silence as she says to the cousin next to her, "I love your jacket. So colorful!"

Dad makes it to the turn and steadily goes around it, with no slipping. He's done it. I feel the air in my lungs escape, along with my worry. And when I breathe in, the air tastes crisp, fresh, and balanced.

Dad drives another hundred feet, passing the two Jeeps that are huddled up close to the rock wall, leaving just enough room for him to get around. He stops when he's no longer driving on packed, icy snow.

We all let out a sigh of relief and begin carefully running down the steep hill toward him. As he gets out of the Bronco, he smiles a toothy grin of relief and gives us a thumbs up! He is celebrated with high fives, pats on the back, taps on the shoulder, and congratulatory smiles. I give him a big hug and say nothing, as there are no words. I think he is brave.

A few minutes later, everyone gets back into their Jeeps and the Bronco so we can finish our sightseeing of old buildings that used to be used by people who are now dead. The rest of the trip is uneventful.

I'm not sure why Mom came into my head as I lay on the cold marble steps of the State Capitol, holding the hand of a woman who just minutes earlier had described to the crowd how much she misses her daughter. She'd been killed in another school shooting.

Maybe it was because I was once again feeling frustrated with and let down by Mom—partly because she wouldn't read my book ("It's just too sad," she told me), and partly because she wasn't here to watch me, in this important and historic moment, as I led a community in mourning. Or maybe it was because I was

dumb girl

having an emotional and connective moment with a woman I didn't know, a woman who would have given anything to be with her daughter.

I suppose in that moment I wished Mom was there with me—experiencing what I was experiencing, understanding what drove me, witnessing the person I was becoming.

chapter 19

virginia tech

On a cold April morning in 2007, a gunman shot and killed thirty-two people and wounded seventeen others at Virginia Tech University. Like the Columbine massacre eight years earlier, the police response was shown on live TV, and I watched as much of it as I could in between volunteering at my son's elementary school, driving the swim-practice carpool, and making a quick grocery store run.

Experiencing many of the same feelings of disbelief I'd had after the Columbine massacre, I once again felt a push to do something. There had been other massacres since 1999, but there was something about these thirty-two dead students and faculty that hit me hard. Perhaps it was because the Columbine shooting had been the worst high school shooting in US history, and now Virginia Tech had become the worst college shooting in US history. Certainly, the fact that things had not improved in the last eight years incensed me.

After seeing the Virginia Tech Portland chapter alumni president interviewed on a local TV station, I decided to organize a vigil for the VT community. No one else seemed to be organizing anything, and I wanted to give them, and the larger community, a place to mourn the dead and gather in community to grieve.

dumb girl

It was Tuesday night. I decided to hold the vigil on Friday night, which gave me only three days to organize it—perhaps a good thing, because that wasn't enough time for me to consider the questions that would usually take space in my head: *Are you the best person to do this? Why do you think you can pull this off? Who are you to think you can do this successfully?*

Pushing my impostor syndrome aside, I started by calling the alumni president I'd seen on TV, who enthusiastically agreed to speak and promised to get the word out to the hundreds of alumni in the area. I followed up by inviting the Vancouver mayor, a local minister, the TIP executive director, and two local high school and college musicians who I hoped could set the emotional tone of the event. Getting a permit to use the gazebo at a local park and ordering porta-potties was much easier than I thought. The final touch was setting up a table with a large paper roll with markers for people to write messages to the victims and express their feelings.

Around 250 people attended the vigil, along with four local TV stations and three metro newspapers. I stepped up to the podium to deliver some opening remarks, then stood aside as a talented soloist from the local community college came to the stage to sing a song.

I stood quietly, tears running down my cheeks, as she sang an emotional rendition of a haunting song Philip used to play on our family piano late at night.

I'm thirteen, and I wake to loud piano music. *The Tonight Show Starring Johnny Carson* ended hours ago, and I can hear the oddly soothing hum of black-and-white static that flickers on the TV in Mom and Dad's room. The sound of the piano and Philip singing irritates me because I don't want to be awake, and I don't want to have to listen to figure out how his date went. He plays Wayne Watson, Christian music, fast, safe. He sings loudly and passionately; the vibration of the piano through the floor shifts my bedside table lamp.

Philip is the musician in our family. We have a player piano in our living room that Philip plays all the time. He's a talented musician and is praised frequently by Mom and Dad for his playing ability and his exceptional singing voice. They love having him play and lead family sing-alongs on holidays like Thanksgiving and Christmas. On weekends he'll start playing and we all magically float to the living room to participate in a spontaneous von Trapp Family–like sing-along.

He plays when he gets home from school, he plays before going to soccer practice, he plays when he's bored, he plays when we have guests and parties, and he plays when he gets home from dates.

At breakfast the morning after Philip's had a date, Mom and Dad laugh and gush about how they know how his date went from what he plays. A slow country song means the date didn't go well. An upbeat, uplifting contemporary Christian song means the date was good.

I also connect his piano playing with the success of his date, but for different reasons. To me, a good date means he had fun, the girl liked him, they kissed—he'll leave me alone.

Tonight, as I lie here listening to the familiar words of Wayne Watson's "One Day," mouthing along because I can't seem not to, I wonder why Mom and Dad let him sing and play so loud so late at night. But the upbeat song makes me relax a little. Tonight, I can go back to sleep as soon as the noise ends.

But at the same time, as I listen to him sing of God's forgiveness and everlasting love, I feel a peculiar loneliness and longing: a longing to be loved, to be valued, to be wanted. I want to be left alone but I want to matter. The internal conflict hurts deep in my stomach.

Most nights, I make access to my "parts" difficult by wrapping the covers tightly around and in between my legs. I somehow

dumb girl

know I'm less tempting that way. But this night, caving to my need to feel valued, I undress. I push the covers to the side and lie in a "girlfriend" pose, pretending to have fallen asleep. If I offer myself, he won't be able to stop himself, and then I'll matter. I'll be loved and I'll have use.

I wait.

I listen as he plays his last note and sings his last word. I listen as he closes the lid of the piano. I listen to his footsteps hitting each stair as he climbs closer to me. I listen in the darkness as he walks from the top of the stairway to my room. I feel his presence fill my room. I feel his eyes on my body, staring, scanning, deciding. I hold my breath. Then, surprisingly, he walks away, taking with him my essence, my use, my ability to predict.

The room suddenly feels dark, cold, lonely, and void of meaning. I feel a surge of gratefulness for being left alone, but that feeling is quickly replaced by an overwhelming feeling of filth and shame and stupidity. Stupidity that I would put myself in that situation and that I would allow myself to be that vulnerable and needy.

Never again.

The shame of the moment is crushing. I quickly put my ruffled pink Strawberry Shortcake nightgown with matching underpants back on and cry myself to sleep as shame and humiliation engulf me.

The memory of that night disappeared from my mind. It didn't enter it again until a therapist coaxed it out of me ten years later.

And now, at the Virginia Tech vigil I'd carefully organized, it returned for a second time.

My tears were, in part, a reaction to the still-unfolding tragedy of the Virginia Tech carnage, but they were also due to my frustration at my inability to keep Philip out of my head. The shame of that night once again engulfed me, along with images

virginia tech

of dead college students lying in a classroom that was now tainted with tragedy. My tears were physical expressions of my grief for students who were robbed of their innocence and the mourning of my own innocence, which was also stolen.

Intermixed with the grief and mourning, I was proud of myself for recognizing the needs of a hurting community—their needs to express their grief, their anger, and their emotional pain. I had found a way to meet those needs, for them and for me.

chapter 20

the scare

When I'm thirteen, in seventh grade, I miss my period. At first, I don't think much about it, but as the days and weeks pass, I become increasingly worried. I'm old enough now to understand that Philip's boyfriend/girlfriend game, which he still insists on playing regularly, could cause a pregnancy.

A couple of years ago, our teachers purposefully separated the girls from the boys to talk about "the birds and the bees." They taught us girls about periods, hormones, body odor, and the proper names for female body parts. I'm not sure what they taught the boys, outside of how their penises work, which I overheard them giggling about at recess.

I already knew about penises and what they look like and that I didn't like them, especially Philip's. I was glad to learn about my own body parts. My teachers touched lightly on pregnancy, but I'd already learned about that when Mom and Dad sat me down and read me the 1968 book *How Babies Are Made* by Andrew C. Andry and Steven Schepp.

It was filled with paper cutout illustrations by Blake Hampton of plants and animals reproducing and ended with an image of a smiling woman under the covers in bed with a man on top of her, "reproducing." The caption next to the image said "The father

the scare

and mother lie down facing each other and the father places his penis in the mother's vagina."

After reading the book, Mom and Dad told me that if I ever got pregnant, I could go to them, and we'd make a decision about what to do. Mom said she was pro-choice, so I decided I was too, even though I didn't really know what that meant. I appreciated their non-emotional, candid, and practical information, but somehow I knew that if a girl got pregnant out of wedlock, her life and future were basically over.

And now I'm worried *I'm* going to be that girl. It's been weeks since my period was supposed to come.

I race home from school to check my underwear for blood.

Nothing.

Deep dread sets in. Praying to God I'll get my period is the only thing I can think to do.

So I pray. Hard.

Still nothing.

I try to figure out what I should do if I am pregnant. I'm pretty sure I am, because the lady on the film strip said very matter-of-factly, "Your period comes every twenty-eight days, unless you are pregnant." I feel my stomach to see if it's gotten bigger.

It seems like it has.

I think about how I'll tell Mom, and I obsessively practice the conversation in my head but can't seem to come up with the right words.

I try, "Mom, I'm pregnant and Philip's the dad." That doesn't feel right.

I try, "Mom, you know how you told me that if I ever got pregnant, we'd figure out what to do?"

No, that's not right either.

Besides, even though I'm totally sure I am, I have no idea how to find out if I am, in fact, pregnant. I don't even know who to ask to find out how to find out. The only person I can think of who might know what to do is Philip. *He's the one who made me pregnant (if I am pregnant), so he'll probably know what to do*, I think as I lie in bed petting Tigger, who sits on my chest.

But I'm terrified to ask him.

I wait a couple more days, building up courage. Then one day when he's in his room putting away the clean clothes Mom put on his dresser, I slowly walk in and hesitantly mumble, "Philip, um, I missed my period and, um, I think I'm pregnant."

He quickly turns around and looks at me, his eyes wide and narrow. "What?"

I know he heard me, and I'm irritated that I have to say it again. "I missed my period and I think I might be pregnant."

"It's not *my* problem," he snaps as he storms out of the room.

So I do nothing. I continue to pray and bargain with God and just wish it away.

A few days later, forty-two days after I'm supposed to get my period, I find blood in my underwear. I'm overcome with relief. I've never been so happy to see blood in my underwear and feel the familiar and brutal pain of period cramps. I never tell anyone but profusely thank God in my prayers that night for not making me pregnant with my brother's baby.

A week later the boyfriend/girlfriend game continues.

And my period pain continues. Every month, I have debilitating cramps that Midol can't touch. I go to school in pain, I play sports in pain, and when I get home, I curl up and cry, praying the pain will stop. Mom says, "Oh, I never had period cramps, so I don't know what to tell you."

Dad tells me the pain is all in my head and advises me that if I don't think about it, it won't hurt. I resent him for thinking I've made up my own pain and plead with him that I'm not faking it. He tells me, "DBADG."

the scare

∾

One day the following summer, Philip and I are watching TV, and during a commercial, he tells me to meet him in his room to play boyfriend/girlfriend. I'm having a particularly heavy period and can't figure out how it's going to work without making a mess. I tell him to give me a minute, go up into my room, sit on my bed, and pet Tigger as I try to figure out what to do.

"Heidi, come on!" he impatiently yells from his room.

I give Tigger a kiss on the head, slowly walk out of my room into his room, and sit on his bed next to where he stands.

"Um . . . I'm not sure how we're going to play, cuz I got my period," I carefully confess.

He looks down at me. "That's so gross!" he hisses.

I sit stunned, unable to say anything, and patiently wait for his instructions.

He gives no instructions. He abruptly turns and walks out of his room in disgust.

Feelings of overwhelming inadequacy, shame, and humiliation flood me as I absorb Philip's disappointment and anger.

And then suddenly a wave of relief hits me. I've figured out a way to stop *the game*. Why hadn't I thought of it before? I've done everything I can to stop it. I've avoided Philip. I've tried to be gone when he's home. I've busied myself with chores. I've told him I don't want to play. I've even told Robby that Philip has been "touching me," but he's three years younger and can't do anything about it.

Nothing's worked. That is, until I tell him, "I'm having my period." It grosses him out so much that he no longer wants to play boyfriend/girlfriend.

I worry he might want to play in between my periods. He doesn't. That is the end.

Period.

dumb girl

He never touches me again. I quickly and unconsciously block out all memory of *the game*, putting it in a deep and hidden place in my mind I can't access . . . until I'm triggered a few years later.

PART FOUR

chapter 21

board

I was in the middle of unloading the dishwasher and helping my thirteen-year-old son, Aaron, with his science project in 2010 when I got the call.

"Congratulations, Heidi," said the woman on the other end of the line, "we have received ballots from all of the Brady chapters around the country, and they have overwhelmingly voted for you to represent them on the Brady Campaign board."

"Really?" I asked.

"Yeah, it wasn't even close. And the board is thrilled to have you join them. We're hoping you can make the next meeting in DC in two weeks."

"Of course, I can't wait. Thank you so much!" I said before hanging up and then literally jumped up and down.

When the Million Mom March and Brady merged in 2001, an agreement had been made that the Million Mom March chapters could elect one grassroots advocate to sit on the board. I was now that grassroots advocate.

I was ecstatic! Brady was the biggest, most powerful, and oldest national gun violence prevention organization in the country, and being on its board was the highest position one could hold in the gun violence prevention arena. What made the win even more special was that it was my peers, Million

dumb girl

Mom March chapter leaders from around the country, who'd voted for me.

As I prepared for my first board meeting in Washington, DC, I was consumed with fear and worry that I wouldn't be accepted or be able to contribute in the way I was expected. The board was filled with East Coast lawyers, famous people, former congressional aids, and financial industry executives—people I perceived to be better, smarter, and more accomplished than me. My impostor syndrome was on high alert.

And not for the first time.

I'm sitting on the middle of the Columbine High School gym floor along with twenty other basketball players, anxiously waiting to hear if we made the varsity basketball team. Only ten girls will make the team and I'm a long shot because varsity is usually filled with juniors and seniors.

I'm only a sophomore.

I'm wearing gray shorts that say "REBOUND" on the butt and a blue "Columbine Rebels" T-shirt, and I begin to shiver from either my nervousness or the sweat that's cooling on my skin after a two-hour practice, or both. And then I hear it: "Heidi—varsity." Julie, my friend next to me squeals in delight and tackles me with a huge hug.

Yes! I think, doing an internal victory dance. I'm determined to earn a varsity letter in three sports each year of high school, a goal inspired by Linda Parker's success as an athlete. And this puts me on track. I earned the prestigious Ninth Grade Athlete of the Year award in my freshman year, and I intend on earning the All-around Athlete of the Year award in my senior year.

My ball-handling skills are not great, and my jump shot isn't exactly dependable—I miss more shots than I make—which means I'm not good enough to earn a starting spot. I depend on my positive attitude and hustle to get playing time; I'm always

board

the first one back from a drink break and never complain about extra wind sprints. I earn a de facto starting spot because one of the starters, Lori, who can effortlessly dribble behind her back and in between her legs and has an incredible vertical jump and jump shot, is extremely combative with the coach, who deems her to have an "attitude problem."

It feels like Lori is consistently defiant and does things just to piss off the coach. She ignores directions, refuses to run the play, and sometimes just walks out of the gym when she's mad. The coach develops a dislike for Lori and pulls her off the floor after she makes the smallest of mistakes in a game—accidentally passing the ball to the wrong player or doing a crossover when dribbling and losing the ball.

I only have to wait a few minutes before Lori screws up and the coach looks at me on the bench and yells in her southern drawl, "Heidi, get out there for Lori and run the goddamn play!"

Our coach, who is from somewhere in the South, has small eyes, a rigid posture, and a face that rarely smiles. She is extremely negative, constantly angry, and yells at us, a lot. She's the female version of Bobby Knight, the infamous Indiana University basketball coach. She terrifies me. I try really hard not to be in her way or make mistakes, but pleasing her is almost impossible.

When we practice our full-court press, she screams at our offense for not scoring when our defense stops them. "What in tarnation are y'all doin' out there? Yer dribblin' like a chicken tryin' to cross the friggin' road."

If our offense "breaks" our full-court press and scores, she screams at our defense. "Quit playin' goddamn patty-cake out there. Put a hand in their face and make 'em work. We ain't lettin' 'em have no free sweet-tea shots!" It's an impossible situation. Unlike Dad, whose anger comes and goes, she is *always* angry and difficult to read.

Still, I fail to understand why Lori doesn't just do what the

dumb girl

coach says. I know from my experience with Dad what she should be doing. *She'll have a much better time if she just lets the coach be right, lets her win the fight, or does what she says, even if she doesn't want to*, I think. *It's not that hard.*

Months of being yelled at ultimately unites me and my teammates against our coach. The ten of us talk about her and bitch to each other about how horrible she is after every game and after every practice. We laugh as we imitate her southern drawl and the way she says "You just need to have more pride," when what we desperately need is instruction and a game plan.

By March of my sophomore year, I've made the varsity volleyball and basketball teams, replicating Linda Parker's athletic prowess. All I need to do is make the varsity tennis team. The problem is I've missed most of the preseason because our basketball team makes the playoffs, extending the season.

The tennis coach, an old hippie with a scraggly red mustache and beard, uncombed hair, and an unusual coaching outfit that consists of baggy jeans and heavy hiking boots, graciously allows me to try out two weeks into the preseason, once basketball is over. He is kind, funny, and has a carefree attitude, which I find disarming.

The tennis team has gone to state the previous seven years and many of the previous year's players are returning, making me unsure if I'll be good enough to make it. The tryout requires me to play a match on a partially snow-covered court against another incoming sophomore. I easily beat her 6–1, 6–0. The coach approaches me as I'm walking off the court and enthusiastically announces: "Welcome to varsity! You'll be playing number three doubles."

My whole body tingles with excitement. *I did it!*

Over the next three years, I proudly wear my varsity letter jacket everywhere I go so everyone can see the bars, letters, stars, and awards I've worked hard to earn. I literally wear my pride on my

board

chest. I wear it to church, to the cabin, to the mall, to the movies, to after-school games, to Denver Broncos games, while skiing, on family trips, and to school, every day, no matter the temperature.

In my senior year I win the All-around Athlete of the Year award—the final feather in my cap and the ultimate way for me to pay homage to Linda. This is the first time in my life I've felt this way—like I have the ability to reach my goals and control my own destiny. The sense of power it gives me is exhilarating.

I overheard Sarah Brady question my being on the board to one of the board members during a break. I could tell she'd asked a little louder than she meant by the reaction of the woman she'd asked and the fact that I'd heard her from across the room.

Sarah had become involved in gun control after her husband, Jim, President Reagan's press secretary, survived a gunshot to the head during the 1981 attempted assassination of the President.

It was my first board meeting; I felt way out of my depth and had a strong need to prove I belonged. Sarah's question didn't help.

Hyperaware that I'd been elected to the board and feeling like an impostor, I tried to only say things that would add to the discussion, and I was viciously, almost brutally, hypercritical of myself if I said something that didn't get a reaction or at least a nod from the board chair. I noticed how the men "manterrupted" (interrupted women who were talking), mansplained, or took credit for a female board member's idea, and I felt like I was a second-class citizen among DC's elite. I learned that's common in many boardrooms.

I'd been a volunteer for the organization for ten years, but the organizational jargon, with all its acronyms—GVP, AWB, BAGD, FTJ, CCRs, PLCAA, CAP, the list went on—was often unintelligible and more than intimidating. And there was no orientation, so it was a sink or swim situation.

dumb girl

I worked hard to contribute in a meaningful way at each meeting and eventually gained more confidence. And it was noticed. Three years into my tenure, the board chair pulled me aside at a break and said: "You have been doing such a wonderful job, and we think you're ready for a leadership position on the board. Would you consider chairing the governance committee in the fall?"

It was hard for me to believe that they really wanted me to chair a committee. *I don't really even know what the governance committee does*, I thought. *They probably just don't have anyone else to do it.* Despite my nagging impostor syndrome, I said yes.

And am I glad I did! It turned out the governance committee was the perfect committee for me.

After reading the governance handbook three times and bylaws five times, I told Dave, "This is the best job ever! I get to save lives and be in charge of the rules of the board. I'll get to create stability and structure for the board and put in rules and consequences for board members. I get to create cool and fun opportunities for board members to interact with each other outside of the boardroom, and I get to establish and maintain boundaries. It's like all the things I wanted when I was a kid."

"You know you're a complete nerd, right?" he asked before folding me in his arms. "But you're a cute nerd."

I created a board orientation process that ultimately helped change the culture of the board. I told new board members to be on time, come prepared, and stay until the end of the meeting. And I organized a lunch where they got to know other new board members—seeds that built friendships and ultimately established a stronger, more effective board.

There were still challenges, of course. I'm a female introvert with impostor syndrome, so making space for myself in a predominately male meeting was more than challenging, and I knew I wasn't the only one. Maneuvering through manterrupting and "manologues" was a persistent and grating problem.

board

As I became more confident and assertive in my leadership role, it became important to me to make space for other people on the board who were being unconsciously left out by the more domineering members. I kept track of who was, and who wasn't, speaking up in meetings and then subtly created space for them to participate. When making a comment or asking a question, I'd say something like, "Yes, I agree with Frank's point and have a question, but then I'm wondering what Kate thinks about this issue."

It was super effective, and I started using it on other boards and in non-board-related meetings. It's a technique that's probably taught in facilitation classes, but I was never trained. I just did what I wished people would do for me: give me space and time to think, process, and be heard.

chapter 22

not-cancer

While I was finding my confidence in the boardroom, my homelife began to unravel.

Dave's gallbladder needed to come out. His yellow skin, yellow eyes, and uncharacteristic lethargy told us it needed to come out, so did two doctors. He was ready; I was ready—ready for him to feel better.

It was a typical Northwest cold and gray spring day in 2012. He sat in a hospital bed in a small room covered by a thin forced-air warming blanket, waiting for the nurse to roll him into the operating room. I sat next to the bed on a small couch by the window. The room smelled of antiseptic and anxiety.

"I'm not worried," he said.

I was but decided to push my worry aside and match his indifference. He was good at that, not worrying about things I worried about but probably shouldn't.

There was a cheery "Hello? Knock, knock" from behind the curtain. The split between the curtains widened and a woman appeared. I didn't immediately recognize her. She was out of context. She was unexpected, didn't belong in this room, the room that was dedicated to Dave. She wasn't part of his surgical team or one of the nurses who oversaw prepping him.

She was there for me.

not-cancer

She introduced herself to Dave. "Hi, I'm Dr. Keller and this is my trainee, Jordan. Can we come in?"

I knew what this was about. An hour earlier I'd stopped by her OB-GYN office on the other side of the hospital, which was painted with muted pastels and decorated with soft paintings of mothers holding and caressing newborns.

I'd told the woman, fortyish with kind eyes, at the reception desk to let Dr. Keller know I'd be spending the afternoon in the waiting room on the other side of the hospital while my husband had his gall bladder removed. "I'm expecting the results from a biopsy taken last week and not sure she'll be able to reach me on my phone. Can you tell her to go ahead and leave a message when she gets the results?"

Dr. Keller was there to give me the results.

When I'd found the lump on my right breast two weeks earlier, I'd told myself it was probably nothing. When I got the first mammogram, I'd told myself it was probably nothing. When I got the second mammogram, after a lady called me to come back because they needed to redo it, I'd told myself it was probably nothing. When a serious and unfriendly doctor dug a needle into my breast to take a biopsy, I'd told myself it was probably nothing. And now, as I sat with my ob-gyn and her trainee in what felt like Dave's sacred surgery prep room, I told myself it was probably nothing.

It wasn't nothing. It was breast cancer.

She called it "pre-cancer" because the tumor cells were contained inside the ducts of my right breast. It felt like she was minimizing the diagnosis.

"I wouldn't even call it cancer," she said with a flippant tone, "but it's not not-cancer."

What are you talking about? I thought.

She continued in a forced optimistic tone, "I mean, it's stage zero. You caught it early, so I wouldn't even tell people you have

dumb girl

cancer." Then she said a bunch of other things I couldn't hear or process before giving me a piece of paper with a phone number of a local cancer treatment clinic that could help me with my not-cancer that wasn't not-cancer. Then she left.

The air in the room left with her. In an instant, my life suddenly felt out of control, uncertain, and full of worry. Feelings I'd hoped I'd left behind in my youth resurfaced—with a vengeance.

"I have something I need to tell you all," Dad announces one night after coming home late from work.

It's my sophomore year, and Philip is home from college. It's weird how Dad says this, and I'm instantly worried.

He gathers Robby, Philip, Mom, and me in a small hallway that is decorated in 1970s-style silver wallpaper with odd-looking golden aspen trees, which gives all our faces a spooky silver-and-yellow glow. It feels strange to meet in the hallway, and I can't read Dad's mood. He isn't angry or happy. His shoulders hang low, his tie is loose, and his energy is low.

He tells us he went to a psychologist after work and, following what he calls an "enlightening conversation," has decided he's no longer going to hit us kids.

"I learned from the psychologist that when I have a bad day at work, I come home and take my anger out on you guys," he explains. "He told me when I'm angry, it's like I come home and kick the dog, and you guys are the dog."

The five of us stand there in awkward silence, our eyes scanning the burnt-orange carpet.

"Things are going to change, starting now," Dad promises. "I'll never hit any of you ever again."

We're all still frozen in place, searching for what this news means. Dad's delivered this announcement in a way that feels inconsequential—kind of like learning we are switching to a different brand of laundry detergent.

not-cancer

I don't trust it.

There is no apology, no discussion, no debate, and no questions, just the nodding of our heads in acknowledgment. Then we all go back to what we'd been doing before the gathering in the weird aspen tree hallway.

Dad's true to his word about the hitting: It does stop.

But the yelling, emotional intimidation, and fear continue. And after The Fireplace House eventually closes, things get worse.

Dad gets a job with two businessmen who do something that involves "limited partnerships" and "property investments." It seems complicated and no matter how many times he explains it, I fail to understand what it is and what he does.

What I do know is that his "partners" have fancy offices on the second floor of a nondescript office building with big windows, live plants, and a pretty receptionist who smiles and offers me pieces of candy from the crystal bowl sitting on her desk whenever I visit. Dad's office is in the same building but in the dimly lit and sparsely decorated basement, which makes me feel sad for him.

At The Fireplace House, he was the boss and in charge of dozens of employees, and I can feel the dramatic change in Dad's stature from having the big office and being the president and owner of a business with three stores to now being relegated to a weird, smelly, and lonely basement office.

"Why don't you have an office up in the main part with your partners?" I ask.

He replies quickly, with a slight hint of defensiveness, "I love it down here in the basement where I get to do my own thing."

I don't believe him, and it soon becomes clear that his new job is only making him more angry and temperamental. In particular, his impatience and frustrations with Mom seem to be intensifying. I don't know what it is or why it is, but I can feel his aggravation with her and his annoyance from having to deal with family stuff when he gets home from work every day.

Three weeks after the "I'm not going to hit you anymore" talk in the weird silver aspen tree hallway, we are having a tense and typical dinner where Dad yells about something that's upset him earlier in the day, Mom cries, and Robby and I sit eating quietly and as quickly as we can.

This time, after Mom sits down with the toasted and buttered hotdog buns to go with the spaghetti she's made, Dad abruptly pounds his fist on the table, looks directly at Mom, and declares, "I'm done with your drinking, and I'm done covering for you!"

Nervous to draw any kind of attention to myself, I carefully move my fork around on my plate, gathering the noodles together and then spreading them around, keeping my eyes down. I'm suddenly not hungry, even for spaghetti, which I love.

"You are a drunk and I'm no longer going to be embarrassed by you!" he screams.

He warns her that if she gets drunk in public, he's going to tell her, out loud, that she's drunk and is embarrassing him, and he'll announce to the group they're with that they're leaving, and it doesn't matter who they're with or where they are, he'll take her home immediately. He further warns her, "If you can't control your drinking, I will! Because you're acting like a child, I'm forced to treat you like a child."

And then he sits down and takes a big bite of the slightly burnt toasted hotdog bun. The crunch echoes in the silence and crumbs explode onto his plate and lap.

I sit with my mouth open, wishing I could melt into my chair. Dad has warned me about her drinking, worried she might eventually want me to drink with her, but he's never been confrontational with her about it before. Not in front of me, at least.

not-cancer

The dinner abruptly ends with Mom running upstairs in tears and the rest of us awkwardly doing the dishes in silence.

A few weeks later, up at the cabin, we're invited to go out to dinner with some friends who live in a cabin near ours. Mom, Dad, Robby, Philip, and I pile into the blue-and-white Ford Bronco and head into town for what is supposed to be an enjoyable evening of good food and catching up with friends.

Mom has been drinking a lot today; she's already drunk when we get to the restaurant, and she orders a glass of wine as soon as we sit down at the table. She is silly and loud and embarrassing.

Mom trips as she goes to hug the neighbor lady and almost knocks her over. It's a small restaurant, and I can feel everyone looking at us. I'm embarrassed and silently wish Mom would stop being so loud. In these moments, I shrink and attempt to make myself as little as possible so as not to add to the hubbub.

As we order our dinner, I can sense Dad's tension. Mom is having the time of her life, oblivious of the awkward glances our dinner guests keep giving each other as she wildly swings her arms, telling a story a little louder than it needs to be told.

Dad is not laughing; his body screams of anger and agitation.

After two more glasses of white wine and more over-the-top laughter from Mom, Dad stands up abruptly, his chair squeaking loudly as it strains against the wood floor and his weight.

"I'm sorry, but Betty is drunk, and I need to take her home," he loudly announces to the table.

Mom, being in the middle of telling her dramatic and spirited story, doesn't really hear what he says.

She turns toward him and sputters, "Huh?"

"Betty!" he yells as he looks directly at her. "You are drunk, and I told you that if you get drunk in public, I'm going to call you on it, and I'm going to take you home," he explains. "So get

dumb girl

your purse. We're going back to the cabin!" he loudly instructs, as if she's a child.

The small restaurant goes silent. Everyone is looking at him. I try to make myself as small as I can. Dad has warned her, and here she is, acting like a total idiot.

Mom's face drops. Then she looks at the lady she's been talking to and then at the lady's husband, as if searching for reassurance that what is happening is, in fact, not happening. But everyone is frozen in place.

"Let's go!" Dad barks, breaking the spell.

There is a quick scurry as we grab our coats, Dad throws some cash on the table, and Philip leads Mom, who is barely able to walk and confused and dumbstruck, out the door. Robby, Dad, and I head to the Bronco, which is still warm from our drive to the restaurant just twenty minutes ago.

The drive to the cabin is painfully silent and awkward and feels like forever. It reminds me of the night we drove home from the Mexican restaurant after Dad found out I had an F on my report card.

I'm not sure what's going to happen next. I start to worry.

After Dr. Keller delivered her diagnosis of me not having not-cancer and left, I stared at the paper she gave me and absentmindedly rubbed my thumb over the words "cancer center," trying to magically rub them away while Dave and I talked about . . . I have no idea what we talked about.

Ten minutes later, a nurse in blue scrubs and a hairnet appeared at the curtain to wheel Dave into surgery. We looked at each other and panic set in. He pulled me into his arms where he held me in what felt like a universe of gravity, desperation, fear, confusion, and love. We held the hug for longer than was normal for us.

not-cancer

As he let me go, he looked me in the eyes and said, "I love you. It's going to be okay." It was unclear whether he was talking about his surgery or my not not-cancer. And then the nurse rolled him out of the room.

The remaining air in the room left with him.

chapter 23

chaos

After Dave was wheeled out, I walked over to the waiting room and sat.
Alone.

Alone with my thoughts, trying to come up with a plan. Dave was in surgery, Sami and Aaron were at school, and I couldn't think. I couldn't think of a plan.

So I sat and watched the rhythmic pitter-patter of rain collide with the large east-facing window that overlooked a grove of trees in the distance. I concentrated on individual droplets, watching them race down, down, down to the bottom black-steel ledge, where they pooled together before descending into a suspended freefall, landing in clusters of newly bloomed yellow daffodils.

My life felt like it was teetering on the edge; uncertainty loomed. How was I going to manage these racing feelings of fear and hopelessness?

You've done it before, I reminded myself. *The year Mom went into rehab.*

It's raining, so luckily Dad and I only have to wait a few minutes for Mom to arrive. She comes roaring around the corner and drives over the curb of the tennis center's parking lot. Robby is as white as a ghost as he climbs out of the Bronco.

chaos

The four of us have a brief conversation about leftovers at home and car logistics before Robby resumes his seat in the Bronco and Mom and Dad head to their car. They're going out to dinner; Robby and I are headed home. On our way there, Robby, on the edge of tears, divulges, "Oh my God, Heidi! I have never been that scared in my entire life! I really thought I was going to die. She was so drunk and was all over the road. We went through two red lights!" He adds, "You're only sixteen and you're a better driver than her."

I grit my teeth, pissed that she endangered him like that.

I need to show Dad just who she is, I decide.

That night, I get a green marker out of my marker box and draw a half-inch line on the back of Mom's four-liter green Chablis bottle in the refrigerator, marking the amount of wine that's in the bottle. For a moment I hesitate, thinking she might see it, but then I remember how oblivious she is to pretty much everything.

"Mom won't notice this, will she?" I ask Robby, showing him the little green mark.

He shakes his head. "No way."

For the next two nights, I sneak to the refrigerator with my green marker and mark the level of wine left in the bottle. Each night, my mark is three inches lower than the previous night's mark.

On the third night, when Dad gets home, I show him.

The color drains from his face when he sees the small green marks. Combined with the white glow coming from the refrigerator light, he looks like a ghost. His mouth ajar, he stands motionless, taking it in. Unable to read this particular expression, I doubt this is enough to convince him to do something and suddenly wish Mom had drunk more.

He points to the first and then the second mark before muttering, "This is one day?"

dumb girl

"Yep," I say.

"I had no idea she was drinking this much," he says slowly. "We need to do something." He shuts the refrigerator door and turns to me. "Thanks for showing this to me, Heidi."

And then he turns and walks out of the kitchen.

A few days later—the morning after Dad takes Mom to Raleigh Hills Alcohol and Drug Treatment Center—I wake up worried. I don't really know what rehab is, how long it takes, or how it works. Robby and I tiptoe into Dad's room, unsure of his mood but desperate for information about Mom.

The slight creak of the door as I push it open wakes him up, or maybe he has just been lying there thinking with his eyes closed. He motions for us to join him on the bed. He looks terrible. And he looks small and sad. He has bags under his bloodshot eyes, and the wrinkles in his forehead seem more pronounced than usual.

The air is still and smells like bad breath.

"Mom's in a special hospital for drunks, and they have a type of treatment called aversion therapy, which will make her dislike alcohol," he explains.

"How does it work?" Robby asks.

"They'll give Mom three shots, one that closes her stomach, one that makes her feel drunk, and one that makes her throw up. Then they'll take her into a fake bar in the hospital where she'll drink her favorite drink. The 'bar' has mirrors on all the walls, so she'll see what she looks like when she's drunk, and she'll see how embarrassing she is. Her throwing up will give her a negative association with booze."

I listen, eyes wide, trying to imagine Mom in the fake bar he's describing.

"They'll make her do this several times over the next several months, and by the time they're done, she'll hate wine and the smell of wine and won't want anything to do with booze."

chaos

I feel a slight twinge of anger in his voice, but mostly he sounds defeated and sad. His explanation seems simple and straightforward, but I have a feeling that what Mom is going through is more complicated and horrible than how he's explained it.

The weekend family therapy sessions start just a week later.

When we arrive at the rehab center for the first family session, we're led to a community room by a soft-spoken, gentle-natured man who has a weathered face that makes me think he's had a hard life and has lots of stories. He leads us to a large room that has faded floral wallpaper, worn-out armchairs, and four rows of gray metal fold-up chairs that are carefully placed in a semicircle. The room smells of antiseptic and stale coffee, creating an atmosphere that feels both clinical and weirdly welcoming.

Dad, Philip, Robby, Doug and his new wife, and I make our way over to a row of fold-up chairs in the center of the room as we anxiously wait for Mom and the other patients to join us. As we wait, other families filter in, all with bewildered looks on their faces, just like we probably have. The air is thick with nervous anticipation.

As the minutes tick by, the anticipation grows, and finally, the door creaks open and Mom enters along with the other addicts, looking both fragile and determined. She wears a simple, loose-fitting outfit, and her eyes carry a mix of shame and hope. When she sees us, she offers a weak smile. Robby and I glance at each other, understanding the significance of this moment, and I feel his need to lighten the mood with a funny face. He refrains.

Mom sits next to Dad and places her hand in his, and he curls his fingers around hers in a tight white-knuckle grip that feels both desperate and reassuring. A counselor with a kind and empathetic demeanor starts the session, encouraging patients to share their experiences and hopes for the future. When it's Mom's

dumb girl

turn, she introduces herself by saying, "I'm Betty, and I'm an alcoholic." The other patients respond in unison, "Hello, Betty."

Tears start to roll down her cheeks, and I feel her embarrassment and shame.

She tells the room about blackouts, lying, hidden bottles, missed dinners, and morning hangovers. It's the morning hangover confession where I realize, *Oh, that's why she never eats breakfast with us.* I never understood why she wouldn't eat the most delicious meal of the day—cereal, pancakes, waffles, and porridge with spoonfuls of brown sugar on top.

She looks directly at me and Robby, and then at Doug and Philip, and says, "I know that I've hurt you, not been the best mom, and for that, I'm sorry." And then she sobs.

I feel a mixture of heartbreak and a small amount of admiration for her strength in confronting her addiction and admitting her shortcomings. I try to hold back tears as sympathy encroaches on the strong feelings of irritation and anger I came here with today. I feel a small shift.

"Your family member has a disease; it's called alcoholism," the counselor explains to the room. "It's important that you know it's not your fault or your family member's fault. Alcoholism is a family disease, and full recovery will require support from the whole family."

I take what he says literally and interpret his explanation to mean "You have no right to be angry at her because she has a disease, like cancer, and it's not her fault." It doesn't quite sit right, but I go with it and lean into trying to support her as best as I can.

For three weeks, Dad tries to play the mom and dad roles, getting us off to school, helping with homework, and making dinner. He's not great at any of it, and we basically go into a holding pattern until she gets home. I find it hard to concentrate on anything—school, tennis, or grades—while Mom is gone.

chaos

I'm glad Mom is getting help and am hopeful that when she gets home she'll be the kind of mom I desperately want, a mom who makes me a priority, like I see on TV with Mrs. Brady on *The Brady Bunch*, Ma on *Little House on the Prairie*, or Abby on *Eight is Enough*.

Once Mom gets home from Raleigh Hills, everything does change. But not in a good way. She doesn't become Carol Brady or Ma Ingles or Abby Bradford. I don't become a priority, and we don't become the communicative and honest family I thought we'd suddenly become.

Instead, we walk on eggshells.

Robby and I live in fear that if we do something wrong, like forget to unload the dishwasher, we'll somehow cause Mom to start drinking again. Dad acts like he's a guest in his own house, asking Mom if he can do simple chores around the house, which he never did before, and talking about surface topics like the weather and upcoming church events, clearly worried he'll misstep and she'll start drinking. The house suddenly feels foreign and dark, and everything appears to be a trigger for Mom. She becomes absent, going to Alcoholics Anonymous (AA) meetings every night after her new job as a travel agent, leaving us to our own devices for dinner. We eat a lot of TV dinners.

Life eventually folds back to a sort-of new normal. Mom focuses on her life as a recovering alcoholic, and I resume my teenage life of school, sports, and work at my first job at The Donut Hut.

It's not what I'd hoped for, but at least it's not as chaotic as before.

A few hours after Dave was wheeled out of the room for surgery, he was wheeled back in, minus one gall bladder. When I gently kissed him on the forehead, he looked at me, groggy from the anesthetic, and asked, "You okay?"

dumb girl

Tears flowed down my cheeks in relief that he was okay and in astonishment that his first thought after surgery, where an organ was removed, was about me and not himself. Not for the first time, I marveled at the unending selflessness of the man I married.

Our lives were about to become complicated, scary, and sad. But for the time being, I was happy to just sit in a boring, pastel-painted, perfectly nice hospital room with Dave, holding hands, delaying the huge storm that we were about to enter.

chapter 24

sad

My ob-gyn was right: I'd found the cancer early. But what neither of us knew until I went in for a follow-up was that three more tumors were growing inside my right breast. I had ductal carcinoma in situ (DCIS), a form of early breast cancer where some of the cells lining the breast's milk ducts start to turn into cancer cells.

To avoid radiation and chemotherapy—and to ensure I would never ever get breast cancer again—I opted for a double mastectomy. It felt like the least worst option available to me.

I was terrified. Sadness immediately enveloped and suffocated me as I tried to wrap my head around the fact that I had a disease that was trying to kill me.

As my days filled with doctor appointments and surgery prep, I shifted from gun violence prevention advocate to Heidi cancer victim advocate. The kids were seventeen and fourteen—Sami finishing up her senior year and Aaron getting ready to start high school—and they needed me. But being an attentive and thoughtful mom went by the wayside. In the blink of an eye, I turned into a broken woman who cried all the time—and I do mean *all* the time. I woke up crying, I cried all day, I cried while falling asleep, and I woke up in the middle of the night, crying.

dumb girl

I cried all the tears I was never allowed to cry when I was a child. Out in the open. Hiding nothing.

Jeff is tall, with wavy blond hair and an athletic body. I'm completely infatuated with him, and we "go together" for five months the winter of my junior year after we meet at a basketball game at his school. We are both sixteen.

Jeff and I go to basketball games, dances, movies, and hang out at the mall. He works at a T-shirt screening and engraving store at the mall near my house. I get butterflies every time I see him, so I try to see him as much as I can, stealing kisses when I get there and when I leave, hoping it won't get him fired.

A few weeks into our relationship, he comes over to my house on a cold Saturday afternoon when no one is home. I invite him up to my room to show him all my ribbons and trophies I've earned over the years—ribbons and trophies that I replaced the wall of F papers with a few years earlier.

He and I sit on my bed, and we begin kissing. Butterflies explode in my stomach, and a sense of euphoria takes over. Our kissing turns into passion. We begin French-kissing and then lie down as our hands begin to explore above and then under our clothing.

As we lie together, kissing, bodies intertwined, an unexpected flash of an image comes into my head. It's vague and fuzzy. Not so much an image, more a thought or feeling. It's of Philip on top of me. He is naked. I shiver. Then suddenly, I see him sitting on me.

I scrunch my already closed eyes, trying to get rid of the image, but it just stays.

Jeff and I continue kissing as I desperately try not to see Philip. I focus on Jeff, on our tongues, on our exploring hands, on anything besides Philip. It doesn't work.

I stop kissing him and sit up as I adjust my shirt. I tell him, "I

sad

have to get ready for basketball practice."

A lie.

He believes me. We go downstairs and give each other a quick kiss. He walks out the front door to his car and drives away.

As more fuzzy images come in the next several days, I desperately try to push them away. I don't understand where these images are coming from, and I don't understand what they are. I don't remember doing any of the things I'm seeing.

I make myself busy with homework, basketball practice, hanging out with Jeff at the mall—anything to keep my memory from opening up.

It does not work.

I see Philip on me in the basement, I see him reaching for me in the pool, I see us in his bed and on my bed. Each image fills me with despair and dread. I know what I'm seeing is something bad and I feel deep shame but don't have words for it or understand it.

One night, Dad picks me up from basketball practice, and as we drive home in the dark, I ask, "Dad, can I ask you a question?"

"Sure." He sounds distracted.

"What's incest?"

He thinks for a minute and says, "It's when two people from the same family have sex."

"Does it have to be a father and daughter, or can it be cousins or what?" I don't want him to guess what I'm talking about, so I make sure not to say "brother and sister."

"It just has to be the same family. The reason is because the genes in one family are too similar and if a baby is made, it will have deformities."

Suddenly the pregnancy scare four years ago flashes into my head.

"Is it illegal? Can you get into trouble for it?"

"That depends on if the father forced the daughter to have sex."

dumb girl

"Is molestation the same as incest?"

He hesitates. "I don't know. Why are you asking about this?"

Panic sets in. "Oh, for a school project in social studies class," I lie.

"Oh, okay," he says.

And that's the end of the conversation.

I feel a sense of relief that he doesn't figure out that I'm talking about me. I also feel disappointed that he doesn't ask more questions. I'm prepared to tell him the truth if he pushes me. Part of me wants to tell him, to relieve myself of this secret that has suddenly become exhausting. The images that float into my mind are becoming stronger and more clear, and the burden of my shame is growing heavy.

But Dad doesn't push, isn't curious, is probably thinking about work, and doesn't want to know more. I now know the definition of incest, but it doesn't make me feel any better.

I don't know what to do with the ever-growing shame that's building inside of me. But it's clear I'll continue keeping the secret—and the shame. What other choice do I have?

As a kid, I became an expert at stuffing sadness down deep inside. If I did any crying at all, I did it secretly, in my room with Tigger. But this time I was determined to deal with it differently—in the open, not in secrecy, shame, or seclusion.

The devastation, confusion, and fear I was experiencing in the wake of my breast cancer diagnosis felt similar to what I'd felt at sixteen remembering my sexual abuse. There were no easy solutions, I lacked the ability to think or concentrate on anything else, and both felt like a burden I couldn't possibly carry.

The difference was that this time I got to choose how to deal with the shock, fear, and sadness. And I got to choose not to do it alone. This time, I let sadness take hold of me, going against the family norm of my childhood. I rejected the idea that crying made me a DBADG.

I'd seen the "pink washing" that happens every October for National Breast Cancer Awareness month. I saw it in the grocery store, at the mall, and on TV. But it was the NFL games where I noticed it most. They turned their penalty flags pink. Players wore pink sweatbands, pink cleats, pink socks, and pink gloves. And the sidelines were pink. Commercials featured women who used war metaphors like "fight," "warrior," "brave," "enemy," and "survivor."

Once cancer became part of my life story, the slew of phrases I heard, like "keep fighting" and "you can beat this," annoyed me. I was sad, not mad, and "fighting" was not something I identified with. Besides, being in "battle" denotes aggression, fighting, and yelling—all things that scarred me as a kid. It also required putting on a brave face. I didn't want to put on a brave face, and I didn't want to have a positive attitude. The difference was that I recognized I now had the ability to react to what I was facing, any way I wanted.

So I chose sad.

I didn't try to comfort people who were upset that I had cancer. I went to doctor appointments and didn't try to be their best and most positive patient. And I called it cancer, not not-cancer.

Taking this approach—my approach—made me feel honest, genuine, and authentic. It was the first time I felt like I was making decisions and acting on behalf of me and not those around me. I disrupted my need to people please, and it gave me energy and the motivation I needed to heal and recover. Fortunately, Dave completely supported me and just let me be who I needed to be and act the way I needed to act. I don't think he liked it—who would like their spouse crying twenty-two hours a day?—but he fully backed my need for genuineness and my need not to minimize the diagnosis.

dumb girl

☙

Seven weeks after my diagnosis, my surgeon successfully cut four cancerous tumors—along with my breasts—out of my body. My sadness continued through the three additional reconstructive surgeries over the following eight months, but it eventually abated as I slowly reclaimed my body and my optimistic and forward-thinking nature.

I strongly believe that giving myself the space and time to mourn the loss of my breasts empowered me to make difficult and timely decisions, cope with the pain, and recover without "battle fatigue" or PTSD.

I don't begrudge women who wear pink or NFL players whose loved ones have "fought" breast cancer. It simply wasn't for me; it conjured up too many memories of the toxic positivity that was forced on me as a child—the "never let them see you cry" attitude that robbed me of mourning my eleven-year-old friend Michelle, my mentor and hero Linda, and my innocence.

chapter 25

conference

A week before my double mastectomy surgery, a friend of mine emailed me and said "Maybe this is a blessing in disguise. Now you can stop doing the gun thing and breast cancer can be your new thing."

What is she talking about? I thought. *Gun violence prevention isn't some small pet project I've been doing to fill time, it's my life's passion—and I need to get back to stopping all these tragic gun deaths ASAP!*

In that moment, I realized just how deep my devotion to saving lives from gun violence ran. Nothing, aside from my family, mattered more to me. Cancer was just a temporary setback; gun violence would continue to be my "thing."

I'd become an expert, and my impostor syndrome was beginning to melt, but I needed more. I wanted to make a bigger difference, save more lives. My efforts were being noticed by state and national gun violence prevention groups, and I was frequently asked to speak at their conferences and events. Each time, I gladly said yes.

I felt challenged, important, relevant, and finally able to answer the question many stay-at-home moms, like me, struggle to answer when asked by their hairdresser or someone at their spouse's holiday party, "So what do you do?"

dumb girl

"I'm raising two kids and saving lives."

And it seemed I was making a difference locally. Women periodically stopped me in the grocery store to tell me they'd heard me speak and explain how they now ask about guns when sending their kids on a playdate. One woman grabbed my arm in the cereal aisle and told me, "Because of you, I finally convinced my husband to buy a safe and lock up his guns. Thank you so much for making me understand why it matters. You truly are making a difference."

It felt great—until the higher-ups at Brady called me one day in 2013.

"The team here in DC has been putting together the program for the annual summit, and we think you should moderate the main plenary session," Brian said with a tone that was more of a demand than an ask.

"Are you serious?" I said in disbelief.

"Yeah, we think you'd be perfect. You're a board member, a longtime activist, and you're highly regarded in the organization."

Moderate? How do you even do that? Isn't that a job for a trained facilitator? I'd never moderated anything before.

"It'll be a great panel that'll include all the superstars in the movement, and the panel will follow President Bush's Secretary of Homeland Security, Tom Ridge, so it should be well attended," Brian explained.

Giving a speech was one thing; overseeing eight opinionated, passionate, smart, and respected experts in front of over three hundred grassroots and national leaders was quite another. It felt way out of my skill set and comfort zone.

Like that, my growing confidence deflated completely. I'd been on the Brady board for two years but was still dumbfounded that, one, they would even think of me, and two, they would think I would be the right person to lead the session.

So I said no.

conference

I wasn't about to put myself in a situation where I'd fail or be in a situation where people might question whether I belonged.

My impostor syndrome rocketed me back to 1985.

Dad and I pull up to the white fifteen-passenger van filled with ten Amateur Athletic Union (AAU) club basketball players. He says, "Grab your stuff, I'll talk to the coach." I can feel the girls in the van watching me, judging me as I walk reluctantly toward them with my duffel bag, a bag I packed only a half hour earlier. I can't hear what Dad is saying to the coach, but I can see him pointing, insisting, and badgering him into letting me go with the team to California for a weeklong basketball tournament.

I'm mortified.

I don't belong here; I'm not on the team, and I haven't been to any of their practices or games. But for some reason Dad believes I deserve to go on the thousand-mile road trip from Denver to San Diego with the team.

The AAU team consists of the ten top high school basketball players in the area, four of whom are on my high school team. I probably could be on the team if I'd committed to playing basketball year-round, but I haven't. I play volleyball and tennis in the offseason, and I ski on the weekends (which is forbidden in AAU). Summer weekends, I'm often at the cabin. I can't commit to a team that requires that level of dedication, time commitment, and sacrifice.

That doesn't stop Dad from forcing me onto the team.

He told me on the drive here, "I was talking to Lori's dad, and he said that the only way you can get a basketball scholarship is if a college coach sees you play at an AAU tournament. A lot of college coaches go to this tournament in San Diego to find players, so you need to be there if you're going to get noticed. This is your last chance, since it's the last summer before you graduate."

"Yeah, but Dad, I'm not on the team," I reminded him.

dumb girl

"Not yet. Besides, you don't have to be on the team, you just have to go to this tournament," he insisted.

Now, standing next to the van, I see the coach and Dad shake hands. Dad smiles.

The coach shakes his head in defeat as he walks over to me and instructs me to get in the van. He then opens the passenger side door and grudgingly announces to the team, "Heidi is joining us."

I feel the collective aggrievement from the team as I crawl to the back seat and hear whispers and giggles at my expense. They are right to be annoyed; I'd feel the same way if someone who hadn't worked hard or sacrificed suddenly got to go with my team on a trip to a prestigious tournament.

I don't belong in the van.

The week ends up being a disaster. I'm ignored or barely tolerated during the twenty-hour drive to San Diego, and on the drive back to Denver, I sit alone with my bag. I don't know the inside jokes and can't contribute to stories of clutch plays and funny things that happened over the course of the season. At the tournament, I'm out of shape and don't know the plays, so when the coach puts me in, I'm sluggish, can't catch my breath, can't hit a shot to save my life, and make mistakes like dribbling off my foot and accidentally passing the ball to the other team. The harder I try, the worse I get. If a college coach does see me, there is no way they are interested.

I come home frustrated, embarrassed, angry, humiliated, and disgraced. I vow to never again be in a position where I'm not wanted, don't belong, or am destined to fail.

So when, twenty-eight years later, I was asked to moderate a panel at a prestigious conference where I could easily be embarrassed, humiliated, or disgraced, I said no.

But the Brady staff didn't accept my "no."

conference

"Look," Brian said, "I know this seems really scary and big, but the team talked about it, and we really think you'd be the best person to moderate the panel."

"I've never moderated a panel before," I protested. "It's just not something I know how to do—and if this is such a big deal, shouldn't you get someone who knows what they're doing?"

"Tell you what, you agree to do it, and I'll coach you through it so you'll be comfortable," he promised.

I could not talk them out of their horrible idea.

I sighed. "Okay, I'll do it." *But if I'm going to do it*, I thought, *I'm going to do it well and leave nothing to chance.* I wasn't about to repeat the AAU trip.

As soon as I hung up, I called every facilitator I knew for advice and came up with a game plan. In the ensuing week, I set up an initial call with each person on the panel to introduce myself, get a feel for who they were and what they'd talk about, and familiarize myself with their speaking style. Then I set up two additional calls where all eight panelists met each other and got a sense of what to expect, including the questions I'd be asking and how we as a group would manage the time allotted to us.

Just like when I prepared to debate the NRA guy, my dining room table was pushed aside and replaced by my kids' stuffed animals, who sat attentively in their dining room chairs while I asked them questions and practiced how I'd respond if they cut each other off, got emotional, or became disruptive and argumentative.

I practiced with Dave for every scenario where things could go off the rails. I needed to make sure that no matter what went wrong, I'd be prepared.

The day of the panel, I was racked with anxiety. But I knew I was ready to deliver.

What I wasn't ready for was what actually happened: All the members of the panel told their stories in a passionate, compelling, and timely manner. They were respectful of each other's

dumb girl

experiences, adding interesting details of their own trials, and they responded to the nonverbal cue I'd told them I'd give them when their time was up—me leaning forward in my chair—and quickly wrapped up their thoughts each time I did it. My prep calls paid off.

The audience was attentive throughout the panel, and when we were done, they showed their appreciation with a loud and enthusiastic standing ovation. As I stood on the stage, sharing in the praise, I looked directly at a couple standing at a round table just a few feet away. Their daughter had recently been killed in the Aurora, Colorado, movie theater shooting where twelve people were killed and fifty-eight were shot and injured. Tears ran down their faces as they applauded, and it humbled me.

The work I was doing, and the thoughtful effort I put into it on behalf of folks like them, was making a real impact. I felt like I deserved respect, admiration, and appreciation. I felt I belonged.

chapter 26

tennis

The woman on the other side of the court was not that good. Her serve had no pace, she wasn't particularly athletic, and her forehand was a weird slice that made it hard to predict where the ball would land. As soon as I saw her in her neon-green tennis skirt with matching visor and shoes, the word "Tennis" bedazzled on her bright-pink tank top, I knew I'd come away with a win.

But when I lost the first set (2–6) and was down in the second set (3–4), I knew I'd miscalculated. I'd done everything I could think of—hit to her backhand, charged the net, made her move around the court—but none of it worked. She was like a backboard, always getting the ball back to me and waiting for me to make an error.

And I was making a lot of errors. The problem was that every error came with Dad's voice: "That was a dumb shot," "Double faults are unacceptable," "Why would you try a drop shot now," and "Get your head in the game."

I was a forty-year-old woman playing in a recreational women's league a thousand miles from Dad. How was he still in my head?

It's my senior year, and I've won the district championship and will now go to the state tournament as the number three singles

dumb girl

tennis player from Columbine High. Mom and Dad are over-the-moon happy, which feels nice.

It doesn't matter what sport it is, volleyball, basketball, tennis, soccer, gymnastics, swimming, or diving, Dad fully supports my athletic drive and seems to enjoy my success as much as I do.

The problem is that sometimes he wants it more than I do.

He seems particularly invested in my tennis matches. He's developed elaborate systems for keeping statistics on my match play—tracking my winning shots, shot selection, and mistakes. The actual score of the match doesn't seem to matter. What matters is whether I come up with a positive number on Dad's stat sheet, which is hard to do because it's skewed toward errors. A winning shot is worth one point and an error is worth minus two. I don't understand his system or how he calculates points, but he enjoys making up a system. He lectures me when I lose and gives me a point-by-point analysis after every match, which is hard to digest along with the intense feelings of elation from a win or despair from a loss.

I appreciate his support and interest, but his enthusiasm and pushing for me to win have begun to feel oppressive. Every mistake is emotionally excruciating and winning has become convoluted. I've begun to resent the lack of trust he has in me to dig myself out of losing a match or not lose momentum when winning a match.

Dad is a self-taught player who learned the game of tennis by watching the University of Colorado varsity players practice when he was in college. His dorm room was next to the tennis courts. He tells me, "When they finished their practice, I'd pepper them with questions and then practice what I saw and what they told me." Years later, he combined that with Vic Braden's PBS instructional series, *Tennis for the Future*, and taught me how to play, and how to win.

But he also is the reason that my backhand is the weakest part

tennis

of my game. He taught me a one-handed backhand and told me, "Most girls have two-handed backhands, and they are a bunch of DBADGs. Also, a one-handed backhand gives you a wider reach." The problem is I don't have the strength in my upper body to pull it off, so my backhand has become a defensive shot and a liability. Somehow, in the district match, I masked that weakness. But I'm not sure I'll be able to do it again at state.

I win my first match at state (6–2, 6–2), and I've started fantasizing about playing in the finals for the state title. I think about the big crowds, playing with ball girls who retrieve and supply me with new balls—like at Wimbledon—and winning the large trophy. But the dream is short-lived.

My second match is a disaster. The girl I play against figures out my weakness right away and hits exclusively to my backhand. There is nothing I can do. I try and run around my backhand, I try to come to the net so I don't have to hit a backhand, and when all else fails, I try to pretend I have a good backhand. Nothing works. I want to quit.

Which is weird, because I love tennis and I love sports. Usually, playing sports gives me a feeling of importance and proficiency I don't feel in the classroom, and I love having the ability and confidence to problem-solve while competing. If I miss a serve, I get to try it again and make adjustments so it goes in.

Being good at sports is proof I'm not a DBADG. But I'm only "good" when I'm winning.

As my opponent in my second match at state continues to pummel my backhand, I grow desperate for advice. I lose the first set (1–6) and head over to Dad, who's sitting next to Mom in a camping chair just outside the fence.

He gives me two pieces of advice, neither of which is helpful. "If the ball is close to the line, call it out." And "You should be returning every one of her serves, whether it's in or out. It's good practice."

dumb girl

I say, "Okay," as I return to the court while I argue with him in my head: *I'm in one of the last matches of my high school career. This is not the time for me to be practicing, and besides, it's considered rude to hit back an obvious fault.*

I worry about getting into trouble with the umpire or my coaches and strictly follow the rules and etiquette of the game of tennis. That's one of the things I like about tennis and sports in general. There are strict rules, everyone knows what they are, and everyone follows them. If they don't, there are clear consequences and penalties.

My internal dialogue shifts from problem-solving in the match to arguments with Dad. He's all I can think of. His negative comments over the years, the frustration of this match, and the fact that I even have a weakness that we've not fixed puts me on the edge of tears.

Feeling no ability to control what is happening and feeling like it's in large part because of Dad, I begin to fantasize about quitting, throwing my racket, and storming off the court in a dramatic fashion. I find power by refusing to look at Dad the few times I have a good shot and refusing to look at him when I screw up. It feels like a small win and a tiny version of control—not doing what is expected.

I lose badly (1–6, 0–6) and desperately want to cry afterward but don't. I hate it when people cry after losing a game or a match in any sport. I think it's a totally wussy, DBADG thing to do.

Losing at the state championships stung. I convinced myself that I lost because my backhand sucked and Dad kept yelling at me when I made mistakes.

No matter the reason, the joy was gone. So I walked away from competitive tennis when I was eighteen. I periodically hit with Dave and friends over the following years, but I never competed. And I avoided teaching my kids to play tennis, fearing

tennis

I'd sound like Dad when I corrected them or showed them how to hit.

It wasn't until 2006 that I started to pick it up again. I joined a recreational league near my house and played in a few matches and had some success, but still couldn't get Dad's voice out of my head.

Every error I made ushered in his dismay and harsh criticism—and I couldn't seem to turn him off.

Up until that point, I'd describe myself as a "habitual responder." I lived life based on how others were acting, feeling, and doing; my needs, wants, and desires were always last—part of being a people pleaser.

And I played tennis the same way. I'd adjust my play to accommodate my opponent's style of play. If they liked to lob, I'd lob. If they liked to hit short shots, I'd hit short shots. And if they had a slow pace, I'd play a slow-paced game.

But I wasn't having fun and I didn't know who I was on the court.

Then a coach I'd been working with asked, "Why are you always responding to your opponent? You have a powerful serve, a scary approach shot, and you're super agile. Why aren't you making them play your game?" He gave me a stern look. "Find their weaknesses and then pounce. If they aren't agile, make them move around the court; if their backhand sucks, go to it over and over and over again until they adjust or you've won the match."

"Yeah," I said, "but I start to feel bad when they get upset at themselves and are losing."

He laughed. "Are you here to make friends or win matches?"

He had a point. So I started playing more aggressively. I missed more shots and lost matches, but I was having more fun. I went to the net, taking advantage of my height. I hit to their weakness, I hit harder, I served harder, and I played the way I wanted to play.

dumb girl

I was playing tennis on my terms.

With time, Dad's voice started to diminish as I worked to slowly replace it with my internal laughter at my mistakes and a softening of my anger when I lost a match.

I honestly don't know if I won all that much, but it didn't really matter. I found my love of the game again. What I didn't anticipate was how it would spill off the court and into my life. The tennis court became my practice field for my life.

On the court I practiced being super nice to my competitor before the match to see what that felt like and how it impacted my play. And then I practiced doing the opposite, being quiet and refusing to engage in idle chitchat before and during the match. I practiced calling balls out when I was unsure whether they were in or out, because my tendency was to always give my opponent the benefit of the doubt. I practiced not consoling my opponent after the match when I beat her. And I practiced having a forgiving and kind inner monologue.

Off the court I decided how I wanted to show up in a meeting, not withholding my ideas and suggestions. I picked up Panda Express instead of making a well-balanced and nutritious dinner for my family, like I was supposed to. I showed up late for soccer practice pickup one afternoon because I wanted to finish reading the last chapter of *The Notebook*. I booked later, more convenient flights even though it was more expensive. And I didn't engage in idle chitchat with the grocery store clerk when I didn't want to.

They were little things, but ultimately these changes led me to having fun on the court and gave me more power and agency in my life. Prioritizing my needs over what others needed and expected from me was a new concept and felt liberating.

chapter 27

arizona

As I unpack my suitcase, I notice a small magazine in the top drawer of the bedside table next to the Bible. I flip through the magazine, noticing pictures of topless women, some in sexy sheer lingerie. There are pictures of dildos and phone sex numbers and women holding dildos up to their bright-red puckered lips. And there are articles. As I read a couple of sentences in one of the articles, my face turns red realizing it's a detailed account of a man and woman having oral sex.

I know this is bad and want to share the strange discovery with someone, anyone, so I show it to Mom, who's standing on the other side of our hotel room. She flips through it and dismisses it as "a load of crap," curtly handing it back to me.

Mom and I are on a long weekend trip in Tucson, Arizona, to begin healing our very broken mother-daughter relationship. Mom's living her new life as a recovering alcoholic and has just received her one-year AA sobriety chip. I'm seventeen and don't feel like we have a lot in common or anything to talk about, but I agreed to go on the trip because being on vacation sounded better than staying home.

I flick through the magazine, noticing that the penises are much larger than any I've ever seen. In fact, they are huge—some black, some white—but mostly they're interesting because I've never seen anything like it.

dumb girl

Mom clearly has no interest in the magazine. I don't want her to think I'm a freak, despite my curiosity to look at it more thoroughly, so I throw it in the trash can.

Mom and I continue unpacking and getting dressed to go out to the pool while we talk.

"Those kinds of magazines make women look bad and make everything we've worked so hard for on the ERA [Equal Rights Amendment] meaningless," she explains. "Sex is a wonderful thing that a husband and wife do together to express their love."

She continues talking about how "making love" is a natural, loving thing that God created . . .

I stop listening after she says "making love." I hate that phrase. It's "sex." I don't know at the time that finding that magazine and having a conversation about sex and a sex magazine is only the beginning of several sexual encounters, conversations, and revelations she and I will have that weekend.

It's awkward dressing in front of Mom. I don't want to look at her naked body, and I don't want her looking at mine. I'm aware that it'd be weird to change in the bathroom like in the locker room at school before and after gym class, so I face the opposite wall as she undresses and puts on her traditional flowery, brightly colored one piece Lands' End swimsuit with a built-in support bra that doesn't hide her fat or stretch marks.

I quickly put on my pink high-cut Cheryl Tiegs bikini. I think it accentuates my long and muscular legs and showcases my flat stomach, which I'm proud of.

Once at the pool, we stake out a couple of lounge chairs, positioning them to get full sun exposure, and then put sunscreen on each other's backs. Once settled, we talk about everything, including basketball, my frustrations with my coach, our family, alcoholism, Dad, my past boyfriends, and my future. It feels really nice to have a "girlfriend" conversation with Mom. It's the first time it's ever happened.

There are several people sunbathing near us but only one catches my eye, a forty-something-year-old guy sunbathing thirty feet from us. He's out of earshot and is lying on his stomach with his hands under his hips while wriggling around on his lounge chair. It's weird, so I point him out to Mom. "Look at the guy over there. I think he fell asleep and is having a dream. How weird!"

She doesn't take much notice, and we both quickly forget about him and continue talking.

After a while, Mom goes back to the room to get us something to drink and to use the bathroom. The guy I noticed earlier and pointed out to Mom suddenly appears next to me.

"I came to apologize," he says as I hold my hand up to block the sun from my eyes.

He's about five foot seven, dirty blond hair, medium build, with a small forehead and indistinct features. He looks like a guy who'd be cast as the janitor in a 1980s Molly Ringwald movie.

"You were probably wondering what I was doing over there on my chair earlier."

No, not really, I think to myself.

He continues, "I have to tell you, you are a beautiful woman. How old are you?"

"Seventeen," I reply.

"I would have guessed early twenties. I was lying in the sun, I saw you, and then fell asleep. As I was sleeping, I had the most delicious dream about you, and I was trying to stop myself from doing something embarrassing."

I have no idea what he's talking about. What would be embarrassing? But I am flattered that he thinks I'm older than seventeen, and I don't want him to know that I have no idea what he's talking about, so I nod and say, "It's okay."

He continues, "I just think you're so beautiful. I would love to get together with you later to make up for my bad behavior before."

dumb girl

Just then, Mom appears. She introduces herself to him. His demeanor immediately changes. His shoulders slump and he looks at the ground as he explains that he's just come over to say hi. Then he quickly leaves, walking back to his lounge chair.

"What was that all about?" Mom asks.

I explain what he said to me and how he seems nice. She tells me he's a "weirdo" and I should stay away from him. "If he comes over again, you need to come and get me." She continues, "Actually, I don't want you to be here by yourself. If I have to go to the room or you need to go to the room, we should go together."

I feel her fear and protectiveness, and it feels nice.

I look over to his chair. He's gone.

The next morning as I'm setting out our towels on a couple of lounge chairs, he appears again.

"I know your mom doesn't want you talking to me, but I want to let you know that I had the most beautiful dream about you and me last night. I'm very tired today from spending so much time pleasuring myself as I thought of you over and over last night. I know it's weird to hear this, but I think it's important that you know. I'll probably never see you again but want you to know that for the rest of my life, every single time I pleasure myself, I'll have you in my mind." He repeats himself, "I'll make love to you in my mind every day, for the rest of my life."

I'm grossed out, slightly flattered, but mostly confused. He feels dangerous, and I don't know what to do. I desperately look around for Mom and wish I had not come out alone. I tell him, "I have to go," and run as quickly as I can back to the room, where I tell Mom what happened and promise not to go out without her again.

Later that afternoon, Mom and I read books by the pool and talk about boys—specifically, my boyfriend, Jeff. She's on a lounge

arizona

chair and I'm on my towel on the grass next to her. "Mom, I really, really, really like Jeff. He is a total hunk and I love being around him. I get huge butterflies in my stomach whenever I kiss him, and that's why I try and see him at his job at the mall whenever I can."

Her listening to details of my teenage romance feels safe and like something a TV teenager would share with her TV mom.

The conversation suddenly shifts as I remember the feelings of confusion and bewilderment I felt the last time Jeff and I made out in my room. For some reason, I suddenly feel a deep and burning need to tell Mom about Philip and the boyfriend/girlfriend game. I've never told anyone, and I need to tell someone. Mostly because I need someone to tell me if what I'm remembering about Philip is my fault. It feels like it is.

The sun is warm on my skin and beads of sweat begin to form on my forehead. I'm anxious and calm at the same time, and I take a deep breath. I lie flat on my back with my eyes closed as I begin to unload my secret onto Mom.

Initially, Mom holds her book above her stomach, half reading and half listening.

"There's something I want to tell you about Philip and me." I gulp, trying to find the courage to continue. "We did sex things together and I just started remembering it a few months ago."

She puts her book down on her stomach, removes her sunglasses, and repositions herself in her lounge chair. I have her full attention now.

I tell her how it started when I was ten. I describe the things he did to me. I flip over onto my stomach and focus on a blade of grass I've picked. I play with it as I continue the story, unable to look Mom in the face. "There were other times too, in my bed and in his, but mostly it was in the basement when no one was home."

"Is he still doing it?" she reluctantly asks.

dumb girl

"No. It stopped a while ago, but I forgot about it. I just started to remember it and wanted to tell you."

She asks me several questions and I answer as honestly as I can. I don't remember the specifics of the questions, and my memory of what happened with Philip, at that point, is spotty and fuzzy, which makes it hard to explain. A feeling of lightness engulfs me after each question is asked and answered. At the same time, my anxiousness grows, and I become unable to sit still.

Mom's temperament changes too. She becomes very still and serious with each question.

Our moods and demeanors seem to gravitate in polar-opposite directions. She radiates sadness, gravity, and concern as I become increasingly animated, light, and untroubled.

"Heidi," she says, "I need you to know you've done nothing wrong and that what Philip did was wrong and bad and in no way your fault."

I believe her.

When I finish telling her everything I can remember, and she has no more questions to ask, there is silence. A long silence.

"I feel like I've had a ton of bricks lifted off my shoulders," I confess. "I feel so relieved telling you this, Mom."

"I feel like you just gave me a ton of bricks to carry. I really could use a drink right now," she jokes.

We laugh. The break from the tension in the air is a relief.

"I'm really glad you told me about this, Heidi," she confides. "It must have been hard. I need to think about it and think about what to do. I think Dad needs to know and I think I'm going to talk to our therapist about what to do." She takes off her glasses, looks me in the eyes, and says, "You don't need to worry about it anymore," and she ends with an impassioned, "I'm sorry." She reaches over to my hand, holds it in hers, looks into my eyes, and says, "Thank you for telling me."

arizona

For the rest of the afternoon, I feel light, I feel invincible, I feel free, and I feel like everything is going to be okay.

Then I remember that we're going home to Colorado on Sunday, and I start to worry.

When we pull up to the house after our two-hour flight, Philip walks out the front door. He's supposed to be away at school.

I look at Mom. She looks back in surprise and mumbles, "He must have come home for the weekend."

She told me on the plane, "I don't want to talk to Dad about this until we're with our therapist on Thursday. I'm worried about his reaction, worried that he'll drive up to Philip's dorm and kill him for what he's done to you."

Her worry made me feel loved.

"Just pretend everything's normal," Mom whispers as we get out of the car.

I've been doing that for a long time, so it's not going to be a problem.

Luckily, Philip is getting ready to go back up to school, so he's only there for a quick five minutes of packing his stuff into his yellow pickup truck and saying goodbye.

We all gather—me, Mom, Dad, and Robby—to say goodbye to him on the front stoop of the house. He hugs Robby, hugs Mom, and then hugs Dad.

I really don't want to hug him goodbye or even touch him. Now that my secret is out, he repulses me in a way that is fresh, profound, and all-consuming. I don't want his body, his penis, his anything pressing against me, but I'm being asked to pretend everything is normal.

Mom is watching intently.

I brace for his hug when all of a sudden he kisses me hard, his mouth partially open as his tongue finds my tightly clenched

dumb girl

lips. I forget about his body as my focus pivots to his mouth on mine. He holds the kiss while I struggle to push him away. My resistance makes him press harder.

Then suddenly, he releases me.

I can't believe he just did that! He has never kissed me before, ever!

Of all the times to do something like this—his timing could not be worse. He did it to get a laugh, but only Robby, now fourteen, laughs hysterically.

I'm humiliated and embarrassed, but also strangely feel vindicated. Mom has just witnessed what I've been dealing with for years. He's just never been so public about it.

As he drives away and honks twice, we all wave on cue.

Two weeks after I tell Mom, a week after Mom tells Dad, and two days after Mom and Dad tell Philip they know *the secret*, we all find ourselves in Mom and Dad's therapist's office. We are there to talk about *the secret* and to talk about our feelings about it.

This is the first time Philip and I have been in the same room since *the secret* came out, and I'm terrified, calm, and anxious all at the same time.

Mom drives me to the meeting and Dad drives Philip down from his college. I decide not to hug Philip when he enters the room with Dad, which feels awkward. We always hug when we see each other, especially since he left for college. Instead, we awkwardly glance at each other and quickly sit down on opposite sides of the room, on the cold metal folding chairs that make the already small room, filled with a desk, couch, and chair for therapist Stan, feel overcrowded.

And then, once again, I leave my body and float above the group as they discuss "the telling of *the secret*." Feelings do not register.

"Your mom told your dad about the incest last week during

arizona

their weekly marriage counseling session, and it's important that we talk about what happened," Stan begins.

As I float, Mom explains how she and Dad told Philip that they knew.

They tell me they are proud of me for telling.

They say they are feeling very angry with Philip.

Philip says he's sorry.

I don't remember a lot of the meeting.

I float, I observe, and I listen, but what's said doesn't stick.

I cry. Philip cries. Mom cries. Dad cries. Dad crying makes me sad—it feels like it's my fault.

It's decided that Philip will go to counseling up at his college and I will go to counseling in Denver. Stan and Mom and Dad will arrange it.

Later that week, Mom tells me that because she told Dad about *the secret* in front of a therapist, Stan is bound by the laws of Colorado to report the incest to the state.

There will be an investigation and I will have to tell my story to a government official. I feel validation that the state cares enough about me that they want to investigate. At the same time, I don't want to explain what happened to a stranger and I worry I won't be believed. And I still don't remember everything that happened and find it really embarrassing to talk about.

As Mom drives me to the scary, plain-looking large government offices two weeks later, she instructs me to be honest with my recollection of what happened but warns me in a very serious and grave tone, "If they think you were physically hurt or experienced pain or think you are still in danger, they'll put Philip in jail."

So I carefully word what I say, making sure to downplay anything I think would put Philip in jail. I'm really nervous to talk to the agent at the office and tremble as I tell him what I remember up to that point.

dumb girl

I guess I did a good job because Philip does not go to jail and I become a statistic, just one more girl molested by a family member in Colorado in the '80s.

I spend the summer between my junior and senior years driving across town each week to talk to a therapist.

It's hard to tell her everything. I struggle to come up with the right words for the feelings I have and the descriptions of what I can barely remember. The memories are still fuzzy and not clear.

My goal is to trust her, tell her everything, and then have it go away. I view it like basketball wind sprints and "suicides." They're hard, I hate them, but I do them knowing I'll play better if I'm in shape and not struggling to catch my breath in the middle of a game.

I know doing things that are hard makes you better in the end.

The story of *the secret* feels jumbled as it comes out. It's out of order and has too many feelings attached to it. I feel crazy, dumb, and irrational. My memories are sketchy and incomplete, so I tell her the little I have remembered up to that point, and share with her the conclusion I've come to: "I never want to have sex, ever!" I tell her, "I'm not interested in boys, and they all gross me out, especially their penises."

She looks at me and says, "You might be gay."

Two weeks later, I'm sitting in front of a new therapist.

This one listens better and is far more patient with me.

"It's normal to be grossed out by penises and not to remember everything that happened," she explains. "The memories will most likely come back, it just takes time." She lets me talk about the intense sadness, vulnerability, and ups and downs that are part sexual abuse and part being seventeen.

I tell her, "I just feel so alone. No one seems to understand what I'm going through and it's not like I can talk to my friends about it."

She suggests, "There's an incest group that meets every Wednesday night that I think would be perfect for you."

The following week, two days after my eighteenth birthday, I drive to the address my therapist gave me and go to my first incest group meeting. It's a group of ten older women. I'm the only teenager.

I sit week after week listening to their stories of fear, depression, and unmanageable lives. I don't feel like them, look like them, or act like them. I don't belong. I listen to stories of devil-worship and of being caged and beaten and being forced to perform sexual acts to entice the devil. Many of their stories I don't understand. My stories are pale in comparison, not horrifying or bloodcurdling or sadistic, and make me feel like what I've experienced is inconsequential and not deserving of sympathy.

After being prompted several times to share my story or tell the group about myself, I finally agree. After talking about Philip, I also tell them about how frustrated I am when Dad comes in and watches me take a bath every night.

The therapist looks at me with great concern and asks me to tell her more about it. I tell the group how he comes in when I'm in the bath, sits on the closed toilet seat or stands, and just looks at me as he talks to me. I tell the group how I put my leg up to try and cover my vagina and fold my arms to cover my breasts.

The therapist asks, "Have you ever asked him to leave or told him he makes you uncomfortable?"

"Sort of," I admit. "I've asked him if I can just be alone, and most of the time he says no because he has things he needs to tell me or talk to me about. I don't feel like I can just make him leave," I explain.

dumb girl

"I'm concerned about your safety," she says gently. "It's not okay for him to be in the bathroom while you are taking a bath."

I don't quite understand what she's talking about. Lots of things Dad does irritate me, and I don't see this as that much different.

"What he's doing is extremely inappropriate," she insists, "and it's my duty to make sure you're safe."

"But he's not touching me or anything like that," I protest.

"It doesn't matter. You have a right to take a bath by yourself, and him being in there is incestuous behavior. I'm going to check with the state to see what the age limit is on incest and incestual behavior. If the state defines incest as eighteen and under, then I'll have no choice but to report it, and he will most likely be removed from the home or you will be removed from the home."

Holy shit! I think. *This is for real.* I can't believe that this is that big of a deal. It's so much less than what the other women in my group have been describing. Nobody's raping me, or forcing me to worship the devil, or beating me. But they all look at me with sadness and astonishment for what I'm going through.

I don't feel deserving of their attention and concern.

The week goes by excruciatingly slowly. All week I picture over and over what Dad being removed from the house looks like. I envision cops coming to the door and handcuffing him and putting him in the back of a police car as he sadly looks at me, Robby, and Mom on the front doorstep. I have difficulty sleeping and frantically pray every night, pleading with God that Dad is not removed. I don't want our family to be a bad family or for people to think we're weird.

The following week, I'm anxious to get to group knowing I'll find out from my therapist if Dad's going to jail.

My prayers are answered.

Because I'm eighteen, it's not a crime for Dad to watch me

bathe. I guess Colorado thinks I'm old enough to fend for myself. I'm relieved, but my therapist passionately explains to me how important it is for me to stop Dad from doing what he's doing, and the group helps me figure out how to confront him through role play.

I know she's right, but I also know there's no way I can confront Dad; I am not willing to test his unpredictable outrage.

Instead, I switch to taking showers instead of baths, and make sure to only take baths when he's not home.

"I just told him, like we practiced, and he just stopped coming in," I tell the group at our next session.

They tell me how proud they are of me. I try to ignore how ashamed I feel for lying to them.

chapter 28

month with a gun

On December 13, 2012, a man walked into Sandy Hook Elementary School and shot and killed twenty-six seven-year-olds, along with six adult staff members.

Three days after the massacre, before all the little bodies were buried, the NRA's spokesperson, Wayne LaPierre, went on the offensive and told the country, "The only thing that stops a bad guy with a gun is a good guy with a gun."

What does that even mean? I thought when I heard the audio clip. His rationale was confusing and distressing—and, most importantly, untrue. I knew, from the ASK campaign, that a gun in the home is twenty-two times more likely to injure a friend or family member than an intruder.

His simplistic and inaccurate rationale brought up the same feelings of confusion and irritation I had when I couldn't understand Dad's logic. And the guys who were showing up to my events with guns on their hips were equally confusing to me. I knew they were doing it in part to intimidate me and the other organizers, but I didn't understand why they felt the need to have a gun with them everywhere they went. Were we really all that unsafe at the park or in the State Capitol building?

As usual, I wanted to understand their perspective. *What would it be like to be that good guy with a gun?* I wondered. *What*

month with a gun

would it be like to get that gun, live with that gun, and be out and about with that gun?

I decided to find out.

So I did something that was completely against everything I stood for: I bought a gun, a 9mm Glock. And I decided to carry it everywhere I went for a month—the grocery store, business meetings, the bank, parties, yoga, tennis, and church—to see how it made me feel. Then I contacted *Ms. Magazine* and asked if they'd be interested in publishing a four-part article I planned on writing called "My Month with a Gun."

They said yes.

Two days into my experiment, I went to breakfast with my two kids and some friends. After eating and shopping, my gun with me in my purse the entire time, I was anxious to get home to enjoy the warm weather. I put my purse on the counter and then spent the next hour out on the back deck.

Walking into the kitchen to refresh our drinks, I noticed my purse sitting there—and realized the 9mm Glock was still inside it.

I'd forgotten to lock it up in the safe!

Panic set in as I realized fifteen-year-old Aaron was playing video games just ten feet away. What if he'd decided to get the socks I'd bought for him from my purse while I was out on the deck?

Thoughts raced through my mind, and I pondered how I'd just crossed the fine line between being a responsible gun owner and being an irresponsible idiot whose fifteen-year-old might have accidentally shot himself or someone else—with my gun.

A week later, I was in downtown Seattle in a dimly lit parking lot that reeked of urine. I was late for a meeting and was distracted, so I barely noticed the large man enter the stairwell behind me.

I heard his footsteps about halfway down to the third floor.

dumb girl

When I got to the second floor, I became nervous, and the *Oprah* episode where a man attacks a woman alone in a situation just like this played in my head. I thought about the 9mm Glock in my purse as I clumsily continued down the stairs in my skirt and heels.

He followed me. I looked back at him, so he knew I knew he was there (like Oprah's expert suggested). Then I thought, *Should I pull the gun out? Should I point it at him?*

I put my hand in my purse and wrapped my fingers around the cold metal grip but realized the gun wouldn't do me any good because he was a couple of steps above me and behind me. And besides, *What if he's just an innocent guy going down the stairs?* I thought.

My heart racing, we finally got to the street-level door, where the man simply passed by me, on his way to . . . somewhere. I let out a sigh of relief as I let go of the gun. I'd grown paranoid. He wasn't the bad guy I perceived him to be, and the gun hadn't made me safe.

Deep down, my goal was to try to understand my nemesis. I figured that if I could walk in the gun guys' shoes, I might be able to understand them, know why guns are so central to their identity, understand why they always seem so angry, and just maybe figure out a way to find common ground so we could stop gun violence together.

Naive? Probably.

I just didn't like being scared of them and wanted them to stop hating me. I thought writing about my feelings, my perspective, and the vulnerabilities I experienced as a gun owner might be a way to achieve that.

As a teenager, I embraced the power of being honest, straightforward, and sharing my vulnerabilities, believing—naively—that baring my soul would somehow protect me.

month with a gun

༃

I meet James on the airplane when Mom and I are returning from Arizona, the same trip where I tell her about *the secret*. I'm seventeen. He's a thirty-one-year-old high school football and track coach at a school across town. I first notice him when Mom and I are finding our seats on the plane. He looks at me and smiles as he passes by; I smile back. He's kinda cute in a blond, tan, muscular, older guy kind of way.

Thirty minutes into our flight, he walks down the aisle and introduces himself. "Excuse me," he says as he leans over, looking directly at me. "I noticed your letter jacket when we were at the boarding gate. Do you go to Columbine?"

I nod, feeling proud that he's noticed.

Looking at the large gray "C" on my jacket that's filled with shiny gold bars, stars, and patches, he asks, "So I see from your jacket that you play volleyball, basketball, and tennis at Columbine. And I assume you're what, a junior, from all your hardware?"

I blush and respond, "Yeah, and I'm in the middle of my tennis season." He smiles and nods and seems genuinely impressed. He introduces himself to Mom, and they talk as I internally gloat, thinking about how much I love my letter jacket and how it's gotten a cute guy to talk to me.

After about fifteen minutes, and two warnings by the flight attendant that he needs to clear the aisle, he walks back to his seat, but not before giving me his phone number.

Despite him being nearly twice my age, Mom really likes him and tells me, "Wow, what an impressive guy! You should call him when we get home. I think he'd be a good person for you to be around."

I agree.

Mom sees James as an adult, I see him as a guy, a guy who's cute, tall, blond, and muscular, but most important, he thinks I'm impressive.

dumb girl

∽

I spend a large part of the following Saturday afternoon making my hair look perfect and making sure that I put just enough blue eye makeup and pink lip gloss on. James is taking me to the movies.

I know he has arrived when Robby runs into my room yelling, "Oh my gosh, he drives a Corvette!" Then he looks at me with jealousy and says, "Lucky!"

Mom, Dad, and Robby come out with me to greet him as he gets out of his brand-new bright-cherry-red Corvette Convertible. Dad shakes his hand and says, "Betty's told me all about you."

I can tell he really likes him as he and Mom enthusiastically talk about Doug and Philip and sports and all the people the three of them know. As I stand next to Robby, I feel like we are little kids at church watching Mom and Dad talk to one of their good friends about adult things.

Once they finally run out of common acquaintances to talk about, James opens the passenger side door. I slip in and wave as they watch us drive away. I feel like a princess riding away in a chariot. I love how proud Mom and Dad are that I'm with a really cool guy who impresses them.

Ten minutes into the trip, sitting at a stoplight holding hands, James nervously looks around and tells me, "You look amazing and so beautiful."

I blush.

Then he cautiously explains, "Hey look, I could get into a lot of trouble if someone I work with sees me in my car with you. They just wouldn't get it."

He's a track coach at a local high school, but I don't see what that has to do with me. He doesn't work at *my* school.

"Because of our age difference, people might not like that we're together, so can you keep your head down so nobody can see you? I'll let you know when it's okay to sit back up."

month with a gun

I still don't quite understand why he doesn't want people to see me, but it seems important to him, and I desperately want him to keep liking me. So that's what I do, I put my head down between my knees and stare at my shoes while he drives, so nobody can see me.

Now I feel less like a princess and more like a secret.

After we've been dating for several months, James invites me to his house for dinner. As I drive across Denver to his place, I gleefully sing to the car radio, looking forward to him making me dinner and not having to hide from people seeing me. I love the attention he gives me and how I feel when I'm around him. I dream about how we will kiss and how he'll hold me and how I'll get butterflies while lying safely in his arms.

When he answers the door, he gives me a big hug and a small kiss on the lips. Butterflies fill my stomach and I'm consumed with euphoria. He makes me pork chops, carrots, and breadsticks, and we eat in the living room while we watch TV. Afterward, we sit on the couch holding hands and making small talk about track and basketball.

We start to kiss, and I feel a familiar and uncomfortable pressure begin to form in the air. I just want to kiss but I can tell he wants more. As he starts to put his hand down the front of my jeans, I squirm away and tell him I want to tell him something.

He leans back on the couch and waits for me to talk.

I take a big breath and cautiously begin, "Well, I think you should know something about me, something I don't really ever talk about."

"Okay?" he says with a hint of impatience.

"I wanted to tell you that . . . I was . . . 'incested' by my brother when I was younger."

He's the first person I've told outside of my family or in a therapist's office, and it feels safe. It feels good to say it out loud, especially since he's an adult and it feels like it's the perfect thing

dumb girl

to say to get him to stop. I want to continue kissing, I just don't want to go further than that. For some reason, saying "I don't want to go further" doesn't feel like a good enough reason, but telling him that I am flawed and fragile and broken because of what happened with Philip does feel like a good enough reason.

He listens patiently to what I say and then responds with, "Okay . . . I'm sorry that happened, but there's something I want to show you in the other room." He gives me a loving, gentle kiss on the forehead.

I feel lighter, heard, and understood . . . until we get into his bedroom.

As we stand next to his bed, he starts kissing me and I kiss back. I'm certain it isn't going any further because of what I have just told him. He gently lays me on the bed as he slowly moves his hand under my shirt and cups my breast. It feels good and I groan. We continue kissing as he moves his hand to the front clasp of my bra and unhitches it. I'm surprised by how easily he does this with one hand when it always takes me two hands and a mirror to unhook.

Then his hand makes it down to my jeans, where he effortlessly undoes the five buttons on my Levi's 501s, and I say to him, "I don't want to do this."

He ignores me and continues as I stare at the white popcorn ceiling and the square translucent light cover that doesn't align with the room.

I start to get mad. I've told him about Philip and explained how I want to take it slow, but he seems to be ignoring all that. My attempt at getting him to have sympathy and understanding for why I don't want what is happening is futile.

I plead, "Please stop!"

He ignores me and continues.

While I lie there looking at the white popcorn ceiling, I begin to float away to the corner of the room, just like I did with Philip.

month with a gun

I feel powerless and small and watch from above, disconnected. He grows frustrated, and I can tell he's getting mad that I'm not participating. His movements become faster and faster as he tries and fails to get me to like it.

He finally gives up and leaves the room in a huff. I float back into myself and then pull my underwear and pants back up, hook my bra, and sit on the edge of the bed as I try to figure out what I'm going to do next. I sit for what feels like a long time.

I slowly walk into the kitchen to find him doing dishes. The air is thick with awkwardness and tension. I carefully say, "Well, I better go, I've got practice early tomorrow."

He picks up a dish and dries it with the red-and-white striped towel that was on his shoulder. He responds, "Yeah, you should go."

That's the last I'll ever see of James.

I cry as I drive home, thinking, *How could I have been so stupid?*

"Stupid," "immoral," "dangerous," and "coward" were just a few of the words the gun-rights advocates used for me after the *My Month with a Gun* article was published on the *Ms. Magazine* website. One guy suggested I put the gun in my mouth and pull the trigger.

The day after Part One was published, a *Ms.* editor contacted me to inform me they weren't going to publish the other three parts of the four-part series.

I was dumbfounded.

"The article has generated over thirty thousand hits and two thousand comments in the first twenty-four hours," she said. "We can't keep up with the response."

Confused, I said, "I thought getting a lot of hits was a good thing?"

"Most of the comments are from angry gun-rights advocates threatening me and my small staff, which we can't manage," she

dumb girl

explained. "Also, they keep trying to post your home address."

That, apparently, was the last straw.

Joe Nocera, an acclaimed op-ed columnist at *The New York Times*, found out about the situation and wrote a column about it. He contacted the *Ms.* editor to find out what happened and ask why they canceled the series; in his column he wrote "*Ms.* allowed itself to be censored by Second Amendment absolutists."

The editor wouldn't respond on the record but disagreed with his assessment. Nocera concluded in his column, "I don't see how you could view it in any other way. *Ms.* published something the NRA-types didn't like; they responded by bullying *Ms.* online, and *Ms.* folded."

"NRA 1, *Ms. Magazine* 0."

In the meantime, I reached out to *The Daily Beast*, the online version of *Newsweek*, and they were more than happy to publish the rest of the series. I was relieved that my thirty-day experiment was going to be available to the public.

Gun advocates "yelling" at me online didn't bother me as much as I thought it would. As I told a friend of mine who was worried about my safety, "There are a bunch of gun control advocates that are far more prominent than me and nobody's tried to take them out, so I'm not really all that worried. They're just bored and lonely men who like to spew hate behind the safety of their computer screens."

The controversy was picked up by other news outlets, and I spent the next month being interviewed on numerous radio and TV programs. Then, to my surprise, *Ms.* cofounder Gloria Steinem weighed in and *Ms.* published the full series after all.

I would have loved to have been a fly on that editorial meeting wall.

Joe Nocera effectively standing up for me, a stranger, was some-

month with a gun

thing I'd never experienced. I did a thing, it was noticed by bullies, they bullied me, someone didn't stand up for me when they should have, and then someone of importance did stand up for me. I felt vindicated and accepted in a way I'd always longed for.

Besides making me feel good, being seen and heard in that way gave me the confidence to tackle my next project: making a film.

PART FIVE

chapter 29

fundraising

"So how much money do you still need to raise?" Kenny asked as we sipped our warm Cokes and waited for the tired and overworked manager with dark bags under his eyes to call out our order number.

It was the spring of 2017, and we were waiting for what we already knew would be suspect burgers and overcooked fries at a shitty little burger place outside of Miami. Kenny and I, along with my coproducer, had just interviewed and filmed a woman who'd attempted suicide with a gun, and we had an hour to grab a bite to eat before our next interview, with the doctor who'd perform her fifty-third surgery on her face. Kenny was one of the two cameramen I'd hired to travel with me to film the interviews and supporting footage for my documentary.

After the success of *Beyond the Bullet* and the *My Month with a Gun* series, I'd been hungry to do something else that looked at gun violence in a different way.

"I don't understand why when a child finds his parent's gun and shoots and kills a sibling, we call it an accident and don't prosecute the parent, but when a parent leaves a child in a hot car and they die, we call it involuntary manslaughter and put them in jail," one mother I'd talked to a year earlier had said to me.

dumb girl

It was these kinds of conversations that had inspired me to find new and different types of projects that challenged the way we think about gun violence.

Initially I wanted to write another book, a book about people who'd pulled the trigger. I wanted to explore the complications of being "the good guy with a gun" and then living with the ramifications and consequences of being that guy. But gradually I realized a book wasn't going to capture the internal conflict a person must feel after they shoot and kill someone, even when it's justified. We needed to see their face, not just read their words.

I needed to make a documentary, not write another book.

"Money?" I asked Kenny, a little confused by the question. Then I realized what he meant. "Oh!" I said. "I've already raised it all."

There was a slight pause.

"What?" he said, perhaps a little louder than he meant. "What do you mean you've raised it all? All of it?"

"Um . . . of course I raised all of it." I cocked my head to the side, bewildered. "How could I have done the film without raising all the money first?"

"That's amazing." He chuckled. "Nobody does that."

"What do you mean nobody does that?"

"It's really hard to raise money," he explained, "so most filmmakers raise a little bit, and then film, and then raise a little more, and then film a little more, and do it that way until the film's done. That's why it takes so long."

"Oh, I didn't know that was an option." I shrugged. "I just thought that if you wanted to do a film, you had to raise all the money before you started."

"Nope, that's definitely not what most people do. But yeah, that's great that you've already raised it all," he said, sounding astonished.

"Number fifty-eight!" yelled the manager.

Kenny smiled at me and then got up to go get our food.

fundraising

I thought back to the dozens of calls and meetings I'd had with people to raise the $250,000 I was told I'd need to make the film. The first couple of meetings hadn't gone well. I'd never done a film before, so I struggled to explain what I was trying to do and why it would make a difference, and I failed to illustrate the quality of imagery and storytelling I was going for. I left those initial meetings feeling as downtrodden as Dad did, when I was fourteen years old, when he had trouble raising money for his limited partnership deals.

"Wish me luck," Dad says as he walks out the door on his way to ask Mr. Turner for $15,000. Mom, Robby, and I watch him walk down our walkway, across the street, and onto Mr. Turner's doorstep where he rings the doorbell. His rounded shoulders and hanging head evaporate as he juts his chin forward, pulls his shoulders back, and inhales deeply.

We hold our collective breath as we see Mr. Turner open the door and then the two of them disappear inside.

I've never seen Dad this nervous before. But then there's a lot on the line. Earlier this afternoon he explained, "Mr. Holter and Mr. Wright and I are trying to buy an apartment, and we each need to get twenty people to invest $15,000. The deadline is midnight tonight and I only need one more person. If I don't get one more investor, the whole deal falls through." He adds, "I've asked everyone I know and I'm running out of time. Mr. Turner is my last hope."

I feel scared for him. Mr. Turner is terrifying. His house is directly across the street from ours and he is the crabbiest man I know. He never smiles but grunts when Robby and I play in the street. When I wave and say, "Hi, Mr. Turner," he looks away and ignores me. When I was twelve, he yelled at me for the sin of making a snow angel on his yard in the fresh eight inches of snow that had fallen the previous night.

dumb girl

I don't know how long it takes to ask for money, but it feels like Dad's been in there for an awfully long time. Robby and I sit on the bright-yellow corduroy couch in the living room staring at Mr. Turner's boring brown front door, willing Dad to victoriously appear.

Suddenly the door swings open and Dad walks onto the porch, shakes hands with Mr. Turner, and heads home. I can't tell whether he got the money or not.

"Mom!" I yell, "Dad's on his way home." Robby and I jump off the couch and head over to the hallway where Mom meets us to greet him.

The doorknob turns and Dad walks in. His face is white as a ghost, and he is trembling. I wonder if Mr. Turner yelled at him. He loosens his blue striped tie and steadies himself on the half wall that separates the hallway from the living room. He looks humiliated.

"He wouldn't give me the money," he says matter-of-factly. "He said he doesn't invest in these kinds of things, and when I explained how he could double his money by investing in this apartment building, he said, 'I'm not a risk taker,' which is total baloney. It's a sure thing!"

He shakes his head in disbelief, takes his tie off, and starts unbuttoning his shirt while heading up the stairs. His embarrassment follows him. I feel sorry for him. I don't know the details of how the "deal" works and I'm not sure if this is just a small setback or if maybe he's just not that good at fundraising, or his job.

After seeing Dad come home empty-handed and humiliated from Mr. Turner's that day, I decided never to work in a job that requires fundraising.

Then I came up with a passion project that demanded just that.

The first pitch I made was over lunch with a friend in New York City who was heavily involved in gun violence prevention,

fundraising

had funded many independent films, and had an empathetic heart.

I thought she was a shoo-in.

After I gave her a long and rambling explanation of the film and told her the five different directions I might go in, she had questions: "Will you have a narrator? Who? Where will it be seen? HBO? Netflix? How many people will be in it? How long will it be? Who else is providing funding? Are you partnering with any organizations?"

She knew what she was asking. I didn't know what I was talking about.

Because I literally didn't know the answers to her questions and hate to lie, I answered most of her questions with "I haven't decided yet" and then agreed with every small suggestion she made, matching her enthusiasm for each idea.

"So, it's a movie about forgiveness?" she asked.

"Totally!" I said, a little too eagerly.

"What about religion? Will you bring that into it?"

"Oh, absolutely." I nodded.

By the end of the lunch, she just looked confused and a little irritated that I'd wasted her time.

After that meal, I felt that old impostor syndrome creeping in . . . but it wasn't the same as it was when I first became an advocate. It wasn't as intense, and it didn't stop me like it used to. This time, I acknowledged it and then said to myself, *Okay, how do I move forward? How do I prove to her and the other people I plan to ask for money that I'm not an impostor?*

I needed something to help me sell the idea. I needed a proof of concept or a visual "product" I could show.

At the suggestion of a local filmmaker whom I brought on as my coproducer, we created an emotional and compelling five-minute film about two people who'd shot and killed someone—a sizzle reel.

dumb girl

The first person was a woman who shot and killed her abusive husband a few seconds before he was going to shoot and kill her and, this being before domestic violence laws were enacted in California, was sent to prison for twenty years. The other story was about a teenager who was playing with a shotgun while sitting next to his best friend when he accidentally pulled the trigger, instantly killing him.

Both stories were heartbreaking and tragic, and fundraising got a lot easier after I made that reel. I simply showed it to potential donors, explained how the film would allow gun owners to see what being "the good guy with a gun" actually feels like, and invited them to be a part of this nuanced piece of storytelling.

When they needed a minute to collect themselves and wipe away the tears after watching the last (especially emotional) thirty seconds of the sizzle reel, I knew I'd get a yes.

Fortunately, after years of working in gun violence prevention, I knew a lot of people who'd funded other films or were passionate about the topic.

Until Kenny and I sat in that shitty burger joint in Miami, I had no idea it wasn't normal to raise the entire budget for a documentary before filming. I just knew I needed to do it and figured it out.

The fact that I'd pulled it off signaled to me that I was starting to shed my long-held belief that I was incapable and undeserving.

chapter 30

truth and trust

Kevin was my first interview for my documentary. I cold-called him in 2016. I wanted to speak with someone who'd shot a robber or intruder in their home and I didn't know where to start, so I started where most searches start, Google. Yep, I Googled "man shoots intruder." That led me to an NRA website that, to use their vernacular, listed dozens of "heroes" who'd used their "God-given Second Amendment right in the way our Lord intended."

I started by calling a veterinarian in rural Washington State who'd shot and killed a man who had broken into his home to steal veterinary pharmaceuticals.

He hung up on me.

Then I called a man who'd accidentally shot and killed his teenage daughter when she snuck back into their home after slipping out earlier that evening to hang out with her friends.

He also hung up on me.

Kevin was my third call. I told him, "I'd like to help you tell your story."

He reluctantly agreed to meet with me in his home—without cameras.

dumb girl

∽

The following Tuesday, I drove 156 miles to his modest-looking house in rural Washington.

Kevin was a living stereotype. He was a sixty-something rail-thin man with a weathered face who wore loose-fitting jeans, an oversized checkered shirt, an old baseball hat to cover his receding hairline, and a gun on his hip he never took off.

He lived with his wife in a double-wide trailer on a couple of acres. The trailer backed up to a forest where he'd set trip wires because, as he explained, "You never know." His backyard contained a chicken coop, a small shed with an electric stove he called "my man cave," a tractor, and a couple of broken-down pickup trucks he clearly stopped working on years earlier.

Long guns were strategically placed by both the front and back doors and hung on the wall above the TV, which played Fox News nonstop. A sign on the front of the house read "There is nothing in here worth dying for" on top of an image of a revolver and five bullets.

He scared the shit out of me.

I had nothing in common with Kevin, yet I was there to gain his trust and ask him about the worst day of his life: the day two guys broke into his house and he shot them both, killing one of them.

As we sat together at his kitchen table and he told me his story, I listened attentively and took a few notes. It wasn't long before I began to notice a softening in my body. I was conditioned to hate him, hate his politics, and hate his way of life. He was an NRA member who owned several guns, after all. But my fear and dread and uneasiness began to melt as he explained what had gone down three years earlier, when he shot the two intruders. He wasn't the monster I'd envisioned and, like most things in life, his story was more complicated than it appeared in media reports and on the NRA website.

truth and trust

That said, he wasn't exactly turning into my best friend. He still scared me, especially when on the first day of filming he dropped the shotgun he was holding—the same gun he had used to kill the intruder—and it landed on the floor between us, the muzzle facing me.

I jumped to the side, convinced I was about to be shot.

"Whoops!" he said, laughing at his carelessness. "Don't worry, I took all the shells out."

What the hell am I doing here? I thought in that moment. But deep inside, I knew why I was there. I was there to experience and explore what scared me, find empathy for someone who is crude, and earn trust without lying. I was unconsciously trying to redo the afternoon Dad made me lie to the man at the door.

A couple of months after The Fireplace Store—also known as Thermo-Rite Sales (TRS)—shuts its doors for the last time, there is a knock on our front door. Dad is sitting at his desk in the living room when a gray-and-white Oldsmobile Cutlass pulls up and parks in front of our house. I'm busy in my room doing thirteen-year-old things, organizing my books in alphabetical order.

I hear him scramble to the foot of the stairs and yell, "Heidi, come down here—immediately!"

I dash down the stairs, feeling the urgency in his voice.

"The man walking up to the door is trying to find me and I need you to be the one who answers the door," Dad explains. "He's going to ask you if the owner of TRS is home. I'm no longer the owner of TRS and have not been for months, so you need to tell him that you don't know the owner of TRS and he does not live here."

I stare at his neatly trimmed mustache feeling a pit grow in my stomach as I try to figure out why I'm the one who has to lie to the man walking up to the door.

"You're not lying, because I'm not the owner of TRS, and so the owner of TRS does not live here," he pleads.

dumb girl

He's interrupted by a loud and impatient knock from the other side of the door.

Dad motions with his hand and raised eyebrows for me to answer the door, then goes to hide in the next room.

I slowly turn the knob and swing the door open, bracing myself.

"Hi, I'm looking for the owner of TRS," the man announces. For some reason he doesn't know Dad's name.

"There is no owner of TRS here," I explain, exactly as Dad has instructed. I think I sound like a robot.

"Do you know TRS?"

"No."

"Is your dad here?"

"No," I lie again.

"Is he the owner of TRS?"

"No, he's not," I answer, trying to say it with confidence, the way Dad did.

He looks around as he runs his hand through his curly blond hair, trying to figure out his next question or next move. He looks at me in desperation. He knows I'm lying.

I avoid his gaze; I can't look him in the eyes. Instead, I look at his feet, absorbing his frustration. I desperately want to tell him what he wants to know, make him happy—save him. But I can't go against Dad.

Finally, he loudly exhales, slowly turns around, and walks back to his car in defeat.

Deflated but relieved I only had to tell a few lies, I carefully shut the door. Dad comes out from hiding, lifts his eyebrows, and wrinkles his forehead, forming a question with his face.

"He didn't figure it out," I huff before turning to run up the stairs to my room.

Once in my room, I flop onto my bed and cry. Lying is agonizing. It's one of the Ten Commandments, and I just violated

truth and trust

them, so now I'll have to ask for God's forgiveness. Besides, I'm not very good at it. He definitely knew I was lying, which is embarrassing and humiliating.

I'll never lie to a stranger again, I vow to myself. It's not worth the stress or agony it causes me.

I ended up meeting with Kevin five times. The last time, I sat on his worn and uncomfortable couch with him and his wife, and we watched the finished film together.

When I arrived, he proudly presented me with a freshly grilled pink salmon he'd caught the day before. He'd lovingly seasoned it with parsley and lemon, which gave it an acidic bite. It was his way of thanking me for taking an interest in him and for helping to tell his story. I didn't have the heart to tell him I hate the taste of fish, so I slowly ate the flaky fish and controlled my gag reflex while we watched the movie together.

What I learned from Kevin is that trust is based on authenticity, graciousness, and honesty. It was clear that he and I differed vastly on our views around gun ownership and gun regulations, but that's not what we talked about. He never asked what I thought about the NRA, gun control, or Fox News, and I never asked him. We talked about family, and safety, and regret, and emotional pain. It was a big deal to ask complete strangers to tell me the details of the worst day of their life, and I took the responsibility seriously. With him, as with everyone else I interviewed for the film, I tried to be as authentic and honest as I could be in all of our conversations.

I tried my best to relate to my interview subject by putting myself in their shoes and giving them the respect they deserved, which, really, was the only thing I knew to do.

chapter 31

christian

Taylor was eight when he found his mom's loaded gun and accidentally shot and killed his five-year-old little brother. Ten years after the shooting, I sat next to eighteen-year-old Taylor and his dad in a church pew in North Carolina, reciting the Lord's Prayer, trying to prove to them that they could trust me.

I first found out about Taylor when reading an online article on a Christian website titled "A Grief Shared." In the article, Taylor's dad wrote about how he chose to grieve after Taylor killed his youngest son.

It had been ten years since the accident, and I wanted to include their family's tragic story in my documentary because it illustrated how easily a responsible gun owner can turn into an irresponsible gun owner. I thought Taylor, now that he was eighteen, could talk about how the shooting had impacted him—both in the immediate aftermath and in the decade since.

Taylor's family was an evangelical patriarchal family, and they reminded me of my family and my Christian upbringing. When I interviewed them, it had been twelve years since I'd been to church, and I had worked hard during that time to make peace with the idea that I could be happy without Jesus being in my heart and church being the center of my identity. But with

christian

Taylor's family, I easily reverted back to a younger version of myself where Christian-speak and my fundamental Christian knowledge were still present. I easily sang the words to the hymn "Holy, Holy, Holy" from memory when I attended church with them, which Taylor's dad noticed. My Christian roots helped me gain the family's trust, and also gave me insight into their handling of their loss.

As my cameramen were setting up their cameras and microphones before I interviewed Taylor's grandparents in their empty, sunlit Baptist church sanctuary, Taylor's grandmother warily asked me, "Are you a Christian?"

I'd worried someone would ask me that question. I knew that confessing "No, I'm no longer a Christian" might jeopardize their trust in me, but I didn't want to lie.

"I grew up in a Presbyterian church and have fond memories of weekends spent at youth group retreats and going to Bible studies," I told her, and her face lit up, all skepticism gone.

I'd honored my desire to be truthful without telling all the truth—just as I'd done with my family's minister decades earlier.

Pastor Keith, the minister of our church, is kind and warm as he greets me with an open hug. I sit down on a cold black fake-leather chair that makes me lean back more than I want to, while he walks around his desk and sits in his large wooden chair, a heavy chair that's fitting for an important person like him.

He asks, "So what do you want to talk to me about?"

His large brown wood desk separates us and makes my visit feel official, almost businesslike—unlike a therapist's office, which feels open and warm, an inviting place to explore feelings.

I decide to talk more about facts and less about feelings.

Two weeks ago, I listened to his Sunday morning sermon about people who were experiencing a "crisis of faith." He told the congregation, "God is always with you, even at your darkest

dumb girl

times." His message did not feel true, so I've decided to talk to him about how I believe I've been abandoned by God.

I want to know why I don't feel God's presence and feel so alone. I'm eighteen, I'm depressed, and it's getting worse. I need help. It's a huge risk, though, because he and his wife are friends with Mom and Dad, and he is mentoring Philip. I'm worried about how Pastor Keith will react. Will he believe me? Will he still like Philip? Will he judge our family?

The other part is that he's an adult who I've known throughout my entire childhood but have never had a one-on-one conversation with. I don't know if I can trust him. *He's a minister, of course you can trust him*, I scold myself. *Ministers are kind of like counselors, right?* I'm pretty sure he's bound by law to keep all conversations confidential.

I decide to limit the chitchat up front and just blurt out, "Philip 'incested' me and I think God left me because of it."

He doesn't really react. At least, not in a way that is visible.

A long ten seconds later, he blinks and then says, "I'm sorry."

I tell him what happened in the same way I told Mom in Arizona, but this time it's not just to get it off my chest. I continue and explain how long *the game* went on, how I'm still remembering things, how I have a counselor, and how I pray all the time but it really feels like God is not there and I wonder if he is mad at me for this happening.

He listens to it all and then again says, "I'm sorry." He then asks, "Have you ever thought about the possibility that it was you who left God?"

At first I just blink, unsure of how to respond. Then I say, slowly, "No. That has never occurred to me."

"What I think is that in your desperation to feel better about what happened and make sense of it all," he explains, "you stopped letting Christ be a part of your life and journey. You shut God out and feel alone because of it."

christian

And then he opens the large black leather-bound Bible that sits on his desk and begins to read. I listen patiently as he reads verses while I desperately try to understand his logic.

Before I know it, the hour is up.

I leave his office feeling like I still have no clue how to get Christ to love me again and be a part of my life. All I know is that Pastor Keith is right about it probably being my fault that God is not in my life. I just can't figure out how I shut God out in the first place, or when.

That night I pray and ask God to come back.

I meet with Pastor Keith one more time, about a week later. I'm anxious to ask more questions and share my thoughts from the previous week's session. His wanting to meet with me a second time gives me assurance that my story is believable and that my healing is more important to him than his mentorship with Philip.

I start the second session by telling him more about Philip's and my history and feel the need to go a little deeper with feelings than what we talked about in the first session. I tell him, "Mom's focused on her recovery, Dad's distant and angry, Robby's always in trouble, and sports aren't fun like they used to be. I feel really alone, in a way I haven't felt before. Also, I keep remembering things from *the game* and they freak me out."

A confidence grows in me as I share intimate details about my insecurities around my faith and my awkwardness around Philip. And I feel proud that I've gotten past my fear of trusting Pastor Keith.

About a half hour in, I ask, "How will I know when I've opened my heart back up to Jesus?"

He doesn't answer.

I ask it again a little louder, thinking he must not have heard me. Still nothing.

dumb girl

The reflection of light on his brown tinted glasses makes it so I can't see his eyes. I think, *Are his eyes even open?*

Then, he starts snoring.

I sit in disbelief. *Is my story not compelling enough to keep someone awake?* I feel awkward, intrusive on his space and time, small, unsure. *Do I wake him? Do I just leave? Do I just sit here and wait? What do I do if he wakes up? Pretend I never noticed and keep talking?*

Time stands still. I wait. I'm not sure how long. Maybe a minute? Five minutes? It feels like five minutes.

He wakes with a startle and mumbles something I can't hear as he wipes his mouth. "I have to go. I have a bunch of homework I gotta go do," I lie. I lie in part to save me but also to save him from embarrassment when he realizes he fell asleep.

He bows and begins to pray for me. I bow with him. And then I leave.

I never meet with him again to talk about Philip or God. But I do continue going to youth group, looking for answers I can't get from Pastor Keith.

"You're not worthy of God's love," the youth minister tells the small group of us at Wednesday night Bible study. "He only gives love to those who truly want it and work for it. If your life is a mess and you're not getting what you ask God for, it's for one of three reasons: You are not worthy because you don't love Jesus enough, you don't pray enough, or you aren't devout enough. God works in mysterious ways and is not to be questioned."

God never does come back to me, and I believe for a very long time that it's my fault.

Being back in a church talking the Christian talk brought back deep feelings of childhood pain and abandonment, but I knew I needed to put them aside so I could do the job I'd come to do. I found my resolve and steadied myself.

christian

Taylor sat with his dad, two aunts, grandmother, and grandfather around a large dark wooden table I'd moved into the church narthex (lobby), backdropped by six large multicolored stained glass windows telling the story of Jesus's crucifixion and flooding the room with filtered sunlight.

I sat behind a large glass doorway that separated the narthex from the sanctuary, wearing a big black headset with attached microphone as I whispered instructions for the camera shots I wanted my two cameramen to capture.

I invited Taylor's grandfather, who was a minister and the patriarch of the family, to start the family discussion. He began with a short prayer, and they all bowed their heads and held hands. After the prayer and in his southern accent, he said, "This occasion is as special as it is unique. This was a difficult memory for all of us to unpack and to address it. Sometimes it helps to talk about what we were initially concerned about in those early days."

"Close up on Aunt One," I whispered into my microphone as Taylor's aunt, who'd begun crying, wiped away tears and began to share.

"Obviously I had a huge concern about Taylor's age. You know, he was so little, and so what is he going to have to go through?"

Taylor's grandmother added, "I still wanted Taylor to be a happy little boy."

"Shoot stained glass Jesus behind Grandma, then pan down to Grandma, then sweep to Dad," I quickly whispered into my microphone, wanting to capture the emotional image of Jesus dying on the cross behind her as she described her heartache.

"I didn't know how he'd be able to handle it," she continued, then said to Taylor, "I didn't want the memory to haunt you all your life."

As each family member shared what they remembered from that day with Taylor, including their fear, regret, and pain, I felt the familiar tightening in my throat and pressure behind my eyes

dumb girl

as I choked back tears. Pangs of jealousy hit me as I realized I was watching a family that was laying it all on the table, processing their pain, sharing their grief, and healing . . . all things I wished my family could have done.

For three days I'd interviewed Taylor and followed him around along with my two cameramen while he hung out with his friends, took notes in his history class, mowed the lawn, made dinner with his dad, and went to church. All the while, there'd been a hesitation about him; he seemed unable or unwilling to let down his defenses. I'd suggested this family discussion because I hoped Taylor would open up if I created a scene where he could hear, from the people he loved the most, how the shooting impacted them and learn about what they did to protect him from guilt.

To my relief, it did.

Near the end of the emotional discussion, Taylor broke down. "I was young, and I didn't understand what was going on at the time, and it was difficult for me to process. I guess I've been pretty distant from people, and I guess that's the way I've been dealing with it. But . . . through family and everything . . . it's all brought us closer, and I appreciate what you all've done for me. The thing I think about daily is how would Matthew expect me to be an example and how would he want me to live."

I could feel some of his guilt, shame, and burden leave his body as he confessed all this for the first time. Simultaneously, I felt the tension in my own body build. Tears ran down my cheeks as I absorbed the family's visceral pain and the raw emotion on display. My tears were for them and everything they'd been through, but they were also for me. I cried happy tears for the healing moment I'd created for them; tears of gratitude that I'd managed to overcome my own childhood of pain, tragedy, and trauma; and tears of grief for a family I never had.

Near the end of the reunion, Taylor's dad turned to Taylor and, through choked-back tears, said, "You're the kind of big

christian

brother I would have wanted you to be," and then added, "I'm proud of you." Then they hugged a hug that had been held back for ten years, their faces buried in each other's necks, which morphed into uncontrollable sobs.

When I'd interviewed people for my book ten years earlier, I'd worried I was taking from them. I didn't worry about that with this family; it was clear what they were gaining from the experience. I watched, in real time, a family committed to open and honest communication, a family sharing and acknowledging what they'd been through, a family full of love for one another, coming together and healing.

chapter 32

crisis

Of all the people I interviewed for my film, it was Christen, the woman who attempted suicide by shooting herself in the face, whom I related to the most.

Her story was remarkable because over 60 percent of gun deaths in the US are suicides, and I felt it was an important story and perspective to tell. Only 10 percent of people who attempt suicide with a gun survive, so finding someone who was physically able and willing to talk about their attempt was extremely challenging. When Christen agreed, I was thrilled. And that was before I realized how much we had in common.

Christen came from a loving Christian family. "For the most part, I had a charmed life," she told me. "Then in a short period of time, I lost my job along with my health insurance, my grandmother, whom I adored, died, and my dog died. I was forty-one, didn't have a job, my bills were stacking up, and I was facing the threat of being evicted. After months of sleepless nights, I became increasingly unhappy and depressed and felt I'd become a burden to my family and friends. I felt like suicide was my only option."

I knew that feeling.

I've become increasingly unhappy and depressed. It starts with getting a bad case of chicken pox a few weeks after I turn

crisis

eighteen, which takes me out of volleyball and the classroom for two weeks. Missing school puts me behind in my classwork and, more importantly, takes me off the court when I'm desperately trying to earn a volleyball scholarship to a university. I struggle in math and French class and continue to get only mediocre grades by sucking up to the teacher or flat-out cheating on tests. I feel the ever-present pressure of not screwing up my grades and putting in jeopardy a potential volleyball scholarship.

I desperately want a boyfriend, someone to love me, go to school dances with, pay attention to me, and be part of a thing bigger than just me. I'm jealous of girls at my school who have steady boyfriends, and I wonder what's wrong with me, why I can't get a boyfriend. At the same time, I don't know how to deal with the flood of new memories from *the secret* that surface as I balance school, church, sports, my parents, and the numerous extracurricular activities I'm in, like glee club, choir, peer counseling, and a "kindness" club.

Mom (post rehab) and Dad are busy with their stressful jobs. They attend my games and matches as much as they can, but I feel disconnected from both of them. I want to talk about what happened; they don't. And there is often tension and conflict between them as they adjust to Mom's new sobriety and my need to process the fallout from *the secret*.

A few months into Mom's sobriety, she comes up with a new strategy for when she gets angry or has had enough of Dad yelling at or demeaning her. She abruptly announces: "I have an early morning meeting tomorrow and I'm low on gas," and then finishes with, "I'm going to get gas," as she grabs her purse and slams the door, leaving Robby and me to deal with Dad.

I feel alone, misunderstood, and broken. The ups feel muted, and the downs feel crushing. I complain to my diary about constant exhaustion, not being able to sleep, trying and failing to pretend to be happy, and the constant irritation I feel at Mom and

dumb girl

Dad. The wins in volleyball matches and the success our team has in basketball no longer fill me with the joy and contentment they previously did.

My youth group leaders at church offer scripture and messages of everlasting love and peace in heaven with God, who they say can't disappoint. The thought of everlasting love and peace becomes an attractive and plausible solution to my misery. I think, *Why not be with God now, in paradise, where I'm unconditionally loved?*

After one particularly difficult school day and basketball practice where I can't seem to do anything right, I call a suicide hotline. I tell the woman on the phone about *the secret*, how mean Dad is, Mom's drinking, how God has abandoned me, and how misunderstood and lonely I feel. She asks, "Do you have a plan?"

I do.

She asks, "Have you tried before?"

I haven't.

She asks, "Are you in immediate danger?"

I'm not sure.

I ask, "Can you give me a reason why I shouldn't go and be with God, right now?"

She highlights the supportive teammates I have, the college plans I have to look forward to, and the success I'm having in sports. When I eventually get off the phone, I feel stupid. I feel like I've wasted her time, picturing other callers who are in immediate danger, perhaps having the phone in one hand and a gun in the other. But my sadness and loneliness continue.

I sit down and write a suicide note so it will be ready when I finally have enough guts to end it.

Several weeks later, as Robby, Mom, Dad, and I are eating dinner at the kitchen table, I bring up *the secret*.

Dad uncomfortably shifts in his seat. Mom changes the

crisis

subject and says, "I cut these flowers from the garden, aren't they just beautiful?"

I understand I'm making them uncomfortable, but I need to process this stuff, and they told me in front of their therapist that I can talk about it whenever I need to. I press on, talking about a conversation I had with my therapist a couple of days earlier.

Dad begins to scowl. "I was attracted to you too when you started developing, but I stopped myself from having sex with you," he says matter-of-factly. "You don't see me going around telling everyone about it."

My mind floods with flashbacks of him showering with me and watching me bathe, and the many times over the years when he positioned his hand on my bare butt, under my pants and underwear, when I snuggled up to him on the couch or in his bed while we watched TV together.

I drop my fork onto my plate, sit silently for thirty seconds, and think about how I'm going to respond. I stand up and announce, "I have class early tomorrow morning and I'm low on gas. I'm going to get gas!" and I abruptly leave.

As I jump in the Mustang and drive away from the house, I decide, *This is it. This is the day I kill myself. I can't do this anymore.* I speed off to the nearest highway, looking for an overpass and a large cement support column off the side of the road I can slam head-on into. As I drive, I bawl and howl and scream to no one about how I hate Dad and how I hate life. I yell at God about the unfairness of life and question why he's even put me on Earth in the first place, and I cry from the excruciating emotional pain I'm in. I just want it all to end.

I increase my speed, seeing an overpass up ahead. As I get closer, I notice black-and-yellow metal guards around the column and quickly calculate that they will cushion the impact of the crash and I won't die. I continue driving but, overpass after overpass, the support column is protected in the same way.

dumb girl

Not having another plan, I decide to drive to Doug's house a few miles away. I pull in to the driveway and knock on the door. Nobody answers. Defeated, I walk back to the car and decide to try another road that might have something I can crash into. As I drive, my mind fills with images of Dad standing next to the crumpled Mustang Convertible. I envision him heartbroken that his beloved car was totaled. I don't picture him being upset that I died. That makes me even more angry.

I feel stuck and am in pain and feel like a burden and just want it all to end. I drive a little longer and with each mile, unable to find something to crash into, I decide I'll just continue driving until I figure out my next move. I can't bear to go home, at least not yet.

I've recently become close to my math teacher, who has pulled me into a club she and another student created called Magic. We perform random acts of kindness to students we think are having a bad day or just need to be noticed in a positive way. We've been meeting at her house to plan and create our random acts, like anonymous notes we drop in lockers, and I admire her immensely. Her two-year-old tragically died six months before I met her, and she shared some of the details and despair she's experienced. I feel honored that a teacher would confide such painful and private parts of her life to me, her student. She is kind, openhearted, and seems safe.

I drive to her house.

When she answers the door, I'm a mess: Tears are running down my puffy red cheeks, snot is coming out my nose, and my body is shaking uncontrollably. I fall into her arms.

Her husband, also a teacher, recognizes the crisis I'm in and motions to her that she should attend fully to me while he puts their six-year-old son to bed. We sit at her kitchen table as I tell her everything—*the secret*, the physical abuse, Mom's drinking, the depression, and the comment Dad made earlier that evening that put me into this crisis.

crisis

She listens in a way I've never been listened to before. She offers no advice, gives no platitudes, and doesn't discount my experience. And she believes me. We talk until I have nothing left to say and exhaustion takes over.

I stay at her house for hours. Late in the evening, my parents call her house to see if by chance I'm there. They've frantically been calling my friends, teammates, and coaches to find out where I am and make sure I'm okay. It feels nice that they are worried and panicked because until this moment, I've felt dismissed and misunderstood. I'm glad they finally know just how much pain I'm in.

I eventually make my way home, where Mom and Dad meet me with hugs and tears and relief but no discussion. It's past midnight, and we are all exhausted from a long and emotional night.

Today at school, friends and teammates ask what happened and why my parents didn't know where I was. I tell them, "I went driving and then to a friend's house and I forgot to tell my parents," which seems to satisfy their curiosity. Their concern makes me feel appreciated, valued, and wanted.

Mom's reaction is very different. I come home tonight and mention to her the concern I received at school today.

"I don't know why," she says flatly. "If you ask me, it was blown way out of proportion."

Christen was an adult with an apartment and life experience, not an emotional teenager. But her desire to be in heaven with God, have all her problems go away, and simply end her emotional pain was profoundly relatable for me.

When I interviewed her on camera, Christen described how she tidied up her Washington, DC, apartment, then decided to go out on the balcony to minimize the potential injury and mess from the bullet for her upstairs neighbor. "I wanted to shoot myself in

dumb girl

the head," she added, "because I'm an organ donor and wanted to preserve as much of myself as possible, to save someone else."

Christen survived her suicide attempt but suffered greatly in the years following. The bullet had blown off her right jawbone, shattered a third of her teeth, and destroyed her tongue and right sinus before bouncing off the bone of her nose and exploding, smashing her right eye but, surprisingly, failing to pierce her skull. She had daily pain and was constantly preparing for surgery, having surgery, or recovering from surgery.

What was remarkable to me was that despite her daily physical pain, she was the most optimistic, positive, forward-facing, empathetic person I'd ever met. "Surviving suicide," she told me, "gave me a new perspective on life. I survived the unsurvivable. When I wake up in the morning, I wonder, *who am I going to help today?*"

After her suicide attempt, Christen dedicated her life to visiting trauma victims like her to give them hope by sharing her story of survival.

"I tell them I know what it feels like to be in that hospital bed," she shared. "Every time I help someone, part of me heals."

I knew exactly what she meant.

chapter 33

stupid

"So how did you know you could make a film? Did you go to film school?"

It was a simple question. And it seemed like the answer should be "Why yes, of course I went to film school. How else would I know how to direct and produce a full-feature documentary film?"

Beth was creating the DVD cover and promotional poster for the film, and we were on the phone discussing some of the designs she'd sent me. She was an accomplished designer and spent years learning her craft. She wanted to know how I had learned my craft. I didn't have a good answer.

I hesitantly replied, "No, I just wanted to make one, so I found a guy who's made several really good films and asked him to partner with me."

"What about your book? How'd you learn to do that? Were you an English major?" she asked.

"No, I didn't study that in school at all. In fact, I was a PE major." There was no response, so I continued, "I just met all these women who'd lost kids and wanted to help tell their stories."

"So, you didn't have any training for your book or your film?"

"No, not really."

"Who does that? Just writes a book because they want to,

dumb girl

or makes a film with no experience or training?" she asked in amazement.

Who does *do that?* I thought.

Beth's questions made me think about what it was in me that made me think I could do such things with no formal training or experience. I didn't view myself as a risk taker or as a creative person; in fact, I still viewed myself as dumb. Inside, I was still that girl who had to cheat in school in order to pass tests.

The days and weeks after my suicide attempt seem different. I feel a new focus as I make a shift toward finishing up my senior year and looking to the future. I earn a coveted scholarship to play volleyball at the University of Northern Colorado and start earning awards and adulation for my success on the volleyball, basketball, and tennis courts. I'm living up to my goal of achieving Linda Parker success. I also feel a slight difference in Mom and Dad. I can't put my finger on it; they just somehow seem less irritating and are no longer in my way.

I focus on my last requirements: passing all my spring classes and graduating.

I go into my French final knowing nothing but confident I'll do well, since I plan to cheat. The teacher, Mrs. McFee, likes me. She enthusiastically greets me when I walk into her class and always asks how I did in my game or match the night before. She seems to like that I'm a leader in the school and am nice to people in class and that I don't goof off. I feel like she's "pulling for me" and is genuinely happy or relieved for me when I do well on a test. And I've met with her many times after school for extra help, so she thinks I'm trying.

I'm not trying. I hate French. It's hard and confusing. It's hard to memorize words and their meanings and even harder to try and spell them on a vocabulary test. I cheat on most tests. I can't figure out a way to pass them otherwise.

stupid

Senior year French has been especially difficult because we've been learning to conjugate verbs, understand tenses, and figure out if a noun is masculine or feminine. Some of the words are obvious, like pants (*le pantalon*) being masculine and a dress (*la robe*) being feminine. But then there are words that are just wrong. Why would an apple tree (*le pommier*) be masculine and pizza (*la pizza*) be feminine? It makes no sense. On top of that, I can't spell or conjugate English words, so how am I supposed to do it with French words?

I don't like that I cheat. It makes me feel more stupid than I already feel, because when I do get a good grade, I know I haven't earned it. Plus, I constantly worry about getting caught.

This all started after Dad made me put my F papers on my wall when I was eleven. When I don't cheat, I do poorly on the test, and when I cheat, I do well—I get As and Bs with only the occasional C. I want to stop, but I'm addicted. It's all I know. I think about it constantly and pray about my problem every night. I start with asking God's forgiveness and then ask him to help me stop.

But God doesn't seem to be helping me, and even though every time I cheat, I feel more guilt and shame, I feel it's all out of my control. Years of cheating on French vocabulary tests means at this point I lack even a basic level of knowledge in the language. So it's essential that I cheat—or at least that's what I tell myself.

As Mrs. McFee passes out the final tests, she reminds us, "All of your notebooks should be under your desks, and the only things on your desks should be a pencil and the test."

I get out a few blank notebook papers and put my cheat sheet under the top blank paper, next to my test.

I'm about halfway done with the test when she comes up to me to see how I'm doing. I don't see her, and her sudden presence startles me. I quickly cover up the cheat sheet I've put under the blank pieces of paper.

dumb girl

"What are you doing?" she asks quietly to not disturb the other students.

"Just taking my test," I whisper.

"What are all these papers for?"

"I just do better on tests if I have a scratch paper with me in case I need to spell something out or something."

She picks up the papers and rifles through them.

I hold my breath.

I feel her demeanor change and see her shoulders drop as she slowly pulls my cheat sheet out of the group of papers. "What's this?" she asks.

"It's a paper that I'm using cause I didn't think I could do good on the test without it," I quietly confess.

She visibly exhales and time slows down as I feel my heart pound in my chest. She stands there looking down on me for what feels like forever. Her voice full of disappointment, slowly and very quietly, in almost a whisper, she says, "You know the rules of this class. If you're caught cheating on a test, you fail the class, not just the test, but the class."

"Yes, I know," I reply, my head hanging low as tears flood my eyes. "I just didn't think I could pass it without help."

"I'm taking your test away and you need to come see me after school," she instructs before heading back to her desk at the front of the room.

I sit there for the rest of the class period thinking about what's happened and how badly I have messed up. I quietly cry. My only hope is that she likes me so much and pulls for me so much that she'll decide to just fail me on this test, and I'll end up with a D for the quarter.

I pray. Hard.

After my last class, I slowly and nervously walk to Mrs. McFee's office.

stupid

I've never failed a class, and this is the end of my senior year. I've already been accepted into the University of Northern Colorado on a volleyball scholarship, so an F in French will not affect that, but Dad's disappointment, degrading screaming, and verbal insults will be more than I can handle. And besides that, it will be humiliating to have to say I failed a class in high school. I pray she shows mercy.

I knock hesitantly on Mrs. McFee's office door, which she shares with five other foreign language teachers. As the door opens, the two other teachers in the room look at me, gather up their papers, and quickly scoot out of the room. Their faces tell me they have just been discussing me and are disappointed in me.

My plan at this point is to cry, which comes easily in this moment, and beg forgiveness and remind her how worthless and stupid I am and how failing the test will be equally as painful to me as failing the class will be and remind her how bad I am at French and how I have come to her for help and how I really have been trying and how I am really really really sorry and how I will never ever cheat again.

When she turns to face me, her eyes are red and slightly swollen. She wipes her blond bangs from her round face and shifts uncomfortably in her chair. She waits for me to sit in the red plastic chair in front of her before she speaks. "I want you to know, Heidi, how disappointed I am in you. You're a bright girl with a lot going for you. I was really expecting you to do well on this test and was shocked to see you cheating. You're a good student and I really like you," she explains. "However, I want to be fair. I can't have a rule and then just ignore it because I really like a particular student. I've been sitting here debating whether I should fail you on the test or fail you for the quarter."

I hold my breath as she continues, "I've decided that I need to follow my own rules and fail you for the quarter."

The air leaves the room. I start to cry.

dumb girl

Water wells up in her eyes.

"Heidi, this is probably more difficult for me than it is for you. I really like you and wanted you to succeed. This is by far the most difficult decision I've ever had to make as a teacher."

I tell her I understand and explain that I've been struggling with cheating and am worried about it for next year in college. I tell her, "I've been praying for God to help me stop cheating and I guess this is how he's helping."

We both laugh. The laughter breaks the intensity and feels nice.

When I get up to leave, she gives me a hug and says, "I'm sorry."

Mom has thirteen months of sobriety now and is attending AA meetings daily. She works at a travel agency these days, so between that and her meetings, she is rarely home.

When I get home after my meeting with Mrs. McFee, I call her at work and ask, "Can you meet me for dinner somewhere near work because I need to talk to you about something important."

She has no idea what I'm talking about but agrees to meet me.

I'm not worried about her being angry or disappointed with me. I just want to tell her so she'll maybe protect me from Dad's wrath.

My plan is to explain to Mom what happened and tell her about my struggle with cheating and how I have tried and tried to stop and how I have prayed about it for months. I will explain how I've struggled with it ever since I was in fifth grade and cheated in spelling and how I've become addicted. I'll tell her how part of me is glad I got caught because I've been worried that I will cheat in college and now I won't. She'll feel bad for me for making a bad decision and will be glad that I am upfront and thankful that there are no lasting consequences from failing French class. And she will be proud of me for being so mature about it.

And that's exactly what happens.

I cry when I tell her, and she cries with disappointment, but it

stupid

feels like a business meeting where I just have some bad news to tell her. I feel tremendous relief after telling her, similar to when I told her about the boyfriend/girlfriend game.

An hour later, when we are finishing up our desserts, Dad shows up at the restaurant and I reluctantly tell him about what happened. Having already told Mom and having her there with me gives me a sense of safety I didn't feel when I told him about my bad grades in fifth grade. I also have my car to escape to if things get bad.

His response is a predictable anger—tight mouth, furrowed eyebrows, shallow breathing, and clenched fists like he's ready to punch me. I'm relieved that we are in a public place, so he can't yell at me or hit me.

It's different this time, though.

"Mom and I talked about this already and we both agreed that even though it's horrible and I really messed up, it's actually a good thing," I tell him. "It's cured me from cheating. Now I won't cheat in college, which would have huge consequences."

After looking at Mom, who is nodding, his shoulders slump in defeat and he leans back in his chair. "I suppose that's true," he agrees reluctantly.

It's the first time I have really messed up and ended up having a mature, adult discussion about it. There is no yelling, no hitting, minimal crying, and no drama. It feels like I've broken the spell of years of me having no control over Dad's response to bad news.

Despite the emotional roller coaster it's been, I feel like today has actually been a huge win.

Beth was still waiting for my reply.

"I don't know," I finally said. "I guess I just felt like the stories in the book and the stories in the film needed to be told, so I figured it out."

dumb girl

"You're amazing," she said, "I could never do that, do something that big that I don't know how to do."

How *did* I just do these things? And what made me think I could in the first place?

I thought about failing French and my bedroom wall, the wall filled with F papers I fell asleep to every night when I was eleven. They were the last thing I saw when I went to sleep and the first thing I saw every morning when I woke up—for months. Even after I took them down, I still saw them, breathed them, lived with them: *You are dumb, everyone knows you're dumb, and you'll always be dumb.* I fully believed it and lived my life believing I was a DBADG.

I'd always thought the wall took my power, told me who I wasn't and who I could never be. That is, until this moment.

Beth's questions prompted an epiphany for me: The wall didn't take my power, it gave me power.

I discovered I'm able to do things I'm not trained to do or have experience in *because* I feel dumb. Being "dumb" allows me to ask questions, get support, and be comfortable not knowing what I'm doing.

Thinking I'm the dumbest person in the room makes me curious, attentive, and perceptive. It's actually freeing not to hold on to ego or pretend to be something I'm not. In a weird way, believing I'm dumb has become my superpower. It's helped me write a book, serve on two prestigious national boards, and direct and produce an international award-winning documentary despite having no previous experience.

The conversation gave me a new perspective, and a lot of the shame I held and was burdened with suddenly vanished. I started to understand that being "smart" wasn't just about being book smart. Creativity is a form of smart, being a good mom is a form of smart, risking is a form of smart, listening to your intuition is a form of smart, and being empathetic and perceptive of other's needs is a form of smart.

I just wish I'd learned it sooner.

chapter 34

awards

I was sitting with Dave in a large auditorium along with hundreds of other filmmakers. My hands were sweating, and I could feel and hear my heartbeat—which irritated me. Was the pounding in my chest a betrayal of the pride I had in not coveting awards? A defense mechanism in case I didn't win?

It was the last day of the 2020 Las Cruces International Film Festival in New Mexico, and I had to admit, I was hoping to win Best Documentary. As I sat in the softly lit theater, I half practiced a speech—just in case.

My documentary had premiered the previous year at the prestigious Slamdance Film Festival in Park City, Utah. That screening was the beginning of a year of touring around the country, screening the film at film festivals, participating in Q&A sessions, conducting media interviews, and doing talks on how I got strangers to trust me enough to talk about the worst day of their lives on camera. As a first-time filmmaker, I never expected to win any awards, so I'd been shocked when I did—and not just once. *Behind the Bullet* had won Best Documentary at four film festivals in 2019.

As the emcee put the names of the films that had been nominated up on the large screen, I held my breath and clenched Dave's hand. "And the winner for Best Documentary is . . ."

dumb girl

Not me.

Someone else's name and someone else's film were displayed on the screen. Dave squeezed my hand in consolation, and I let out a long exhalation of both disappointment and relief that I wouldn't have to make a speech. My body relaxed and my mind went blank; I no longer needed to hold on to or repeatedly rehearse in my head the just-in-case speech I would have given if I'd won.

I patiently listened to the winner accept his award and then waited for the emcee to announce the winner of the last category, Best Director.

I thought back to *The Killing of Kenneth Chamberlain*, an incredibly moving and important film about a black man in White Plains, New York, who was brutally killed by the police. It was a breathtakingly honest film and was directed by a seasoned filmmaker. I thought about how much skill it must have taken for him to hire, organize, motivate, and direct actors to create such gripping performances. I was glad I didn't have to work with actors. I was sure he'd win.

Again, the nominees' names were listed on the screen, including mine. The emcee leaned into the microphone attached to the podium and said, "The winner of Best Director is . . ."

"Heidi Yewman of *Behind the Bullet*."

I sat in stunned silence, not absorbing his words or my name splashed across the screen. It had never occurred to me that I could win Best Director.

While I was still processing, Dave leaned over to me with a huge smile on his face, grabbed my face with two hands, and kissed me.

The realization of what was happening hit me gradually. As I stood up to thunderous applause, I suddenly realized I didn't know what I was going to say. My just-in-case speech had vanished from my brain. I slowly floated down the auditorium aisle,

awards

up the wooden stairs, across the stage where my heels echoed, and over to the podium. I stood looking out at the crowd—shaking and mute. In that instant I remembered the girl I no longer was, the girl that was voiceless, dumb, ineffectual, and powerless.

And I remembered the first time I began to claim my power.

Doug meets me at a Chili's restaurant on a cold spring day in North Denver, which is only an hour's drive from my college dorm. As I nervously wait for him in a booth in the corner of the restaurant, my hands are sweaty, and I can feel and hear my heartbeat. When he sees me, I stand, and he smiles a big toothy smile and hugs me before we both sit down across from each other.

I ask him about his wife and the kids, he asks me about classes and volleyball, and we order lunch. After the chitchat ends and the waitress leaves to attend to another table, I start shivering. I have suddenly become really cold. I ignore it and say, "Doug, I have something to tell you, something that happened when we were growing up."

Because Doug is eight years older than me, he doesn't know about *the secret* or the fallout from it. He was in college when Philip started the boyfriend/girlfriend game and when the physical abuse from Dad got bad. Our age difference doesn't give us much in common or give us reason to be close. I'm in my second year of college; he has two young kids, a wife, a dog, and is busy running a manufacturing company. Our lives are very different.

But part of my recovery, now that I no longer live at home, is not keeping *the secret* anymore. I'm ashamed about the incest, and I don't want to be. Telling Doug feels like another step toward taking the shame away.

He sits very still and looks at me intently. I decide to be direct and just jump in.

"Philip 'incested' me," I begin as I wrap my hands around the porcelain mug of hot tea in front of me. And then it all spills out,

dumb girl

like a dam that's been lifted. I don't tell him the specifics, which are still surfacing, but I tell him generally how things started in his basement bedroom when he was in college and how things got worse and worse until they stopped. I tell him how Mom and Dad were told about it and how they confronted Philip, how Robby knows too, how I'm in therapy and am getting better, and how I think he should know, since it's his family too.

He is shocked.

Tears form in his eyes as he stares out the window. I take a sip from my mug. Then he looks at me with a heaviness and intensity I've not seen from him before. He leans forward, putting his elbows on the table as he reaches for my hands.

"I'm so sorry that you had to go through this, Heidi," he says. "And I'm so sorry I wasn't there to stop it from happening."

Telling Doug makes me feel validated and cared for. His response, so loving, is just what I need and not what I expect. I fear not being believed or being judged—being told that what happened was not a big deal. But Doug believes me fully and thinks it's a huge deal. It's such a big deal to him, in fact, that at the end of the lunch he proposes sending me money so I can continue going to therapy each week. Dad recently filed for bankruptcy, so he and Mom can't afford it anymore.

I gladly accept his kind offer.

In this moment, telling Doug seems like the final thing I need to do to be free from the shame and heaviness of *the secret*. What I'll eventually understand is that it will actually be a lifelong journey. But right now, walking out of this Chili's with my big brother, all I can feel is the glow of his love and the power that comes with taking control of my own story.

As I stood behind the podium holding my new Best Director glass trophy, a warm sensation engulfed me. It was a feeling of pride, of accomplishment, of pure joy. I was being recognized

awards

not only for making a great film; I was being recognized for my vision, my creativity, my leadership, my ability to empathize, my ability to get people to trust me, and my ability to bring a team together to make a kick-ass documentary. I'd forgotten my just-in-case speech, so I briefly told the tragic story of the film's four subjects, I shared my appreciation for them agreeing to participate in the film, and I thanked the organizers of the festival for showing my film and for awarding me Best Director.

I walked back to my seat to a standing ovation and to Dave, who looked like he was about to burst with pride. He gave me a full-body hug and we cried tears of joy. As we sat down, he leaned over and whispered into my ear, "I've never been so proud of you." I leaned over the armrest, gently putting my head on his chest as he kissed me on the top of my head.

After the ceremony, we attended the after-party held at a restaurant nearby. As I walked into the intimate and tastefully decorated private room filled with filmmakers who were loudly talking, drinking, and celebrating with toasts, high fives, and hugs, I noticed the director of *The Killing of Kenneth Chamberlain*. He was talking to the director of the film festival, who had announced my win. He motioned me over, so I walked over to him, clutching my trophy.

"Congratulations on winning Best Documentary," I said as I shook his hand.

"Thanks," he said, "and congratulations to you for winning Best Director. I gotta tell you, what you did on that film was unbelievable. The way you got the people you interviewed to tell you such intimate details and the way you got them to be comfortable enough to be that vulnerable is a real testament to who you are as a person, not just a filmmaker. Really unbelievable!"

I blushed in amazement that such an accomplished and experienced director would be so impressed by me. I thanked him

dumb girl

before saying, "I loved your movie too. So powerful! I'll bet Kenneth's family is incredibly grateful that you are telling his story."

As we were talking, a short line formed of people wanting to talk to me. One woman said, "Congratulations, I've never seen such a powerful movie."

Another woman confessed, "I have guns at home, and after watching your movie, especially because of how you didn't make me feel attacked for owning guns, I feel like I need to rethink how I store my guns."

And a man whom I'd seen in the theater when my movie was screened a couple of days earlier shook my hand firmly, using both hands, looked into my eyes, and said, "You are one talented filmmaker. I can't believe this is your first film." He looked at Dave standing next to me and said, "You must be so proud of her."

Dave nodded and simply said, "Oh yeah. I sure am."

I was proud of me too, the proudest I'd ever been. This award was validation, evidence, and verification that I, in fact, had made something of my life, despite all I had to overcome. I was not a dumb girl, and I was capable of greatness.

becoming

When I sat down to write this book, I envisioned who I thought would most benefit from reading my story. Ultimately, the person I most wrote for was myself, as a way to honor what I've been through. I hoped that by writing my memories down, I would lessen the sting and weight of all that's happened to me over the course of my life. I hoped I could forgive myself for not standing up to or stopping those who abused me. I hoped I could see the impossible power structure I was in that left me mute and powerless to stop the constantly unfolding tragedy.

I also wrote this book to my nineteen-year-old self, my just-out-of-high-school self who didn't know what had hit her. I wished she'd had a book like this to give her the truth of what happened and the permission to know that despite her depression, confusion, low self-esteem, anger, and sadness, she was going to be okay.

There's so much more I need to say to her that wouldn't fit in the story I've told here, though, so I want to end this book with a letter to her—a letter that is also for every other young woman who needs to hear these words:

Dear Heidi,

Congratulations! You made it out. This is the beginning of the rest of your life; it's on your terms, and you now get to begin the life you want, not the one that was put on you. It's going to take a lot of work to unravel the past nineteen years and come to terms with it, but you will, and you will not only thrive but exceed all your expectations. You will come out of the shadows, and it will be safe to trust yourself and be your own person.

Things are scary right now as you are continuously flooded with images and feelings you don't understand or have context for or know what to do with. From thirty-seven years in your future, I'd like to explain to you what's going to happen and how you'll turn your perceived weaknesses into superpowers. Your spirit has been crushed; you have no idea who you are and what you are capable of. You need time to process and heal. Then you'll slowly use the many survival skills you've developed over the past nineteen years to become so many things—a cherished spouse, an exceptional mom, an award-winning filmmaker, an author, a national expert on the impact of gun violence, and a compassionate person who helps others feel valued. You'll sit on several boards, including two national boards and an international board, and you'll make a significantly positive impact on those organizations. You will be brave, you will be smart, you will be kind, you will be seen, you will be important, you will be safe, and you will be loved.

Here are the specifics:

School and getting good grades will continue to be difficult for you. You will be safe in college but will learn about dysfunctional families in your psychology, sociology, and family systems classes. This will bring up intense and confusing feelings as you discover for the first time that your family was not the perfect family it pretended to be, not the family whose projected image you completely bought into.

This new discovery will make you angry and you'll have no place to put that anger, so you'll focus on putting

becoming

all your energy into volleyball practice. You'll feel proud to be a volleyball player on scholarship, but it'll be harder than you thought. You were the best player on your high school team. The problem will be that everyone on your college team was the best in their high school, so you won't be that impressive. That and your need to please the coach with your strong work ethic will not be noticed or appreciated. You'll go to the exhausting three-hour practices every day and return to the gym for an additional three hours each evening so your depleted self-esteem can be quenched by playing volleyball with regular students who find you talented and skilled.

Going to class will be a struggle; you will frequently opt to sleep in instead, and your grades will suffer. You will struggle daily with depression but won't know that's what it is.

You will have a series of bad boyfriends who are cruel and unsympathetic to your story of past sexual abuse. One will be sensitive to your journey but emotionally abusive on all other fronts. You'll accept the abuse and continue in the relationship because being noticed and seen is better than being lonely and rejected. Besides, you understand how to maneuver and live with anger and abuse. It feels normal. The low point will be when you beg one boyfriend, who's trying to break up with you, to stay by pleading "I'll be whoever you want me to be. Just tell me how you want me to act and who you want me to be," because you don't know who you are, and you are desperate for someone to tell you or show you.

You are in so much pain.

You won't go home in the summers of your college years, knowing it's not a safe place, and instead will work at a summer camp in the Pocono Mountains. You'll feel

dumb girl

important, appreciated, and relevant at the camp and will discover your self-esteem and purpose. The campers will adore you, and your fellow counselors will appreciate your company, humor, and fun personality. Your mission will be to build your resume for a future middle school teaching position, but the three summers you spend at camp will give you far more. You'll learn how to appreciate preteens and all their quirks. You'll learn how to be in healthy relationships with people your own age. You'll learn what it feels like to be safe. And you'll learn what it feels like to thrive outside of a court, field, or gym.

The other thing you will get from camp is a husband. You'll meet him between your third and fourth year of college, fall deeply in love almost immediately, trust him as much as you can, and marry him a year and a month later. Because he met you at camp, when you were emotionally strong, had higher self-esteem, and came off as confident and happy, he'll fall hard for you. He'll see in you what you can't see in yourself. He'll continue to love you unconditionally when you return to regular life (college) and he'll morph into your pseudo counselor and confidant as he lovingly and patiently holds you night after night while you cry and tell him about the abuse and feelings of inadequacy. You'll be unable to convince him that you are unlovable, damaged, and unworthy of his love and devotion. He'll by far be the best thing that has ever happened to you.

Like most marriages, you will have ups and downs, but you'll have one big issue you won't be able to solve, which is common to those with sexual abuse histories. You hate sex and he loves it. At the beginning, he'll be sensitive and understanding, as you have flashbacks and vivid body memories that surface during sex. He'll hold

becoming

you, let you cry, and listen as you process what you're experiencing. He'll write an article for *Beyond Survivors* detailing the challenging nature he finds himself in as he attempts to balance supporting you and your pain with his desire to physically connect with you. He'll make you feel safe in and out of the bedroom, but he'll become frustrated, unable to fully express his love in a way that is natural and reasonable to him. This will, by far, be the most damaging and long-lasting fallout of the sexual abuse you've suffered.

Before you and Dave graduate from college and move to a different state, it will become important to you to confront Mom and Dad to let them know what they did to you and the impact it's having. You'll meet them at their house and cry as you read a list of grievances from a letter you wrote. Dave will hold your hand knowing how hard it is for you. You'll fully anticipate them denying everything you accuse them of, the hitting, the yelling, the molestation, the abandonment, the mistreatment, the cruelty, and the injustice of it all. What you won't expect is their apology and acceptance of everything you tell them they've done. Mom will cry and apologize. Dad will tell you he doesn't remember most of it but believes he did it all and is extremely sorry. You'll feel both vindicated and perplexed. Every book you've read up to this point about sexual abuse and abusive families explains that the vast majority of perpetrators deny accusations of abuse. You'll have been prepared for that but will have to adjust and will lean into their apologies. The night will end with hugs and a deep sense that this chapter of your life is now officially behind you.

After several years of living your dream of teaching PE, coaching high school volleyball and high school

dumb girl

basketball, you'll give birth to your own kids—first a baby girl and then, three years later, a baby boy, an age difference just like the one between you and Robby. You'll eventually transition into being a stay-at-home mom and love the freedom of being at home, managing the kids' activities and organizing all household chores while Dave works at a public relations agency. You'll be immensely happy and satisfied with who you are as a mom and confident in your ability to raise two children who will not feel the way you felt when you were growing up, consistently undervalued.

You'll subconsciously believe you are raising Heidi and Robby the way they should have been raised, and you'll rely on your instincts to do the opposite of what your mom did. You'll focus on making sure your children are confident, especially in school. You'll teach them letters and numbers before they start kindergarten and positively reinforce how smart they are. The foundation, nurturing statements, love, and great care you give them will come with a profound recognition of just how easy it is to be kind and supportive to children; at the same time, you'll feel a sense of jealousy that they get what you didn't, and sadness as you mourn what you could and should have had.

You will conflate your son, Aaron, with Robby and have a great desire to protect him when he does not need to be protected. Dave will require him to do simple chores around the house like taking out the trash or mowing the lawn, or he'll become angry with him for making normal childhood mistakes like losing his coat or breaking a plate, and you'll instinctively come to his rescue, which will confuse Aaron and anger Dave. Ultimately, it will not serve Aaron, but your desire for a "do-over" in unsuccessfully protecting Robby from Dad's vengeful anger will be too strong.

becoming

After a mass shooting at your high school, you will make a life-changing shift toward advocacy for reducing gun violence. This will become your passion for the next twenty-plus years.

You'll start to amaze yourself as you discover an inner strength you didn't know you had. It will surprise you that you are passionate about a topic that is steeped in conflict, anger, and unflinching beliefs. It will surprise you because avoiding confrontation at all costs will still be a big part of you feeling safe. The rallies, vigils, and protests you organize will teach you that being yelled at or hated is not the worst thing, and it's survivable. You'll grow from these experiences and will eventually see your adversaries as human and develop empathy and compassion for those who angrily taunt and ridicule you in person and on social media.

The success you'll have in the gun violence prevention world, the satisfaction you'll get from raising confident, smart, kind, athletic children, and the unconditional love and support you'll get from your husband will not keep away the shadows of depression from a childhood of abuse. You'll struggle with depression over the years, and it will come to a head when your daughter, Sami, turns ten, the same age you were when the sexual abuse by Philip began. The suicidal thoughts and longings will return as you try to cope. You won't know why it's happening, but it will hit you hard and you'll need intense therapy and medication to get through it.

And you'll have to decline going to Doug's daughter's high school graduation, knowing that being around Philip or any of your family members would be intolerable. You'll explain to Doug and Mom and Dad the truth of why you can't attend, and they'll tell you they

dumb girl

understand. You'll believe them but still feel guilty and be confused about why you can't get your shit together. And you'll be angry at your assumption that the impact of the abuse was all behind you.

Like many survivors of childhood abuse, you'll remain in contact with your family, including spending holidays and vacations with them even though you'll live a thousand miles away. This will be a constant source of angst between you and Dave as his desire to physically connect with you becomes a constant reminder of the abuse, fanning the flames of anger that he holds close to the surface. He'll want nothing to do with your parents or brother, while you'll enjoy and revel in the positive parts of the relationships that remind your eight-year-old self that you are loved and appreciated by your parents. You'll be quick to dismiss small hurts, like when Mom dismisses you or Dad drives too fast and in a reckless manner. You'll continue believing in the fantasy that your childhood family was healthy and convince yourself that they have turned a new leaf and the abuse is behind you and has been dealt with properly.

But there will be cracks. One day, Dave will offer to fill Dad's gas tank while Dad cleans the windows. Once the tank is full, Dad will notice that Dave accidentally put premium gas in the tank, making the price more than what he would have paid for regular at a station near his home. He will scream at Dave and belittle him and scorn him. Dave will giggle, do a quick calculation in his head, pull $2.80 out of his pocket, and offer it to Dad to make up for the price difference.

You'll sit in the car shaking, paralyzed with fear as you hear the heated exchange and feel the familiar pangs of guilt you had when Robby was yelled at, because you are not coming to the rescue of Dave. Turns out, Dave won't

becoming

need to be rescued. He won't find Dad intimidating or scary or terrifying and won't cower to the bluster. He'll think it's amusing. You'll think Dave is amazing. This will be the first time you'll see that Dad can be stood up to. It will be life-changing.

Mom's brother, whom you adore, will die in 2017. You'll go to his funeral by yourself while Dave stays home with the kids. You'll attend with your parents and brothers, and when Philip delivers the eulogy from the pulpit, you'll be flooded with excruciating detailed images of him sexually molesting you. You'll cry uncontrollably and those around you will think you are crying for your uncle. You'll be confused and angry that this is happening and annoyed that all these years later, you're still unable to control the feelings and images entering your mind and body.

After the funeral, at your aunt's house, Mom will insist on a family photo, since the six of you so rarely get together. Dad will stand between you and Mom with his hand on your shoulder. Doug will suggest, "Let's take hands off shoulders to make it a better photo." Dad will enthusiastically say, "Good idea, let's put them on fannies instead!" then put one hand on Mom's butt and one on yours, and squeeze. You'll yell at him for being inappropriate and he'll remove his hand, but you'll freeze while more photos are taken. Then you'll go out to your rental car and cry.

Philip will eventually come out and ask if you're okay. You'll tell him no and explain what happened. He'll be mortified and offer to support you. You'll tell him you'll need to confront Dad once he and Mom get back to the hotel before you lose your anger and bravery. He'll offer to stand with you so you don't have to do it alone. You'll feel his kindness and his hesitancy to intrude or

dumb girl

insert himself too much in this delicate and emotionally charged situation.

A few hours later, you'll knock on Mom and Dad's hotel door, with Philip right behind you. You'll have woken them up from a nap and will insist that Dad sit up. Mom will move to a chair in the corner of the room. You'll scream at him, use lots of swear words, and cry. He'll apologize, admit how stupid it was to put his hand on your butt, and explain how he immediately regretted it. You will continue to scream and cry and swear and ask why he would do this, given our family's history. He won't have a satisfying answer. Mom will sit there and say nothing. You'll run out of things to say, and Philip will continue the angry rant. You'll appreciate him being there and will be impressed that he says all the other things you wish you'd said but couldn't think of because you were so mad and emotional.

The discussion will turn to how Dad generally treats women. Mom will finally pipe up and echo Philip's and your perspective that Dad is an unenlightened old pervert. She'll explain to him that women are not to be touched whether his intent is sexual or not. He'll get hung up on *intent* and Philip will become even more angry. You'll get the feeling that Mom sees this kind of behavior from Dad more often than she's willing to admit. Once you've said what you came to say, Dad will again apologize and ask for a hug. You will oblige.

I don't know why.

You and Philip will move into the hallway just outside their room and you will break down. Philip will catch you and you will bawl, letting all your feelings and anger out. You will find it puzzling that earlier that day you were crying while reexperiencing this same person molesting

becoming

you, and now you are in his arms being comforted because your dad sexually assaulted you.

This will forever break the bond you and Dad had. You'll mourn the loss over the next several months and will only have short, small, and inconsequential conversations with him. When you see him next, you'll be cagey and cautious, never have your back to him, and refuse to hug him. He'll feel like a predator.

As you'll learn in your college family systems class and in years of therapy, most survivors of childhood abuse do not become estranged from their abusive family. You will be in that norm. Despite all the pain and suffering your family causes you, it will not be a black-and-white issue for you. You'll find precious moments of love, appreciation, kindness, and support from your family over the years. It will be impossible for you to cast them as 100 percent bad.

The family system you grew up in was dysfunctional and injured you greatly, but along with the pain was fun, love, humility, kindness, gentleness, and care, which makes it difficult to separate from and leave. A large part of you will love your family and believe in what they can be and should be. You'll also tend to downplay the bad things that happened, thinking it's a normal part of all families.

As your parents age and start needing support, you'll find yourself in a strange position where you'll see their weakness, vulnerability, ineptitude, and inability to do things for themselves, especially technological tasks. You'll pride yourself in not treating them the way they treated you, like when Dad becomes confused on how to set up his calendar on his computer. You'll show him and explain how it works gently and slowly and not yell at him or

dumb girl

become short or demean him for asking the same question several times, the way he did when you didn't understand how to solve a fourth-grade math problem. You'll feel a cathartic relief as you demonstrate to them the calmness, understanding, patience, and even-tempered response that was not afforded to you.

And this will feel right.

Lastly, the most important thing you will accomplish, which will bring you the most joy and satisfaction, is the success of raising your children. They will be the Heidi and Robby you wish you were. They will go into adulthood with compassion, empathy, bravery, self-confidence, curiosity, intuitiveness, intelligence, and love in their hearts. They won't spend years trying to unravel a childhood full of chaos and danger. They'll know who they are and will appreciate the life you gave them and the work you did on yourself to stop the cycle of abuse.

You will be proud of yourself—for surviving, for breaking the cycle of abuse common in so many dysfunctional families.

Right now, you may not feel like any of this could possibly happen. But from my fifty-six-year-old perch, I can absolutely say it will.

You are, in fact, NOT a dumb girl.

You are a smart, perceptive, creative, and compassionate girl.

And you always have been.

acknowledgments

This book began as a solo endeavor, but I quickly realized that was the wrong approach. It became so much more honest, thoughtful, and powerful because of these incredible people:

To Liz Green, my book coach, whose unwavering patience and insight not only helped me find my voice but also recognized the importance of my advocacy stories. Her endless compassion and guidance have been invaluable, and I'm forever grateful.

To Krissa Lagos, my editor, whose wisdom and thoughtful guidance taught me to cut what wasn't essential and to begin stories where they truly belong—in the moment. I do love starting a story with context, which is a hard habit to break.

To Brooke Warner, who saw the potential in a raw and undeveloped manuscript and believed in me and my writing when I struggled to believe in myself.

To the entire She Writes Press team for transforming my words into a tangible book, one that people can read, hold, and hopefully find inspiration in.

To my little brother, Robby, who bore witness to the abuse. Your humor, empathy, and friendship were my lifeline. I am forever grateful.

To my kids, Sami and Aaron, my muses of self-compassion and resilience, and the catalysts for my healing. I love you both more than words can express.

And finally, to the love of my life, my husband, Dave, whose

dumb girl

unwavering love, support, and belief in me have been the foundation of my healing. Thank you for reading and editing the manuscript over and over, even when it meant confronting the painful realities of my past. Your ability to love me in a way I now understand I deserve is a gift I will never take for granted.

about the author

Heidi Yewman is a gun control advocate, author, and documentary filmmaker. She's best known for her first book, *Beyond the Bullet*, and her international award-winning film *Behind the Bullet*, which explores the impact of gun violence on individuals and communities. A graduate of Columbine High School, Heidi has dedicated her career to gun violence prevention, including serving on the board of Brady: United Against Gun Violence. As a survivor of childhood abuse, she is driven by a commitment to reducing trauma and gun violence while promoting public safety through education and advocacy. She lives in Portland, Oregon.

Looking for your next great read?

We can help!

Visit www.shewritespress.com/next-read
or scan the QR code below for a list
of our recommended titles.

She Writes Press is an award-winning
independent publishing company founded to
serve women writers everywhere.